STUDIES IN HISTORY, ECONOMICS AND PUBLIC LAW

EDITED BY THE FACULTY OF POLITICAL SCIENCE OF COLUMBIA UNIVERSITY

Number 337

FEDERAL FINANCING

A STUDY OF THE METHODS EMPLOYED BY THE TREASURY IN ITS BORROWING OPERATIONS

FEDERAL FINANCING

A STUDY OF THE METHODS EMPLOYED BY THE TREASURY IN ITS BORROWING OPERATIONS

BY

ROBERT A. LOVE, PH.D.

The School of Business,
City College, New York

NEW YORK
COLUMBIA UNIVERSITY PRESS
LONDON: P. S. KING & SON, LTD.
1931

PRINTED IN THE UNITED STATES OF AMERICA

PREFACE

Probably no part of the government meets more severe criticism than does the Treasury department. Every step it takes has its repercussion on the social and economic structure and invites the attention of individuals who are disturbed. Scarcely any important action, accordingly, escapes the scrutiny of those who search for the effect of the step upon the subject of their interest. Consequently we find whole treatises on the effects of the government's financial policies.

At one time or another, we learn, actions of the Treasury have resulted in undesirable alterations in monetary conditions, they have brought about unjust redistributions in wealth, and they have been responsible for unfair advantages to competitive firms or industries. We find a criticism of the failure to provide a proper arrangement of maturities; we meet the claim that the banking system labored for years under a handicap imposed by a war-time measure; and we are told that the borrowing policy of the war further subjugated the poor to the rich. In view of the fact that such comments cover the results of the government's financial operations from practically every conceivable point of view, it is particularly significant that there seldom appears a discussion in which the writer assumes the point of view of the financier himself. Rarely in all the financial literature, whether official or not, do we find a clear-cut attempt to solve a given financing problem in the light of facts as the Secretary of the Treasury should have been able to see them, as he could have seen them, or even as he actually did see them. On the contrary, attention has ordinarily been given to an analysis of the effects as they were related to events of the time of their occurrence, rather than in their connection with the financing tactics which gave rise to them. As a result the student of financing may fail utterly to gain an appreciation either of the problems of a financier or of his methods of solving them. Consequently the former is not in a position to evaluate financing policies and programs of the past or to project measures for the future.

This situation has supplied us with what may be considered a justification for the selection of our own points of view. We have attempted to look at developments first through the eyes of the financiers who have been responsible for the several financing programs and secondly through those of a contemporary critic who would evaluate actions in the light of actual as well as prospective situations as they were revealed by existing facts.

The discussion of our point of view has indicated that we aspire to study such aspects of financing as will facilitate our understanding of financing policies and programs.

Upon analysis of the situation, however, we find that financing programs are made up of more or less independent policies; that the policies involve a number of separate steps; and that the steps themselves have to do with decisions on a variety of security features and financing devices. Since such features and devices supply the factual framework on which the financial structure is built, it logically follows that they should constitute the subject matter of our study of federal financing.

We may further establish the validity of this choice of subject matter by citing an example of the manner in which specific features and devices serve as the basic material out of which policies are built. Let us consider the problem of inflation. This orgy of war finance comes about not as a result of an announcement that it is to take place, but through a series of steps—definite actions, if you please—each of which involves a choice of alternative measures, and each of which presumably receives legal or official sanction.

There may exist, to be sure, in the minds of legislators and Treasury officials certain general theories or creeds which influence their decisions on specific points. When action is actually taken, however, it has to do with a specific point such as making notes receivable for taxes, reducing the time before redemption, providing for financing or investments out of current bank funds, forcing banks to discriminate in favor of paper secured by government bonds, or even making treasury notes legal tender for all debts—but it never has to do with inflation as a policy.

Because of the situation which this example illustrates we conclude that a study of American financing may advantageously be centered around an analysis of the numerous measures and actions which in truth constitute the tangible manifestations of government policy and practice.

What we now have to say appears to weaken the argument for studying the Treasury's operations by looking at specific financing measures. Nevertheless we must admit that an understanding of a financing device can not be attained by detaching it from its setting. On the contrary, we must consider it one of a group of features, a study of which must be projected against a background of social, industrial, financial, and political conditions. For this reason a topical treatment of financing devices was found impracticable, until we had first reviewed the use of each in connection with the financing programs in which it chanced to play a part. The topical treatment has accordingly been presented in the concluding chapter, while the main part of the text is taken up with a treatment of those coordinated developments which have characterized the various periods of our financial history.

Those phases of the subject which could be reduced to numerical or tabular form, together with a large number of comments having to do primarily with matters of fact, have been relegated to the appendix.

Before taking up developments during the Post-Revolutionary period, we may be permitted to encroach on subject matter which should logically fall in the summary, but which may, if placed at this point, facilitate an appreciation of what is to follow.

In the first place, we may refer to the fact that interesting financial manoeuvers are characteristic of periods of financial stress. Especially in time of war, the Treasury has ordinarily resorted to every known device, not only for the purpose of securing funds but also with the intention of avoiding political criticism and maintaining an appearance of financial strength.[1] The resulting attempts to maintain low nominal interest rates and the effort to build up the demand for government obligations has in turn supplied us with most of the materials for our study.

In the second place we may point out that a study of the financing devices which have appeared in response to varied conditions and diverse political theories discloses the singular fact that most of the financing measures appear and re-appear somewhat disguised, perhaps, but performing essentially the same service as when they were in their old dress.

Finally, we may suggest that universal employment of tax exemption, conversion, receivability, and the like has undoubtedly contributed to a situation which virtually compelled their future use. The truth of this contention becomes apparent when we recall that by virtue of the operation of the various devices, loans were actually placed at a lower nominal rate of interest than they would otherwise have

[1] *Cf.* A. C. Pigou, *A Study of Public Finance* (London, 1928), p. 187.

been. Since the reasons for the low nominal rates of interest were not understood by the public,[1] it is obvious that every loan on such a basis played its part in leaving the public less willing to sanction a remunerative rate on a loan placed on a clear-cut business basis. In other words, the popular idea of a normal rate of interest has ever rested upon the assumption that government securities will have those characteristics which make them sell at lower rates of interest than do comparable obligations of private business firms. To strip the issue of such characteristics would at once invite the criticism of the multitudes who comprehend the increase in the nominal rate, but who are not able to understand that there has really been no increase in the cost of borrowing. True this political pressure may be said to find its origin in the ignorance of the public but it has nevertheless undoubtedly handicapped any Secretary who aspired to introduce business tactics into the Treasury.

If the presence of such political pressure is not sufficient to justify the adoption of the very measures which fed it, a recognition of the facts in the case may at least increase one's understanding of the processes and the actions involved. Perhaps we may even be excused for sympathizing with the Secretary who was able to look out over the financial chaos which followed in the wake of repeated issues of non-interest-bearing legal tenders and boast of "average" interest payments of less than 4%; or with one who over a half century later reinforced his claim for the presidency with a reference to the low interest at which he had placed loans, even though he had disregarded future burdens while he was engaged in the task of equipping the loans with every known effective device for decreasing the nominal rate of interest. Irrespective of the nature of the sympathies aroused it is our

[1] *Cf.* Pigou, *op. cit.*, p. 251.

hope that the accompanying monograph may be recognized as an attempt to view events as they were rather than as they seemed to be and that it will accordingly contribute to an understanding of federal financing.

For assistances in preparing the monograph I am under many obligations.

Professor Edwin R. A. Seligman first directed my attention to the field, later encouraged me in the study of my chosen topic, and finally advised me on the selection of subject matter and the form of its presentation. To Professor Robert M. Haig I am deeply indebted for his sympathetic counsel as well as for his innumerable criticisms and suggestions. His advice has been invaluable in connection with the major task of transforming the raw materials of the study into the monograph as it is here presented. Mr. Ralph W. Souter read the manuscript and made pertinent suggestions. Various other members of the Staff of the Department of Economics and of the School of Business, Columbia University, supplied helpful criticisms on specific points. Mrs. E. M. McGill criticized matters of style and suggested improvements looking toward clarity of expression. To Mr. Gilbert Sussman I am indebted for his work in assembling data, for painstaking checking of references and for suggestions especially on legal aspects of the subject. The encouragement and help received from my wife and friends, is largely responsible for the completion of the study.

School of Business, City College,
New York, January, 1931.

TABLE OF CONTENTS

PAGE

CHAPTER I

The Post-Revolutionary Period

The Heritage of War Psychology 17
Commissions and Other Inducements versus high Interest Rates. 19
Appropriation of Special Revenues. 26
Price Maintenance 28
The Sinking Fund 29
Exemption 30
The First Bank of the United States as an Aid to the Treasury . . 30
Receivability 34
Refunding as "Post-mortem" Conversion 35

CHAPTER II

The 1812 War Period

Financing Policies and Pre-War Conditions 36
Early Efforts to Avoid a Loss from Conversion. 37
Using the Currency Feature in Short-Term Financing 37
Receivability as a Means of Making Notes Current. 40
Difficulties with Conversion. 43
Changes in the Treasury's policy 52
Debt Retirement 53
Relations with Banks 54

CHAPTER III

Short Term Financing and the Resulting Security Features (1837–1857)

Significant Aspects of Financial Theory and Structure 57
The Democrats' Dependence upon Treasury Notes. 59
The Whigs' Attempt to Fund the Debt. 63
Mexican War Financing 69
Security Purchases by the Treasury 70
Miscellaneous Features 71
Significant Developments of the Period 72

PAGE

CHAPTER IV

Civil War: Conditioning Facts and Theories

The Heritage from Pre-War Finance 74
Rate and Terms 77
Bias against Interest Payments 79
Inadequate Taxation 82
The Currency Situation 82
Early Relations with Banks 83
Suspension and its Reaction upon the task of Financing 85
The Treasury's Need of a Currency 86
Elimination of Competing Media 86

CHAPTER V

Civil War—Special Financing Devices

Receivability 89
Payment Upon Demand 93
Payment to Public Creditors 94
Legal Tender. 96
Conversion 100
Temporary Deposits 106
Coin Payments 108
Tax Exemption. 111
National Banks as Outlets for Bonds 114
The Use of Financing Devices as a reflection on Civil War Financing 116

CHAPTER VI

From the Civil War to 1917

Changes in Marketing Technique 118
Coin Payments 120
Bond Purchases. 122
Receivability 123
Foreign Situation. 125
Legal Tender Proposals and the Circulation Privilege 126

CHAPTER VII

Adjustment in the Financial Structure

Deposit of Government Funds in Banks 129
Removal of 10% limit. 133
Preferential Rates on Notes Secured by Government Bonds. . . . 133
Changes in Reserve Requirements. 135
Bond Purchase Requirement Removed. 136

PAGE
Currency and Inflation 137
War Finance Corporation 141

CHAPTER VIII

THE FIRST LIBERTY LOAN

The Appeal to Patriotism 146
Selling Expenses 146
Small Denominations. 147
Sale at Par 148
Circulation Privilege 148
Conversion 149
Tax Exemption. 150
The Rate of Interest and the Treasury's Policy. 151

CHAPTER IX

THE SECOND LIBERTY LOAN

No Sale Below Par. Circulation Privilege. 155
Appropriation for Expenses 155
Conversion 156
The Administration's Change on Exemption. 157
Exemption of Specified Amount. 162
Maturities and the Rate of Interest 164
Summary. 165

CHAPTER X

THE THIRD LIBERTY LOAN

Political Technique Employed in Passing the Act 167
The Abandonment of Conversion 167
The Interest Rate and the Treasury's Policy 168
The Receivability Feature. 170
The Purchase of Bonds by the Government 171
Proposal to Exempt Bank Holdings of Government Bonds. 172
Acceptance of Liberty Bonds as Security. 174
Summary. 174

CHAPTER XI

THE FOURTH LIBERTY LOAN

Market Conditions 176
Contingent Exemption 178
Control of Market Transactions 181
Summary. 183

PAGE

CHAPTER XII

The Victory (Fifth) Loan

Patriotism and the Rate of Interest 185
Obstacles to a Remunerative Rate of Interest 186
Securing Discretionary Power. 187
Political Reasons for Rushing the Measure. 188
Measures Having to do with Price Maintenance 189
Making the New Bonds Attractive 190
The Loan as a Whole. 191

CHAPTER XIII

Significant Post-War Developments

Maintaining the Price of Bonds 193
The War Finance Corporation and Price Maintenance 194
The 5% Purchase Provision 195
The 2½% Sinking Fund 198
Purchases from the Proceeds of the Franchise Tax of the Reserve Banks and from the Repayment of Foreign Loans 199
Acceptance of Liberty Bonds in Payment of Estate Taxes and from Foreign Governments 200
Other Proposals. 203

CHAPTER XIV

Summary and Conclusion

I. Policy and Theory. 208
Rate of Interest. 208
Significance of Sale at Par. 209
II. Preparation of the Field 211
Appeal to Patriotism 211
Manipulating the Currency—Inflation 212
Banking Changes. 213
III. Arrangements for Disposing of Securities 214
Use of Banks. 214
Agents versus Direct Sale. 215
Compulsory Loans 216
IV. Security Features 218
Tax Exemption. 218
Receivability 220
Convertibility. 222
Duration of the Loans. 228

PAGE
V. Assuring Solvency of the Loan 231
Sinking Fund. 231
Specific Appropriations 232
Taxation 233
VI. Price Maintenance. 234
Sinking Fund Operations 234
Direct Purchase and Similar Operations 235
Price Maintenance as a Policy. 236
VII. Conclusions on Financing. 239
Appendix . . . . Inset
Footnotes for Tables 241
Sources. 254
INDEX 257

CHAPTER I

The Post-Revolutionary Period

THE HERITAGE OF WAR PSYCHOLOGY

An understanding of the financing tactics employed during the Post-Revolutionary period presupposes an appreciation first of the legacy of war psychology and secondly of the prevalent economic and financial conditions.

As illustrative of the manner in which war psychology influenced the thought of the time, we may call attention to the disrepute into which the use of bills of credit fell.[1] The origin of the legal limitations on the rate of interest [2] and the restrictions against the sale below par [2] may likewise be explained by reference to the crystalization of official sentiment against a repetition of the costly steps which had characterized Revolutionary finance.

Unfortunately the commendable ideals of low interest costs—the goal of the two types of restrictions just described—and the desire to secure the domestic placement of loans, ran counter to forces which made them incapable of attainment.

When credit conditions and the financial status of the

[1] Hamilton, *Report to Congress*, 1790, Dec. 13, 1790; Report on Bank, vol. i, *Treas. Reports*, p. 64; Matthew St. Clair Clarke, *Legislative and Documentary History of the Bank*, p. 15; John J. Knox, *United States Notes* (New York, 1888), Preface, p. iv.

[2] Data on the loans have been tabulated and the results relegated to the appendix which will hereafter be referred to as the table. In connection with the present topic see Column F in the early loans.

[3] Table, Loans 39 and 47.

Treasury[1] are taken into consideration it becomes apparent that if the investor had received no greater returns than the interest stated in the authorizing acts, the securities would not have been attractive. In addition to this handicap, the government's ability to secure funds from domestic lenders was further limited by the fact that there was a dearth of capital. Even high yields would accordingly have been inadequate to the task of exacting money from these people who had none in their possession.

The existence of such unfavorable conditions gave rise in turn to financing problems not unlike those faced in war periods. It is not surprising, therefore, that financing tactics were employed which are worthy of enumeration along with emergency measures.

One of the steps taken was negative in that it involved the abandonment of a measure instead of its retention. Hamilton relinquished his plan for making the securities[2] redeem-

[1] An indication of the inability of the Treasury to meet the requirements upon it is to be found in the frequent borrowing not only to pay the principal but also to meet the interest on the public debt. (*Am. State Papers*, vol. i, pp. 176 and 658. See also *Act of June 4, 1794*, 1 Stat. at Large 372, ch. 40. *Act of June 8, 1795*, 1 Stat. at Large 409, ch. 2. *Act of Mar. 3, 1795*, 1 Stat. at Large 433, ch. 45, sec. 1. *Act of April 29, 1802*, 2 Stat. at Large 167, ch. 32.)

Other and more forceful proofs of the condition of the Treasury are to be found in the practice of reserving, at the time of issue, a part of the proceeds in order to be able to pay the interest on the loan as it became due (*Act of June 2, 1794*, 1 Stat. at Large 394, ch. 63, sec. 3, p. 395), and in the earlier custom of paying the interest by the issue of new securities, as for example, when Securities were issued in exchange for the indents of interest which had been issued in lieu of interest payments on war obligations. (*Act of Aug. 4, 1790*, 1 Stat. at Large 138, ch. 34, sec. 3, p. 139. Indents, or certificates of interest indebtedness came to be used extensively after March 1, 1782. Previous to that date interest payments had been met. See Dewey, p. 46.)

[2] The writer has used the term "security" to describe any interest-bearing instrument.

In the main, the terminology employed in the text will be found to

able at the convenience of the government in order to render them more attractive by the statement of a definite time for repayment. In other words, prospective future convenience was foregone for the purpose of making the issue attractive at the time of sale.[1]

The convenience of the government during the immediate future, on the contrary, supplied the reasons for Hamilton's well-known provision for a number of types of securities on which total interest payments would be at a minimum for the first few years and then increase gradually.[2]

COMMISSIONS AND OTHER INDUCEMENTS VERSUS HIGH INTEREST RATES

The difficulties of the struggling American government were especially noticeable in connection with the attempts to secure funds from the financial centers of Europe. Among the difficulties one, having to do with an objection to accepting American money in payment of obligations, led to the practice of making interest and principal payable in the cur-

conform to usage of the period. For example long-term obligations are referred to as "stock" in the earlier periods and as "bonds" in the later periods. "Notes" refer to obligations of short duration (ordinarily not over one or two years) but since world-war financiers designated five-year obligations as "notes", we have deemed it wise to retain their terminology. Either an indebtedness of the government or the instrument to which it gives rise may be referred to as an "obligation". Of the more specific terms only Convertability and Receivability require definitions. A security is said to be convertable when the government will accept it in exchange for some other issue. If it is acceptable to the government in payment of taxes it may be said to enjoy the receivability feature. The several manifestations of these two security features will be described later so that a further definition is unnecessary at this point.

[1] Dewey, *op. cit.*, p. 94; and Albert S. Bolles, *The Financial History of the United States from 1789 to 1860* (New York, 1883), pp. 25 *et seq.*

[2] *Act of Aug. 4, 1790,* 1 Stat. at Large 138, ch. 34. *Cf.* Dewey, *op. cit.*, p. 94, and Bolles, *op. cit.*, p. 25.

rency of the country in which the security was sold [1] and to a provision that interest should be payable abroad at specified rates of exchange.[2]

These provisions, while important for the purpose of removing certain objections to American securities, made insignificant headway in rendering the obligations attractive enough to encourage their purchase. Representatives of the Treasury accordingly found it necessary to supplement interest payments on certain loans [3] by other financial inducements which were in turn described as discounts, commissions, bonuses and gratifications.

While it is true that previous to these loans others [4] were taken by France and Spain at par, without deducting discounts or commissions, it is probable that the motives for such actions on the part of these countries cannot be found in the immediate financial returns carried by the loans. In other words the ability of the American States to secure funds was more dependent on good will than upon the pecuniary attractions of the securities. Beginning with the Dutch loans previously referred to, however, we find evidence that the values of the securities as investments were being scrutinized more closely, with the result that a remunerative investment had to be offered. For our purpose, the interesting phase of the transaction had to do with the form which the remuneration took. A 4½% commission was allowed on a 5% security. Under close study, the true nature of the transaction becomes apparent. In the first

[1] See for example Holland Loans of 1784, 1787, 1788, 1790, Sept. 1791, Dec. 1791, 1794. Louisiana Purchase Stock, *Act of Nov. 10, 1803*, ch. 2, 2 Stat. at Large 245, sec. 2, p. 246. Also *Act of Feb. 11, 1807*, ch. 12, 2 Stat. at Large 415, sec. 5, p. 417.

[2] *Act of Feb. 11, 1807*, 2 Stat. at Large 415, ch. 12, sec. 5, p. 417.

[3] For example, the Holland loans of 1782, 1784, 1787, 1788. See table.

[4] The first five loans in the table.

place, it is obvious that the 4½% commission can not be considered a mere allowance for selling costs but that it must be recognized as a means of increasing the attractiveness of the securities. In the second place, since the combined inducement offered by a rate of 5% and a discount of 4½% does not result in a net yield equivalent to the 6% authorized on the eleven-year obligation, it can not be said that the legal limitation actually forced the Treasury to depend upon other inducements. The resort to high commissions accordingly appears as a result of a voluntary choice to grant an inducement in this form rather than in that of a higher rate of stated interest. In other words the motive back of the administration's efforts to minimize the nominal rate of interest apparently found its origin in political rather than in statutory limitations.

In 1784, however, when John Adams came to negotiate a Dutch loan,[1] conditions had changed to the extent that it would have been impossible to secure advances within the 6% limitation. In fact accumulating maturities and other financial difficulties had given the struggling American states such a bad reputation in the world's money market that the two million guilder loan could be obtained only by offering some inducements other than the 4½% commission. He chose to offer such attraction in the form of additional obligations, premiums, and gratifications.[2]

[1] Table, Loan No. 7.

[2] The details are of interest. The bonuses or premiums consisted of 690,000 guilders of additional obligations themselves bearing interest at 4%. These obligations were issued in specified amount every two years from 1785 to 1797 to recipients who were determined by a drawing held three months prior to the issue. The holders of these securities as well as the owners of the original issues also received a gratuity, payable at maturity and saving from 4% on the amount payable in 1801, to 10% of the amount payable in 1807. Payments on this account resulted in an additional aggregate cost of 201,800 guilders.

The details of the transaction can be learned from the following table:

The completed transaction actually included (1) a sale at

(See Rafael A. Bayley, *The National Loans of the United States from July 4, 1776, to June 30, 1880* (Washington, 1881), 2nd ed., pp. 18-19.)

PAYMENTS AND REDEMPTIONS

	Guilders	
Feb. 1, 1801 amount of loan due with	250,000	
obligations issued 1785	50,000	
		300,000
Plus 4% gratification		12,000
		312,000
Feb. 1, 1802 amount of loan due with	250,000	
obligations issued 1787	60,000	
		310,000
Plus 5% gratification		15,500
		325,500
Feb. 1, 1803 amount of loan due with	250,000	
obligations issued 1789	70,000	
		320,000
Plus 6% gratification		19,200
		339,200
Feb. 1, 1804 amount of loan due with	250,000	
obligations issued 1791	90,000	
		340,000
Plus 7% gratification		23,800
		363,800
Feb. 1, 1805 amount of loan due with	250,000	
obligations issued 1793	100,000	
		350,000
Plus 8% gratification		28,000
		378,000
Feb. 1, 1806 amount of loan due with	250,000	
obligations issued 1795	120,000	
		370,000
Plus 9% gratification		33,300
		403,300
Feb. 1, 1807 amount of loan due with	500,000	
obligations issued 1797	200,000	
		700,000
Plus 10% gratification		70,000
		770,000

discount, (2) a lottery of additional securities and (3) a gratuity in the form of an obligation to pay all lenders an augmented principal. As a result of these manoeuvers, Mr. Adams was able to lower rather than raise the nominal rate of interest so that an actual yield which approached 6¾%,[1] appeared as an interest payment of only 4%.[2]

In the two succeeding loans, the rate was placed at 5% with the result that a commission of 8% was necessary in order to sell the bonds.[3]

While these deductions from par ordinarily appeared as commissions, it must have been quite obvious that they were far in excess of the usual selling commissions which, when loans were actually disposed of later on a business basis, ran as low as one eighth of one per cent.[4] The obvious manner in which the prevailing practice opposed the spirit of the limitation on the interest rate, raised the question as to whether the practice was in violation of the law. The case for allowing the charges was argued by Hamilton,[5] and the question was finally answered in an act which followed his line of reasoning to the extent of stipulating that the paying of charges was within the meaning of the limitation clause in the law.[6]

With this point firmly established high discounts came to be the standard means of making foreign loans attractive.

[1] Bayley, *op. cit.*, p. 19.

[2] It may be pointed out that this lowering of immediate disbursements of interest at the expense of increased payments at maturity had the desirable effect of diminishing the outlays during the period when the government was unable to pay, and of increasing them at a time of hoped-for strength.

[3] A full account of Jefferson's plans for issuing the 5% securities, together with his statements of the necessary discount, was aired in one of his letters. (Bayley, *op. cit.*, p. 21.)

[4] See Table.

[5] *American State Papers*, vol. i, no. 28, p. 109.

[6] *Act Mar. 3, 1791*, 1 Stat, at Large 218, ch. 25.

With regard to domestic loans, we must differentiate among four types according to the means for securing their acceptance. First, there were the loans given in exchange for outstanding securities.[1] In the case of these issues the rate as well as the provision for exchange was definitely fixed by law. There was accordingly no question as to interest rates and no possibility of discounts or commissions.

The same argument applies to a second type in which securities were issued in payment of the government's obligations to specified creditors.[2]

A third type of arrangement was made with the banks including both the Bank of North America and the Bank of New York. With the exception of the two million dollars borrowed as a subscription loan from the Bank of the United States in 1791,[3] loans from this source were designated as temporary loans, but were in reality loans of long duration.[4] The rates of interest were either 5% or 6% and the obligations were always placed at par.

A final group of loans consisted of three domestic issues which were apparently placed on the basis of their financial appeal. On one of these, namely, the 6% stock of 1796[5] the nominal rate was limited by Statute to the 6% which it carried but the selling price resulted in proceeds of only

[1] See Table, Loans 21, 22, 23, 36, 37, 45, and 46. (These included (1) the 6% stock of 1790, (2) the deferred 6s of 1790, (3) the 3% stock, (4) the 5½% stock of 1795, (5) the 4½% stock of 1795, (6) the exchanged 6% stock of 1807, and (7) the converted 6% stock of 1807.)

[2] This type is exemplified by the debt due foreign officers; Loan No. 18. (See also *American State Papers*, vol. 1, p. 146) by the Louisiana 6% stock (Loan No. 44), and by the Navy 6% stock (Loan No. 41). Bayley, *op. cit.*, p. 43, attributes to Hamilton the idea of issuing stock in payment for vessels.

[3] Loan No. 24.

[4] See Loans 25 to 35; 38; 39; 47.

[5] Loan 40.

87½. Furthermore although this loan was opened in 1796, (before the sale of the bank stock) no bids were received and almost two years elapsed before the paltry sum of $80,000 was finally realized at a private sale.[1]

In the same year under the authority of an Act in which the rate of interest was not limited, an 8% security was placed at par.[2] In 1900 an 8% stock[3] sold at 105.6. Since this loan was not to be repaid until after fifteen years, the net yield would be in excess of the interest rate appearing in the limitations set in other acts and even farther above the nominal rate of the loans. And yet a report on the financial conditions of the time[4] gives evidence that these figures reflect in a fair way a normal rate of interest for the period. This fact gives telling proof of the effectiveness of the government's efforts to keep the nominal rate of interest down to a low level. We have already observed not a few examples of attempt to achieve this aim. Actual discounts were used in making the foreign loans attractive; lack of a satisfactory alternative induced those who exchanged old securities to accept the new on a non-remunerative basis; the peculiar exigencies of the banking arrangement prevailed upon the banks to absorb the temporary loans, the desirability of making a sale induced France and shipbuilders to accept securities, while only three loans out of the forty-seven which were issued previous to 1812 were really placed upon a commercial basis and at the same time issued without camouflaging the actual rate.

[1] *American State Papers*, Fin., vol. ii, p. 564 f. n.

[2] Loan 42.

[3] Table, Loan 43. See footnote, p. 19.

[4] *Report of Ways and Means Com. on conditions of Treas. Dept.*, Jan. 28, 1801. *American State Papers*, Finance, vol. 1, p. 692.

APPOPRIATION OF SPECIAL REVENUES

The plan of accompanying a bond issue with a provision for using specified revenues for paying interest on the debt or retiring it will be easily recognized as an arrangement which should add to the security of the loan.

Following Hamilton's idea that a debt should be accompanied by the means for its extinguishment,[1] financiers of the period resorted extensively to the practice of thus connecting revenue with financing. The result was that import and tonnage duties were commonly appropriated while proceeds from the sale of public lands,[2] the income from duties on spirits distilled in the United States,[3] dividends on bank stock owned by the government,[4] and even the income from certain building lots,[5] were pledged for the purpose of reenforcing the government's ability to meet specified obligations.

In the course of time, there occured not a few changes in the methods of making appropriations, especially in regard to import and tonnage duties. The blanket appropriation of revenues for payment of interest was at times modified to include a provision that any surplus over and above the amounts necessary for the payment of interest was to be used in extinguishing the principal of the debt. The apparent intention of using any surplus after current expenses of the government had been met was made more concrete by the specific reservation of a definite amount for governmental expenditures,[6] by stipulating that only surplus proceeds

[1] *Treas. Report*, 1790-1814, vol. i, p. 61.

[2] *Act of Aug. 4, 1790*, 1 Stat. at Large 138, ch. 34, sec. 22, p. 144.

[3] *Act of Mar. 3, 1795*, 1 Stat. at Large 433, ch. 45, sec. 7, p. 424.

[4] *Act of June 4, 1794*, 1 Stat. at Large 372, ch. 40, sec. 2.

[5] *Act of May 6, 1796*, 1 Stat. at Large 461, ch. 21, sec. 2.

[6] *Act Aug. 4, 1790*, 1 Stat. at Large 138, ch. 34, sec. 1.

were to be used, or by referring to proceeds not otherwise appropriated.[1]

Since import and tonnage duties constituted the principal source of revenue,[2] one can readily see that these modifications resulted in changing what were ostensibly specific appropriations into the equivalent of a promise that the Treasury would use funds from specified sources only if it proved convenient to do so.[3]

On the other hand such provisions as those pertaining to the use of the proceeds of public lands, and to setting aside the dividends from bank stock, and one stipulating that certain appropriated duties should continue to be collected until the debt was paid[4] undoubtedly supplied a real basis for added confidence in the security of the affected obligations.

Two other developments are of some importance: One had to do with the method of making appropriations and affords an interesting sequel to the story already told. Beginning with the *Act of April 28, 1802*,[5] Congress was authorized to appropriate a definite annual amount to the sinking fund for purposes of debt retirement.

The second development to which we refer was the practice of issuing securities in anticipation of specified revenues and it illustrates the maximum use to which the idea of speci-

[1] *Act Aug. 4, 1791*, 1 Stat. at Large 138, ch. 34, sec. 20, p. 144; *Act Mar. 3, 1791*, 1 Stat. at Large 222, ch. 28, sec. 15, p. 224; *Act May 2, 1792*, 1 Stat. at Large 259, ch. 27, sec. 15, p. 262; *Act Mar. 3, 1791*, 1 Stat. at Large 199, ch. 15, sec. 60, p. 213; *Act May 8, 1792*, 1 Stat, at Large 281, ch. 38, sec. 7, p. 283; *Act Feb. 28, 1795*, 1 Stat. at Large 325, ch. 18, sec. 2, p. 328; *Act May 31, 1794*, 1 Stat. at Large 371, ch. 37, sec. 2; *Act Dec. 18, 1794*, 1 Stat. at Large 404, ch. 4, sec. 1.

[2] See Dewey, *op. cit.*, p. 110 for table.

[3] This truth was virtually admitted on one occasion by Hamilton who stated that the government was pledging its general credit. (*American State Papers*, Finance, vol. i, p. 200.)

[4] *Act of March 3, 1795*, 1 Stat. at Large 433, ch. 45, sec. 6.

[5] 2 Stat. at Large 167, ch. 32, sec. 1.

fic appropriation can be put.[1] This practice is significant because of the manner in which later financiers have resorted to it as a means of giving security to the temporary or floating debt.

PRICE MAINTENANCE

A definite program of price maintenance was instituted by Hamilton in an effort to avoid the depreciation of prices of government securities on the domestic markets, as well as to prevent the purchase of low-priced securities by foreigners. The law in setting up the machinery for carrying out Hamilton's idea provided for the application of all surplus of duties, after meeting appropriations, to the purchase of the debt of the United States at its market price, if not above par or true value. A loan of two million dollars was authorized for the same purpose.[2]

In keeping with the provisions made in this law, periodic purchases were made.[3] The final figures are as of Decem-

[1] Thus, the commissioners of the sinking fund on one occasion were authorized to borrow one million dollars in any year in anticipation of revenues (*Act Mar. 3, 1795*, 1 Stat. at Large 433, ch. 45, sec. 1.) while at another time they were authorized to borrow two million dollars in anticipation of direct taxes. (*Act of July 16, 1798*, 1 Stat. at Large 607, ch. 84.)

[2] *Act of Aug. 12, 1790*, 1 Stat. at Large 186, ch. 47, sec. 4. "It being desirable by all just and proper means, to effect a reduction of the amount of the public debt, and as the application of such surplus of the revenue as may remain after satisfying the purposes for which appropriations shall have been made by law, will not only contribute to that desirable end, but will be beneficial to the creditors of the United States, by raising the price of their stock, and be productive of considerable saving to the United States. Sec. 1. Be it enacted," etc. (*Cf.* Bolles, *op. cit.*, pp. 44-45: "The object of providing the means to buy the debt so early, even though obtainable only by borrowing, was to enhance the value of the debt, and restore the credit of the nation."

[3] *American State Papers*, vol. 1; Dec. 1790, p. 81; Nov. 1791, p. 111; Nov. 1792, p. 162; Dec. 1793, p. 252; Nov. 1794, p. 302; Dec. 1795, p. 366.

ber 18, 1795 and show purchases of $2,307,661.71 par value and of $1,618,936.04 in specie. That the buying represented bona-fide purchases in the market as distinct from redemptions is made clear by the fact that a line of demarcation is drawn between the two. The figure for purchases remains at the level quoted for 1795, whereas redemptions continue to mount up.[1]

This fact serves to mark the buying activities of the early nineties as a clear-cut attempt to influence security prices by means of market operations. Hamilton, looking back on purchases made prior to February 1793, professed to see proof that the attempt had been successful.[2]

THE SINKING FUND

Since the establishment of a sinking fund may be expected to exert some influence upon the public's belief as to the possibility of a loan's being repaid, and since actual purchases may be relied upon to bolster up market prices, we find it necessary to treat the sinking fund in connection with its bearing on financing.

The major development in the period under discussion and one not uncommon in other eras of history, grew out of the inability of the sinking fund to meet its obligations.

The Act itself[3] placed the management of the debt in the hands of the Commissioners who in turn found that revenues were insufficient to meet obligations. It was accordingly necessary to resort to a series of loans.[4]

[1] *American State Papers,* vol. i, p. 465.

[2] "It was important in two relations", he declared in reference to market operations, "as it regarded the advantages to the Government, from redeeming a portion of the debt at low prices; and still more as it regarded the savings to the country from raising the price of stock on foreign purchases; . . . .". *American State Papers,* vol. i, p. 203.

[3] *Act of May 8, 1792,* ch. 38, sec. 6, p. 282.

[4] Thus an *Act of March 3, 1795* (1 Stat. at Large, ch. 45, Sec. 1)

Another development which likewise became common in our financial history grew out of a restriction against the purchase of securities at prices above par.[1] When prices of government securities went above par during the latter part of the period, the Commissioners were consequently paralyzed as far as their ability to reduce the debt was concerned.[2]

This situation elicited from Gallatin a recommendation to the effect that redemptions be allowed at the market price.[3]

Looked at as a whole the purchasing activities of the sinking fund would appear to be of little importance, due at first to a lack of means, and later to a lack of authority to purchase when prices exceeded par. We may accordingly conclude that the reaction of the sinking fund upon the task of financing was largely confined to whatever psychological effect was produced upon the market by the existence of machinery which was supposed to operate but which failed to do so.

EXEMPTION

The Antwerp loan of Nov. 1891, was distinctive in that it was the only loan of the period which expressly stipulated that the securities were to be tax-exempt.

THE FIRST BANK OF THE UNITED STATES AS AN AID TO THE TREASURY

The relations between the treasury and the first bank of the United States can be understood only after an analysis

empowered the Commissioners to borrow for the purpose of paying interest on the public debt an amount not exceeding one million dollars in any one year in anticipation of revenue.

[1] *Act of March 3, 1795,* 1 Stat. at Large 433, ch. 45, sec. 12, p. 437. *Act of April 18, 1806,* 2 Stat, at Large 405, ch. 50.

[2] *Treas. Report,* vol. i, 1790-1814, p. 333 (1806).

[3] See Gallatin's letter to the Committee on Ways and Means, *ibid,* p. 347.

of the basic theory upon which the bank was organized. Hamilton, it will be recalled, saw in the bank possibilities of an organization capable of lending material assistance to the Treasury in its financial operations. In his eyes the bank was a gigantic political machine which could, and perhaps should, be manipulated so as to assist the government in many ways.[1]

Our interest in the bank grows out of the fact that this idea was in a measure carried out—at least to the extent that the bank afforded an important source of revenue.

The story may be taken up with a consideration of certain provisions in the charter itself. The government was to own one-fifth of the stock, but this stock was to be paid for immediately out of the proceeds of a long-time loan. Thus the government was a nominal rather than an actual contributor to the bank.[2]

Every indication points to the fact that even this first transaction was not an even trade. In other words, shares in a strong financial institution must, even at that time, have appeared more attractive than did the government's obligaions. Subsequent developments proved the former investment not only the more secure, but also productive of the

[1] Hamilton's Report on Banks, Dec. 13, 1790 in *Treas. Reports,* vol. 1, p. 54. Also, *American State Papers,* vol. i, Finance, p. 67. That Gallatin was in agreement with Hamilton on many points as regards the desirable relation with the bank is apparent from the writings of the former who declared that the bank (upon recharting) should be compelled to lend as much as three-fifths of the capital to the government. The government's privilege of borrowing from the bank, he declared, was far more valuable than any bonus which could be exacted. (*American State Papers*, Fin., vol. ii, p. 351) Clarke, *op. cit.*, p. 15.

[2] The familiar story of how the government's allotment of stock was paid for by the ingenious method of drawing bills upon the Commissioners in Amsterdam, taking the bills to the bank and having them returned as proceeds of the loan which the bank simultaneously extended to the treasury, discloses the true nature of the transaction. (Report of Hamilton, Jan. 23, 1793. *American State Papers*, Finance, vol. i, p. 193.

higher return. Even in the early years of the bank's history, its dividends were well in excess of the interest which the government was supposed to pay, while the net result of the entire period of operation showed that the government's venture into banking was highly profitable.

Our primary interest in the government as an owner, however, arises out of the fact that it enjoyed certain privileges as a favored stockholder, rather than because of the fact that it found its venture a profitable one. These privileges permitted the Treasury to make periodic calls for financial assistance, and resulted in material help in times of great need.

Although the original charter had placed a limit of one hundred thousand dollars on loans to the government,[1] this restriction could be set aside by an act of Congress. Authorizations [2] were accordingly obtained as often as the weak treasury of a struggling nation felt that it needed the financial support of a strong semi-private institution. Borrowings during the period 1792 to 1798 alone amounted to more than ten million dollars.[3] Furthermore, the records indicate that the officials of the government did not even consider the bank loans as obligations to be met upon maturity. In a statement showing the sums required for meeting maturing obligations Secretary Wolcott excluded all bank maturities and accompanied his action with the following significant statement: "It being evident that these loans, especially those which will fall due in the course of the ensuing year

[1] *Act of Incorporation—Act of Feb. 25, 1791,* 1 Stat. at Large 191, ch. 10, sec. 11, p. 194.

[2] For material which bears on the status of the Treasury, the authorization of loans, and other aspects of the Treasury's relations with the bank, see "Communication of Alexander Hamilton to Randolph and in Turn Submitted to George Washington and the Senate." Jan. 25, 1795. *American State Papers,* Fin., vol. i, pp. 350-351. Holdsworth, *The First Bank of the United States,* pp. 43-44.

[3] Dewey, *op. cit.*, p. 112.

must be continued by new contracts, the annual interest only is introduced into the general statement which is annexed." [1]

Even the plan of commuting the debt to the bank may be looked upon as an attempt to facilitate further loans and thereby to prolong a profitable relationship.[2] In the course of time, however, the one-sided nature of the relationship gave rise to objections from both the bank's president and its board of directors.[3] From this source also came the suggestion that the situation could not be remedied by an authorization which carried the usual restriction against sale below par. Congress compromised by inserting a unique provision that half of the 6% stock could be sold at less than par. Faced with a failure to raise funds from this and other loans,[5] the government had no alternative but that of disposing of its holdings of bank stock. The episode marked the end of one aspect of a relationship which had proved most productive as a means of securing funds for operating the government.

Before leaving the subject, we should refer to an interesting arrangement whereby the government secured a loan from the Bank of North America upon the condition that funds be left on deposit. By resorting to this plan, the Treasury actually accomplished the goal toward which other devices worked but which they never attained—a loan without interest.[6]

By way of summary, we may point out that the first Bank of the United States was designed with the intention that it should be utilized by the Treasury and, furthermore, that

[1] *American State Papers*, vol. i, p. 372, Dec. 31, 1795.

[2] *Ibid.*

[3] *American State Papers*, Finance, vol. i, p. 412.

[4] *Act of May 31, 1796*, 1 Stat. at Large 488, ch. 44, sec. 3, p. 489.

[5] *Supra*, p. 19 *et seq.*

[6] *American State Papers*, vol. i, p. 198.

it had numerous opportunties to display its usefulness. In the words of one writer it appeared that "the Bank of the United States accommodated the Government whenever called upon and continued the loans to suit its convenience." [1] The number and magnitude of the loans lead us to believe that during the period in question the government's power to command the resources of the bank was of more value to the Treasury than were all the technical financing devices at its disposal.

RECEIVABILITY

A step which proved to be the forerunner of numerous measures of similar type was taken in 1797 when an act authorized that payment for public lands could be made in securities of the United States.[2]

An interesting example of an application of the receivability feature is also to be found in the privilege of paying import duties with bank notes. This arrangement at first arose as a consequence of Hamilton's idea that bank notes should be considered as being equivalent to specie, and received authorization in the Bank Act itself.[3]

Still another manifestation of the principle of receivability arose during the early part of the period and again it was in connection with the Bank of the United States. Under the plan for the disposition of the bank stock, government securities were receivable for three fourths of the amount of the subscription.[4]

[1] Holdsworth, *op. cit.*, p. 44.

[2] *Act of Mar. 3*, 1 Stat. at Large 507, ch. 14. The *Act of April 18, 1806* (2 Stat. at Large 405, ch. 50, sec. 1) repealed this measure and provided compensation for purchasers who had been discriminated against in that they had paid specie for bonds instead of taking advantage of the privilege of remitting in the form of depreciated securities.

[3] Holdsworth, *op. cit.*, pp. 49-50. The *Act of Incorporation, Act of Feb. 25, 1791*, 1 Stat. at Large 191, ch. 10, sec. 10, p. 196.

[4] *Act of Incorporation, op. cit.*, sec. 2, p. 192.

REFUNDING AS "POST-MORTEM"[1] CONVERSION

The Post-Revolutionary period with its refunding activities furnished abundant illustrations of the common practice of exchanging new securities for outstanding obligations. The privilege of exchanging old securities for new may be regarded as a type of conversion which is distinguished by the fact that the privilege is accorded to the security not when it is issued but at the time of the emission of the obligation into which it is convertible. The action comes after the convertible securities have been sold and involves looking backward with the aim of reviewing the conditions of the financing contract rather than forward with the intention of influencing the market for the convertible securities. The term "Post-Mortem Convertibility" is accordingly fairly descriptive of the nature of the privilege.

While this type of conversion did not invite the complications which later characterized other varieties, frequent acts[2] providing for extensions of time in which conversions could be made give evidence that even the simple task of securing an exchange of securities was not accomplished without some difficulty.

[1] This term is used by the writer to cover the type of conversion described.

[2] *Act of May 8, 1792,* 1 Stat. at Large 281, ch. 38, sec. 1; *Act of Mar. 2, 1793,* 1 Stat. at Large, 338. ch. 26, sec. 1; *Act of May 30, 1794,* 1 Stat. at Large 370, ch. 36; *Act Jan. 28, 1795,* 1 Stat. at Large 410, ch. 13; *Act Feb. 19, 1796,* 1 Stat. at Large 448, ch. 2; *Act Mar. 3, 1797,* 1 Stat. at Large 516, ch. 25; *Act June 12, 1798,* 1 Stat. at Large 562, ch. 51. *Act Mar. 2, 1795,* 1 Stat. at Large 338, ch. 26. Also, Bayley, *op. cit.*, p. 115, and *Act of April 13, 1818,* 3 Stat. at Large 425, ch. 56; *Act of July 14, 1832,* 4 Stat. at Large 602, ch. 245. Also, *Act of May 7, 1822,* 3 Stat. at Large 696, ch. 112.

CHAPTER II

The 1812 Period

FINANCING POLICIES AND PRE-WAR CONDITIONS

GALLATIN'S early confidence in loans as a means of financing government operations was undoubtedly due to pre-war conditions, among them a market in which government securities were above par.[1]

The Secretary's views in this matter, although modified later,[2] continued to determine the actions of the Treasury to the extent that the department could be[3] influenced by political and official pressure toward avoiding taxation and depending upon loans. The various aspects of this tendency[4] are so familiar that we need do no more than refer to the subject and point out that the difficult situations into which the government was forced as a result of this preference supplied a fertile breeding ground for financing features and devices. As a result, the history of the period is replete with material pertinent to our topic.

[1] *Treas. Report*, vol. i, p. 333 (1806), p. 359 (1807). *American State Papers*, vol. ii, p. 412 (1810).

[2] *Treas. Reports*, vol. i, p. 449 (1811). *American State Papers*, vol. ii, p. 412 (1801) and p. 523 (1812).

[3] Report of Com. on Ways and Means, Feb. 17, 1812, *American State Papers*, vol. ii, p. 539. In this report the amount of desirable revenue was given as a sum sufficient to meet current expenses plus the interest on the existing debt.

[4] *Abridgement of Debates in Congress*, vol. v, pp. 174 and 221-223. *Treas. Report*, vol. i, p. 491, vol. ii, pp. 6-8.

EARLY EFFORTS TO AVOID A LOSS FROM CONVERSION

Early in 1812, a loan of $11,000,000 was authorized [1] and offered to the public.[2] Little more than $6,000,000 of this amount was subscribed.[3] Soon thereafter the trend of events, including the declaration of war on June 12th, forced the price of government stock down below par.[4] To offer the remaining four and one half million dollars of stock on more favorable terms than had been accorded to the first subscribers would not, according to Gallatin,[5] be desirable because of the consequent obligation [6] to give equivalent terms to the first subscribers. The Secretary accordingly found himself on the horns of a dilemma from which, it must be admitted, he extricated himself in a very graceful manner. He simply refrained from selling any more stock and chose to secure the desired funds by issuing treasury notes which, thanks to his efforts, had been authorized by a new act.[7]

By thus resorting to a new authorization to issue a different form of security, the Treasury avoided conversion claims from holders of convertible stock.

USING THE CURRENCY FEATURE IN SHORT-TERM FINANCING

The situation described above discloses that the switch to treasury notes was motivated primarily by a desire to avoid the payment of bonuses to holders of the old stock. It is accordingly of interest to find that in this case as well as on later occasions the government found it possible to secure

1 *Act of Mar. 14, 1812*, 2 Stat. at Large 694, ch. 41.

2 *American State Papers*, vol. ii, p. 564-565.

3 *Ibid.*

4 *American State Papers*, vol. ii, p. 569.

5 *American State Papers*, Fin., vol. ii, p. 569. *Cf.* Adams, *Public Debts* (New York, 1890), p. 169.

6 *Cf.* Adams, *op. cit.*, p. 169.

Act of June 30, 1812, 2 Stat. at Large 766, ch. 3.

funds from note issues at an interest rate considerably below that of long-term loans. Probably the low rate accounts for the fact that this type of security came to be looked upon as the cornerstone of the financial structure of the period. The evolution of the idea is of some interest.

Even at an early date when Gallatin described treasury notes as a means of anticipating revenue, he proceeded to refer to them as one of three major channels through which funds could be obtained advantageously.[1] Discussions from time to time [2] leave little doubt that he later came to believe in certain advantages of short-term obligations. Not the least among these advantages was that widespread appreciation of the state of affairs made the issue of this type of security politically feasible.[3]

The political aspects of the subject can be appreciated if we refer to some of the ideas which were advanced. One legislator [4] declared that "Any plan (for a bank) will answer my purpose that promises to restore public credit and create a circulating medium." Another defended an ingenious argument based on the view that if the government was going to resort to treasury notes, it might as well issue paper money directly.[5]

[1] *American State Papers*, Fin., vol. ii, p. 412.

[2] *Ibid.*, pp. 523 and 569.

[3] *Abridgement of Debates in Congress*, vol. v, pp. 361 and 383.

[4] Mr. Ingham, *Debates*, vol. v, p. 371.

[5] Former borrowing, it was claimed, had been only from banks or from individuals who made the banks the means of complying with their engagements. Such additional lendings would now be possible only on the condition that United States stock continued to be a fair and safe basis for the banks' issue of paper. Thus, so ran the argument, the entire system was on a tottering fabric of credit, with the government relying on the credit of the banks and the banks on the credit of the government. If confidence was thus to be the basis of operation, it was asked, why not take the more direct route, issue government paper directly, and save the interest?

(*Debates*, vol. v, p. 202, Mr. Montgomery, Feb. 14, 1814.)

Some of these ideas soon received more concrete expression in the form of a series of resolutions introduced by Mr. Hall. One provided for full receivability on the part of treasury notes, and a second declared them legal tender for all debts. The legal tender resolution mustered 42 supporters from the house members who voted. The support which these proposals gained from the left wing brings into bold relief the conservative nature of Gallatin's opinions. On one occasion he declared that treasury notes could be emitted only "to a certain extent".[2] At another time he stated that he preferred to use direct inducements instead of resorting to "any operation which might injuriously affect the circulating medium of the country."[3]

Thus far we have indicated first, that there existed an insistent demand for a circulating medium; secondly, we have shown that there was not a little pressure in favor of impressing short-term obligations into service in this capacity. While we fail to find evidence that the treasury entertained any idea that treasury notes should dominate as a circulating medium, we do find every indication of the presence of a belief that "Treasury notes were in their design and ought to be in their use, a species of circulating media."[4]

In other words, there was a decided tendency to utilize the

[1] *Abridgement of Debates*, vol. v, p. 361, Nov. 12, 1814. (For a significant comment by Mr. Dallas, see *Niles Register*, Oct. 17, 1814. "Whether the issue of a paper currency proceeds from the National Treasury or a National bank, the acceptance of the paper in a course of payment and receipts must be forever optional with the citizens." Later quoted by James Gallatin in a letter to Mr. Hooper under date of April 20, 1864.)

[2] *Abridgement of Debates*, vol. v, p. 361. *Cf.* Dewey, *op. cit.*, p. 135.

[3] *Treas. Report*, vol. i, p. 449.

[4] *American State Papers*, Fin., vol. ii, p. 916. Letter from Dallas to Eppes, Feb. 24, 1815. A claim that treasury notes failed in this purpose is to be found in *Treas. Reports*, 1815-28, p. 25.

existing situation in a way that would facilitate the effort to dispose of notes.[1] This was to be achieved simply by an application of such features as would make the treasury notes occupy the place of the much needed currency.

RECEIVABILITY AS A MEANS OF MAKING NOTES CURRENT

A statement by Gallatin discloses the fact that he looked upon the receivability feature as of more value in placing the notes than was either their security or the interest they bore.[2] One also gains the impression that he depended upon the receivability feature to secure the acceptance of the notes among the circulating media of the country.[3]

A study of prevailing conditions enables us to understand his confidence. Prices, at least after the suspension of specie payment, were judged by the kind of currency to be used as well as by the magnitude of the figure which followed the dollar mark. The government itself discriminated among the currencies and against some of its own obligations.[4]

In the face of such conditions, Gallatin could logically expect the usual advantages of receivability to be emphasized

[1] *American State Papers*, vol. iii, p. 116. Dallas to Calhoun.

[2] *American State Papers*, vol. ii, p. 569. For an earlier statement see *ibid.*, p. 412.

[3] Mr. Hanson later criticized the receivability feature by pointing out that the notes had been made receivable for the very revenue upon which the sinking fund depended. The sinking fund in turn was supposed to impart the value to the securities. (*Abridgement of Debates*, Feb. 14, 1814, vol. v, p. 192.) As a matter of fact his reference to the Sinking Fund's responsibility for the repayment of treasury notes is somewhat misleading. The Act of Dec. 26, 1814 stipulated that both principal and interest of the treasury notes were chargeable against any money in the Treasury not otherwise appropriated. In others words, the Sinking Fund was not charged with the payment. In the main, however, the critic's general argument against receivability is valid. See also *American State Papers*, vol. ii, p. 917, and *Treas. Report*, vol. ii, p. 13.

[4] *American State Papers*, vol. iii, p. 25. *Treas. Report*, vol. ii, p. 25.

at two important points. In the first place, the mere right to dispose of notes at par by using them in payments to the government was of particular value during this time of fluctuating currencies. Secondly, the absence of a satisfactory currency left a vacuum which financiers could attempt to fill with government obligations.

As to ability of the notes to fill the vacuum, we may point out that, thanks to the receivability feature, treasury notes introduced a desirable element of stability at least in a portion of the financial transactions of the country. The satisfactory level at which the market for these obligations was maintained during the entire period,[1] is undoubtedly to be explained by reference to the manner in which they substituted for currency. The same explanation accounts for the ease with which the government placed short-time loans when loans were not obtainable from sales of stock.[2]

Before leaving the subject of receivability, we may give an account of its later progress.

Post-war history witnessed two developments which served to diminish the importance of the feature. In the first place, a depreciated bank currency brought the principal of receivability, at least with regard to bank notes, into disrepute. Secretary Dallas was responsible for a specific proposal to the effect that after a certain date it would be lawful to receive in payment to the United States only coins constituting the national currency and notes of such banks as would pay their notes on demand in the lawful money of the United States.[3] In the second place, the fall of the receivability feature was made complete as a result of the trend of market prices, not only of the notes themselves, but also of

[1] *American State Papers*, Fin., vol. iii, p. 1, Dec. 8, 1815, also Dewey, p. 137.

[2] *American State Papers*, vol. ii, p. 917.

[3] *American State Papers*, vol. iii, p. 116, Mar. 8, 1816.

the stock with which the notes were associated by virtue of the privilege of converting notes into stock.[1]

When stock prices were above par, the privilege of exchanging the notes for stock was of course exercised in preference to the privilege of receiving par credit for notes extended to the government in payment of dues. As a result, proffers of notes in payment of dues ceased.[2] These developments explain why there was an absence of mourners when receivability died at the hands of Congress.[3]

The manner in which one feature thus worked in the direction of making another worthless calls to mind a similar development in connection with attempts to endow treasury notes with the characteristics of acceptable currency. In one of the later authorizations,[4] for treasury notes, the act itself provided for an interesting combination of features. Treasury notes in denominations above a hundred dollars were issued on the usual terms (including the 5⅖% interest) except that the only provision for repayment was through conversion into the 6% treasury note stock of 1815. The notes were payable to order. Under the same act authorization was given for the issue of non-interest bearing notes, in denominations of less than a hundred dollars, payable to bearer, and convertible into the 7% stock of 1815.

The arrangement for ease in transferring, the smallness of the denominations, and the absence of interest, give

[1] The *Act of Nov. 15, 1814*, 3 Stat. at Large 144, ch. 4, made treasury notes due on or before Jan. 1, 1815, receivable in payment for this or future loans.

The *Act of Mar. 3, 1815*, 3 Stat. at Large 227, ch. 87, made any treasury notes actually issued receivable in payment of the loan. The amount of the loan was identical with the amount of the notes outstanding and the purpose of the issue was that of funding the temporary debt.

[2] *Treas. Report* (1817), vol. ii, p. 92.

[3] *Act of May 3, 1822*, 3 Stat. at Large 675, ch. 47.

[4] *Act of Feb. 24, 1815*, 3 Stat. at Large 213, ch. 56.

sufficient evidence to convince us that it was the purpose of the administration to secure the placement of the notes as a circulating medium. It would accordingly seem that the operation of the privilege of converting into 7% stock as well as of using the notes in payment of all dues to the government, was not understood by the Treasury. In any event, these two features led to an almost immediate return of the notes after they were emitted, so that the Treasury was defeated in its attempt to find a permanent place for them among the circulating media of the country.[1]

The experience serves to stamp the act of Feb. 24, 1815 as one of several haphazard attempts to use a number of features without an adequate appreciation of their inter-relationships.

Having discussed treasury notes, their resemblance to currency, and the manner in which the receivability feature made them current, we now turn to a consideration of the long-term loans. Our interest in some of the features developed in connection with this type of financing warrants a somewhat detailed account of the most important borrowing operations.

DIFFICULTIES WITH CONVERSION

An important step in the direction of securing permanent funds was taken early in 1813. By this time, conditions in the money market were such, that it was obviously impossible to sell a 6% stock under the conventional requirement that sales should not be made at less than par. Fortunately for the Treasury however, Congress acceded to Gallatin's request [2] and conveniently omitted all limitations as to rate of interest and terms, settling only the amount to be raised.[3]

[1] *Treas. Report*, vol. ii, 1815-1827, pp. 25-26.

[2] *American State Papers*, vol. ii, p. 523.

[3] *Act of Feb. 8, 1813*, 2 Stat. at Large 798, ch. 21.

Gallatin's victory over Congress was offset, however, by what one might designate as poor judgment in exercising the discretion for which he had fought. The evaluation of demand led to an offer of a thirteen-year annuity as a bonus on a six per cent stock.[1] The offer aroused so little response [2] that the Treasury was led to dicker with the public to the extent of inviting proposals.[3] As a result the terms on the loan were set by two offers to take large blocks of the stock at 88 upon condition that the subscribers be given an option on any terms offered in 1813.[4]

Three significant aspects of the development serve to reflect upon the Secretary's ability to carry out his own ideas of what should be done.

In the first place, the desirability of having outside interests dictate the Treasury's policies might well have been questioned, especially since topics other than price were involved. As a matter of fact it appears that this episode marked the first of three deals in which the independence of the Treasury was undermined.[5]

In the second place, it is obvious that Gallatin's action in issuing $18,000,000 in obligations in order to secure $16,000,000 in funds, ran counter to his earlier contention that attempts to reduce the annual interest payment should never result in the issue of an amount of stock greater than the sum actually borrowed.[6]

Finally, the conversion privilege as dictated by the sub-

[1] *American State Papers*, vol. ii, Finance, p. 622; circular of Feb. 20, 1813. *Treas. Report*, vol. i, p. 493.

[2] *Ibid.*, p. 646. Less than four million dollars were subscribed.

[3] *Ibid.*, p. 626, circular of Mar. 18. *Treas. Report*, vol. i, p. 496.

[4] *Ibid.*, p. 646, also p. 626, notice of April 15. *Treas. Report*, vol. i, p. 497.

[5] *Infra*, pp. 45-46.

[6] *American State Papers*, vol. ii, p. 412.

scribers and accepted by the government must be considered as a material concession to subscribers and as detrimental to the interests of the government. As it happened, the measure was most important in that it later supplied the Treasury with a precedent for a transaction which was ostensibly of the same simple type but which was in reality much more involved.[1] Even so, the subscribers had been given a privilege which was comparable to the right to a bonus.

Any intention of securing such a bonus in connection with the second loan of the year was thwarted by Congress. The authorizing act itself[2] contained the significant provision that the stock should not be sold for less than 88, although there was, to be sure, an apparent loop-hole in that there was no limitation on the rate of interest. Thanks to the courage of Congress and to the Treasury's traditions of a 6% stock, there was accordingly issued an obligation bearing 6% and not to be sold below 88. On the other hand, the financial power of one individual is to be given the credit for having established the price at $88.25.[3] The figure as set by competitive bidding was uncomfortably near the danger mark of 88.

Even this narrow escape, which should have been regarded as supplementing an earlier lesson,[4] did not bring about the abandonment of the policy in question. Moreover, although unwelcome consequences had been averted by narrow margins, the Treasury really had experienced no actual loss from the conversion feature.

[1] *Treas. Report,* vol. i, p. 527. *Infra,* p. 46.

[2] *Act of Aug. 2, 1813,* 3 Stat. at Large 75, ch. 511.

[3] *American State Papers,* Fin., vol. ii, p. 662, Jonathan Smith offered to take three million dollars in stock at that figure. His offer was accepted to the extent of $2,150,000.

[4] Experience of 1812, when Gallatin resorted to treasury notes in order to avoid the paying of a bonus to former subscribers, *supra,* p. 37.

This absence of condemning evidence against the feature left the Secretary free to refer to the precedents. He did so [1] when he came to justify his acceptance of the conversion terms as they applied to the first loan of 1814 and as they were laid down by Jacob Barker, a banker of Philadelphia.[2]

The terms in question stipulated that in return for a price of 88 the subscription was to carry with it an agreement that more advantageous terms were to be received if such were later accorded purchasers of any securities subsequently issued under the same authorization.

On the surface, the agreement did not differ from the now accepted procedure of granting to any subscriber the most favorable terms given to any purchaser. From the standpoint of the practical effects, however, it was much more objectionable because the equality of terms applied not to bids accepted simultaneously, but rather to those to be accepted at some future date when conditions might be distinctly different. The difference between this and the earlier agreements appeared in the fact that a part of the loan remained unissued. Consequently, the provision for simultaneous uniformity was transformed into one for conversion of a more inclusive sort. Since the right to convert applied only to future issues under this authorization, the arrangement was less complicated than that of the first loan of 1813 wherein there appeared a conversion privilege which applied to any loan issued during the year. Differences in the course of subsequent developments, however, again account for variations in practical results. In the earlier period, events were such as to cause the feature to be forgotten. In 1814, on the other hand, conditions ran their course in a way which made it advantageous for former subscribers to avail them-

[1] *Treas. Report*, vol. i, p. 527.

[2] *Treas. Report*, vol. i, p. 536. *Act of Mar. 24, 1814*, 3 Stat. at Large 111, ch. 29.

selves of the privilege which they had wrested from the government. As a result, conversion actually took place, and in a manner and upon such terms as to reflect upon both the wisdom of its proponents and the soundness of its underlying principle.

The details of the transactions are of interest. On the loan of May 2, the net proceeds of subscriptions actually amounted to only $7,936,581.[1] Steps to supplement this sum were taken on August 22, when a loan for six million dollars was opened.[2] Again the Treasury followed the lead set by the bidders and this time the obligations were sold at 80, with the now familiar provision of an option on any terms given to subsequent subscribers.

For our immediate purpose, the second transaction is of course of primary interest by virtue of its connection with the terms of sale on the previous issue of stock. Secretary Campbell opposed the claims of the holders who insisted upon compensation equivalent to the difference between the old price of 88 at which they had bought the stock, and the new price of 80.[3] Upon his assumption of the duties of secretary, Mr. Dallas was quick to accede to their demands. Disagreement on a number of points, however, stood in the way of a final settlement.

An examination of the facts discloses that the controversies arose at one time or another on six major questions.[4]

In the first place, it seems that contractors for the stock (Mr. Barker and others) wanted it stipulated at the time of the first loan that any subsequent bonus was to accrue to them and not to holders of the bonds. The Treasury officials de-

[1] Bayley, *op. cit.*, p. 53.

[2] *Treas. Report*, vol. i, p. 524.

[3] *Brief and Speech of Mr. Jacob Barker, of New Orleans*, N. Y. Public Library, I.A.G., p.v. 54, No. 1.

[4] Mr. Barker, *op. cit.*, *passim*.

sired the opposite arrangement and reenforced their argument by an appeal to patriotism.

The second controversy arose as a result of what was evidently an error in omitting from the shares themselves certain specifications bearing on this point.

Out of these two circumstances and the Treasury officials' realization that the original bargain was a bad one, there accordingly arose the question of whether or not supplemental stock should be issued at all. A fourth topic necessitated a decision as to whether the contractor or the holder of the original stock should receive the supplementary shares when they were issued. The debate hinged on an interpretation of the arrangement which was consummated at the time of earlier discussion of the same topic.

This unsettled nature of the entire proposition paved the way for the Treasury's effort to have those who were pressing their claims give in exchange for the supplementary stock a receipt in full covering all amounts ever to become due on account of the conversion privilege. There also followed the plan of securing from Congress a new authorization and the action of making a new deal with banks.

The sixth decision concerned what would appear to be a minor point but one which was of importance because of the manner in which it served to delay proceedings. The question had to do merely with the date for starting interest payments.

For our purpose it is unnecessary to go into a full account of developments in connection with the settlement of these questions. It is desirable, however, to point out that during the next forty years the difficulties caused by the conversion muddle continued to demand time, energy, and money. Conferences with claimants who had journeyed to Washington for that purpose, study of the problem, correspondence, legal decisions (of which there were a number) and committee work (under authority of Congress) absorbed the time of Treasury and other government officials, not excepting the President.[1]

Having suggested the nature of certain undesirable consequences of the conversion privilege, we now turn to a consideration of the pecuniary cost of the measure. Of the $9,-919,476 [2] recorded as the par value of stock issued on the first loan, $904,076,00.[3] may be taken as the amount issued at the time of the second loan and drawn from the Treasury as a result of the conversion agreement.

When this amount is considered as an additional cost to be charged against the money actually obtained on the second loan,[4] we find that the government paid rather dearly for funds. The cash proceeds of $4,307,307.90 [5] actually occasioned the issue of approximately six and one-quarter million dollars in stock.[6]

[1] A comprehensive summary of developments up to July 1, 1857 can be obtained from Mr. Barker, *op. cit., passim.* *Cf.* Bolles, *op. cit.*, p. 232.

[2] The records of the period afford no conclusive figures as to the facts of the operations under consideration. A comparison of the *Treas. Reports,* vol. i, 1814, p. 537-8, of Bolles (1789-1860), p. 229, and *Annals of Congress,* vol. 28, p. 419, leaves the impression that some of the variations are due to the fact that all of the figures do not represent the completed transactions. We have accordingly accepted he figures of Bayley, p. 52, who compiled his figures at a later date, and whose data correspond very closely with the figures found in the later Treasury Reports (*Cf. Treas. Reports,* 1815, vol. II, p. 17 and 1827, vol. II, p. 390.) From his totals for the issues we have computed the obligations which should have resulted from the conversion feature. The results will be found to differ slightly from some of the incomplete returns mentioned above, but they at least represent a continued process and thus can be used as a fair account of the workings of the feature.

[3] See Table, Loan No. 59.

[4] Subsequent costs might with equal validity be related to the issue which gave rise to them.

[5] Bayley, *op. cit.*, p. 53.

[6] Of this stock, $5,384,135 was issued on the basis of 80, while the remainder was supplementary stock issued for the purpose of satisfying the conversion claims of the holders of the previous issue.

These figures reveal the fact that the conversion agreement forced the government into a position in which the net proceeds of its lending operations were no more than if it had disposed of a share of stock at an approximate price of 66 in a clear-cut sale.

Even this distribution of stock to the earlier subscribers did not complete the transaction which was begun at the time of the original conversion agreement. While, as we have pointed out, Secretary Dallas had insisted that meeting the claims under dispute should free the government from the necessity of paying any subsequent claims of a similar nature, his offer was refused by the stockholders' representative, the same shrewd Mr. Barker who was the instigator of this veritable plot.[1]

As a result, the Treasury faced a situation very similar to the one which Gallatin had met by a switch to treasury notes. Dallas promptly secured a new authorization [2] in an attempt to duplicate the action of his resourceful predecessor. A contract was then made with banks to exchange stock for depreciated bank notes [3] of which the value was equivalent to only 65 in specie.[4]

The manoeuver was unsuccessful even from the standpoint of avoiding demands from old stockholders. The new authorization was, in the words of Bolles, so clearly an attempt to avoid the fulfillment of the conversion contract that previous subscribers hastened to enter their claims.[5] The same author gave a detailed account of how the case was contested until the government finally acknowledged that in floating the November loan at the equivalent of 65 in specie,

[1] Barker, *op. cit., passim; cf.* also Bolles, *op. cit.*, p. 232.

[2] *Act of Nov. 15, 1814,* 3 Stat. at Large 144, ch. 4.

[3] Bayley, *op. cit.*, pp. 55-56.

[4] Barker, *op. cit, passim;* Bolles, *op. cit.*, p 235; Dewey, *op. cit.*, p. 134

[5] *Cf.* also Barker, *op. cit., passim.*

it had obligated itself to place the previous issues of 1814 stock on a comparable basis.[1] Taking Bolles' figure as our basis, the sum which would have been required to meet in full the obligation is readily figured.

Paying the claims of holders of the first loan would require the issue of approximately $2,300,000 in stock. Settling those arising by virtue of the conversion privilege on the second loan would necessitate the issue of an additional one and one-quarter million dollars in new obligations. In other words, a debt of approximately three and one-half million dollars had to be assumed before funds could be obtained on a new contract.

This is especially significant when it is recalled that the net cash proceeds of the new loan amounted to less than one million dollars. Since the receipts of this sum was the immediate occasion for the issue of $1,450,000 in stock, as well as for the assumption of obligations of over three and one-half million dollars on behalf of the previous conversion agreement, it becomes evident that the government increased its obligations by over five million dollars in order to realize a sum of less than one million. In other words, the Treasury, in paying the penalty for its former actions, was securing additional funds at a cost comparable to a discount in excess of 81%. In the language of price, it was selling its securities at the equivalent of the ridiculously low figure of 19.

Since, even the administration's opponents agreed at the time of the loans that borrowing was necessary in order to avoid bankruptcy,[2] the criticism is to be leveled against the original arrangements which made possible the later difficulties, rather than against officialls who were responsible for

[1] Bolles, *op. cit.*, p. 233.

[2] *Annals of Congress*, 13th Cong., 3rd Sess., vol. 28, p. 501, Oct. 4, 1814, Mr. Grosvenor.

the last steps. The difficulties themselves furnish a strong argument against the provision which occasioned them.

CHANGES IN THE TREASURY'S POLICY

At this point it may be appropriate to mention two important changes in the Treasury's policy.

The first occurred during the depth of war-time fiscal difficulties and signalized the virtual collapse of the administration's loan policy.[1] Secretary Campbell went so far as to assert that recent experience had led him to doubt the practicability of continuing the policy of borrowing. Instead, he advocated taxation. If further reliance was to be placed upon loans he urged an increase in the rate of interest and the adoption of other inducements.[2]

The second change serves to mark the turning point away from unfavorable war-time financing as well as to throw into bold relief the difference between Secretary Dallas and his predecessors in office. Under authority of an act [3] which was most liberal in that terms were left to the discretion of the Secretary, Dallas invited bids on an issue of stock. When he found that none of the offers exceeded 89 while some ran below 75, however, the Secretary refused all bids and announced that the securities would be sold at a minimum of 95. The plan succeeded, thanks to his courage and to the arrangement for leaving the loan open in each district until enough had been sold to redeem the treasury notes offered in that locality.[4]

[1] *Treas. Reports*, vol. i, p. 528 and 531; *American State Papers*, Fin., vol. II, p. 840; Bolles, *op. cit.*, p. 235.

[2] *American State Papers*, vol. ii, Finance, p. 840, Sept. 26, 1814. His suggestion was followed by taxes on carriages and harness (*Act of Dec. 15, 1814*, 3 Stat. at Large 144, ch. 12) and duties on distilled spirits and on licenses to distillers. (*Treas. Report*, vol. II, p. 12.)

[3] *Act of Mar. 3, 1815*, 3 Stat. at Large 227, ch. 77.

[4] *Treas. Report*, vol. ii, pp. 26-28; Bolles, *op. cit.*, pp. 240-1.

DEBT RETIREMENT

As early as 1817, attention to the subject of debt retirement [1] had led to provisions for the purchase of securities by the sinking fund at specified rates.[2]

Subsequent developments in connection with such purchases served to cast several reflections upon the wisdom of war-time financing. In the first place, a poor arrangement of maturities interfered with the orderly retirement of the debt in the early twenties and again in 1829. In each instance, market operations on the part of the Treasury were made impossible through a combination of high market prices and restrictions against purchases above par. Developments in the two periods are also similar in that conditions in each gave rise to a request that purchases of securities be permitted above par,[3] and to the desired authorizing acts.[4]

During the latter period the height of market prices and the fact that the 5% stocks subscribed by the banks were subject to redemption, caused the Treasury, according to Secretary Ingham,[5] to refrain from exercising the privilege of buying.

A final chapter in the history of the sinking fund was written in 1836 when an act of July 4 transferred its powers to the Secretary of the Treasury.[6]

[1] Recommendations of Secretary Crawford, Dec. 1816. *Treas. Report*, vol. 11, p. 77.

[2] *Act of Mar. 3, 1817*, 3 Stat. at Large 379, ch. 87.

[3] *Treas. Report*, vol. ii, p. 251. *Treas. Report*, 1829, p. 9.

[4] *Act of Jan. 22, 1824*, 4 Stat. at Large 4, ch. 16. *Act of April 24, 1830*, 4 Stat. at Large 396, ch. 78.

[5] *Treas. Report*, 1830, p. 88.

[6] 5 Stat. at Large 12, ch. 353, sec. 10, p. 115.

RELATIONS WITH BANKS

Proof of the actual dependence upon the Bank of the United States during the latter part of the period is suggested by the number of instances in which this institution was authorized to make loans to the government.[1]

One of these issues [2] was sold to the bank in spite of the fact that higher bids were received elsewhere. The reason assigned for the action was that the government, in its capacity as a stockholder in the bank, stood to gain by the acceptance of what appeared to be the least profitable of two bids.[3]

Such sales to the banks, however, did not represent the customary procedure during the war. The old plan of borrowing direct from the banks was to a large extent displaced by a more roundabout process in which institutions and individuals, including bankers, bid for the stocks. In this connection, it may be pointed out that the large bids from such men as Barker, Smith, Girard, and Astor were quite obviously made by the bidders in their capacities as bankers rather than in their roles as individual investors. We may accordingly ascribe the success (if it may be so called) of the 1813 and 1814 loans to the assistance of the banks as they operated through these financiers.[4]

[1] *Act of May 15, 1820,* 3 Stat. at Large 582, ch. 173; *Act of Mar. 3, 1815,* 3 Stat. at Large 227, ch. 87; *Act of Mar. 3, 1821,* 3 Stat. at Large 635, ch. 38; *Act of May 26, 1824,* 4 Stat. at Large 73, ch. 192; *Act of Mar. 3, 1825,* 4 Stat. at Large 129, ch. 100.

[2] Under the Act of May 26, 1824.

[3] *Treas. Report,* vol. ii, pp. 283-4.

[4] Tribute to the assistance of the banks is to be found in frequent references to the amount of their subscriptions. An example is to be found in a letter to the Ways and Means Committee, in which Gallatin stated that of the first $6,118,900 which was subscribed to the loan of Mar. 1812, $4,190,000 was subscribed by banks. (*American State Papers,* vol. II, p. 564. Bolles, *op. cit.,* p. 222.)

Before leaving the subject of the Treasury's relations with the banks, we may mention that the plan of leaving the amount of the bank's subscription on deposit with the bank was utilized during the period.[1]

Finally, we may point out that while the banks contributed materially to the success of the Treasury's operations, the absence of a government bank during the period of hostilities, prevented the enforced banking support which had characterized the earlier period.[2] Instead of the government being able to enforce its plans upon the bank, therefore, we find the tables turned to the extent that strong institutions are found dictating to the Treasury.

Our survey suggests that many actions of the 1812 period are the result of the administration's false premise regarding the government's ability to borrow.

Thus the placing of notes by endowing them with the features of currency may be considered an outgrowth of the attempt to find a substitute for an expected financial strength which had failed to materialize. Similarly, only the absence of hoped-for strength can explain the Treasury's dependence in allowing outside interests to dictate the financially unfavorable and otherwise undesirable terms which characterize the period.

For our purpose, the most important aspect of the subject is the form which the unfavorable terms took and the nature of the resulting burden. In no other period of our history do we find such interesting developments in connection with the use of the conversion feature. With a record of two narrow escapes from undesirable consequences before them, Treasury officials deliberately chose to grant the conversion privilege in exchange for a slight saving in the rate of interest. Unfortunately, the market trend did not come to

[1] *American State Papers*, vol. i, p. 198 and vol. ii, p. 566.

[2] *Treas. Report*, 1814, p. 528. *Cf.* Dewey, *op. cit.*, p. 133.

their rescue as it had in similar cases. We are accordingly able to refer to the conversion muddle of this period as an outstanding example of the undesirable consequences which may follow in the wake of the unwise use of security features.

CHAPTER III

Short Term Financing and the Resulting Security Features (1837-1857)

SIGNIFICANT ASPECTS OF FINANCIAL THEORY AND STRUCTURE

Events of the period from 1837 to the beginning of the Civil War appear to have been conditioned by the following seven major factors.

1. There was no provision for meeting irregular demands upon the Treasury.

2. Fluctuations in revenue proved particularly embarassing especially when low income was matched with high outlays.[1]

3. A large portion of the Treasury's assets were in the form of deposits with banks and with the states, and were not available for meeting current needs.[2]

4. There existed an antipathy toward borrowing in general and toward funded debts in particular—especially when the proceeds of a loan were to be used in peace times.[3]

5. The objections to banks were utilized for the purpose of strengthening the opposition to loans.[4]

[1] *Treas. Report*, 1837, *passim* and Bolles, *op. cit.*, pp. 554-555.

[2] *Treas. Report*, 1837-1844, p. 8; *Congress Debates*, 25th Cong., 1st Sess., vol. xiv, pt. ii, pp. 1239 and 1259.

[3] *Treas. Report*, vol. iii, p. 361. For an alternative method of meeting deficiencies see *ibid.*, p. 184. For examples of Whig arguments for borrowing to meet the debt which they claimed existed, see *Cong. Globe*, 26th Cong., 1st Sess., pp. 113 and 114 and *ibid.*, p. 147.

[4] *Cong. Globe*, 25th Cong., 2nd Sess., vol. vi, p. 386, May 18, 1838.

6. The ever present prejudice against foreigners was also revived by the opponents of borrowing. Its use in crystallizing popular sentiment is typified by a statement of Mr. Biddle, in which be expressed fear that the notes of 1837 were to find their resting place in London and were to constitute a " new form of loan from the detested Barings ".[1]

This idea of avoiding the taking of loans by foreign capitalists, combined with the desire to reduce annual payments affords an explanation of a proposal to issue treasury notes at low interest or at no interest at all.[2]

7. Political strategy influenced the Treasury's action. The very facts and theories to which we have referred gave rise to converging streams of thought which undoubtedly served to strengthen the flow of opposition to government borrowings. Furthermore, having taken a stand on the subject, the Democratic Party gradually worked itself into a position in which it was forced to defend its every action in the light of the effect upon the public debt situation. Consequently, when the vicissitudes of financial and economic life continued to result in the withholding of sums actually due the government to the extent that the Treasury could not meet its obligations, political pride demanded that the situation be explained away: The government had not gone into debt. The Treasury was simply in need of temporary funds. Revenue was forthcoming in adequate amounts to

Calhoun advanced an ingenious argument to the effect that long-time obligations would represent nothing more or less than an exchange of government credit for bank credit. His conclusion was that the government had better use its own credit.

[1] *Congress Debates*, 25th Cong., 1st Sess., vol. xiv, pt. ii, p. 1224 Oct. 4, 1837.

[2] *Cong. Debates*, 25th Cong., 1st Sess., vol. xiv, pt. i, p. 73. Amendment by Mr. Walker (favored by Mr. Calhoun) doing away with interest, Sept. 18, 1837. *Cf. Cong. Globe*, 25th Cong., 2nd Sess., vol. vi, p. 363, Mr. Cambreling, May 11, 1838; and *ibid.*, 27th Cong., 1st Sess., p. 179, Mr. Gilmer, July 10, 1841.

supply all needs. It was necessary, therefore, only to find a means of obtaining ready cash with which to meet immediate needs.[1]

The government's exclusive use of Treasury notes from 1837 until after the change of administration in 1841, together with the developments which accompanied this use, can be understood only when these facts are utilized as a background.

THE DEMOCRATS' DEPENDENCE UPON TREASURY NOTES

A reference to the authorizing acts will serve the double purpose of disclosing the extent of the Treasury's dependence upon short-term obligations and of making us acquainted with some of the details of financing.

An act of Oct. 12, 1837 [2] started the ball rolling with an authorized issue of $10,000,000. A second authorization was necessary in 1838 [3] this time in order to reissue notes which had been received as payments to the government.[4] Later, the right to issue was simply extended for the purpose of [5] legalizing treasury notes as a source of funds for the fiscal needs of the year 1839. The following year witnessed a slight change in the authorization, in that the measure definitely provided for issue to [6] a specified amount outstanding.

The succeeding law, passed just prior to the exodus of

[1] See *Cong. Debates*, 25th Cong., 1st Sess., vol. xiv, pt. i, p. 1154. *Cong. Globe*, 26th Cong., 2nd Sess., vol. ix, pp. 108 and 109, Jones. *Ibid.*, 25th Cong., 2nd Sess., vol. vi, p. 364, Cambreling.

[2] 5 Stat. at Large 202, ch. 2.

[3] *Act of May 21*, 5 Stat. at Large 222, ch. 82.

[4] *Cong. Globe*, 25th Cong., 2nd Sess., vol. vi, p. 363, May 11, 1838, Mr. Cambreling; p. 387, May 18, 1838, Mr. Calhoun. At first the issue was limited to one year, consequently, allowing a reissue under one act did not dispense with the need of subsequent authorization.

[5] *Act of Mar. 2, 1839*, 5 Stat. at Large 323, ch. 37.

[6] *Act of Mar. 31, 1849*, 5 Stat. at Large 370, ch. 5.

the [1] Democratic Party, retained this provision and increased the amount allowed by five million dollars.

These five acts give abundant evidence of the fact that the equivalent of a permanent claim on the government was being met by repeated borrowing and reborrowing on the basis of short-term obligations. In view of this situation, it is especially significant that the securities continually found their way back to the Treasury, instead of into the hands of investors. One gathers that this situation followed a deliberate choice of financing tactics. It must have been obvious that certain popular security features and financing devices would run counter to the desirable object of securing a permanent lodging place for government obligations. Held up against these disadvantages, however, was the prospect that resorting to such provisions as that making the notes receivable would make of the latter a substitute for currency and consequently facilitate their sale. The short cut to financial strength was evidently looked upon as the more desirable step. In any event we find the utilization of a number of expediency measures. They may be studied to advantage in connection with the central aim of making the notes acceptable as currency.

This idea was brought to the forefront in the early discussions of the problems of financing. In September, 1837, Calhoun declared that the present needs of the Treasury should be raised by a paper which should at the same time have the requisite qualities to enable it to perform the functions of a paper circulation.[2] Calhoun's idea, which was apparently common to other members of his party,[3] was the subject of severe criticism by Webster and others of the opposition.

[1] *Act of Feb. 15, 1841*, 5 Stat. at Large 411, ch. 5.

[2] *Cong. Debates*, 25th Cong., 1st Sess., vol. xiv, pt. i, p. 50 *et seq.*

[3] *Ibid.*, p. 520; also pt. ii, p. 1259; *Cong. Globe*, 25th Cong., 2nd Sess., vol. vi, p. 364; also p. 384.

However, the defenders of a non-borrowing policy were not to be so easily dislodged from a principle which went hand in hand with their scheme for camouflaged borrowing. Their task was rather to advance the means of accomplishing their purpose. Not the least important of these means had to do with the question of interest. A high rate would result in the obligations being held as investments either at home or abroad, while a low interest payment would mean that the circulating [1] media of the country would have to find room for a newcomer.

Calhoun left no doubt as to the nature of his ideas on the subject, when, after he had expounded his beliefs in respect to the desirability of placing the notes as a circulating medium, he voiced his objection to their carrying any interest whatever.[2] He was later instrumental in causing an amendment to be introduced to do away with interest. Although subsequent statements by Calhoun's followers indicate that for practical reasons they were willing to allow interest, it appears that they withdrew their support from the amendment reluctantly.[3]

In spite of the modifications in Calhoun's idea of issuing notes without interest, the administration pushed its efforts

[1] *Cong. Debates*, 25th Cong., 1st Sess., vol. xiv, pt. i, p. 73.

[2] *Cong. Debates*, 25th Cong., 1st Sess., vol. xiv, pt. i, pp. 50 and 73. See also *ibid.*, p. 1155, for statement of Mr. Rhett.

[3] *Cong. Debates*, 25th Cong., 1st Sess., vol. xiv, pt. i, p. 1154. One potential advocate of the policy declared that it would be improper to pay creditors in non-interesting bearing notes. (*Ibid.*, p. 1250, Mr. McKim.) Incidentally, it may be of interest that the use of notes in payment to creditors was itself considered of no little importance; or at least we gain this impression from the administration's opponents who declared that the practice forced on the creditors something of less value than lawful money. (*Cong. Globe*, 25th Cong., 2nd Sess., vol. vi, p. 385, Mr. Webster, May 18, 1836. Also later criticism of Whig measure, *Cong. Globe*, 27th Cong., 2nd Sess., p. 103, Mr. Davis; p. 117, Mr. Underwood on Constitutionality.)

to the point of securing, in the authorization act, a provision that the question [1] of interest was to be left to the Treasury so long as the rate did not exceed 6%. The administration was quick to follow the cue. Notes were issued at interest as low as one-tenth of one percent.[2]

Since 6% was actually paid on a large part of the notes emitted during 1837-1838, any obligations placed at a lower rate, we may assume, must have been materially influenced by the fact that they were more or less acceptable in the place of currency. If this is true, the treasury utilized this factor in placing almost nine million dollars of its obligations at rates of from one mill to 5%.[3] Subsequent measures [4] continued to leave the interest rate to the discretion of the Treasury, with the result that the department took advantage of the opportunity to issue notes at rates which can hardly be considered remunerative.[5] It seems obvious that in thus failing to supply a remunerative rate of return, the administration was anticipating the acceptance of the notes as currency.[6]

In attempting to secure this desired reception for its notes the government made a familiar but important concession in the form of an agreement that the obligations would be accepted at par value in payment of all dues to the government. While this feature might have appeared to be a necessary adjunct to the attempt to secure circulation for the notes and

[1] *Act of Oct. 12, 1837*, 5 Stat. at Large 202, ch. 2.

[2] Table, loan 87; Bolles, *op. cit.*, pp. 577-8.

[3] Knox, *op. cit.*, p. 45; Bolles, *op. cit.*, pp. 577-8.

[4] See *Acts of Mar. 2, 1839, op. cit.*; *Mar. 31, 1840, op. cit.*; *Feb. 15, 1841, op. cit.* and the later *Acts of Jan. 31, 1842*, 5 Stat. at Large 469, ch. 2; *Aug. 31, 1842*, 5 Stat. at Large 581, ch. 287; and *Mar. 3, 1843*, 5 Stat. at Large 614, ch. 81.

[5] See Table, Loans 80, 81, 82, 84.

[6] Knox, *op. cit.*, p. 42; *Treas. Reports*, vol. iii, p. 613.

to give them greater liquidity, in reality it defeated the more basic purpose of the loan. Attainment of liquidity was overdone to the extent that a large portion of the notes were of such transitory nature that they remained in circulation only from the time they left the treasury until they could find their way back as tax payments. Over half of the first issue was thus retired before all were even emitted,[1] with the result that a further call for funds was necessary. That a large part of the operations were of the circuitous nature described, appears evident from the fact that one third of the total of forty-seven million dollars of notes emitted from 1837 to 1843 was in the form of re-issues.[2] We have already pointed out that the proximate aim of gaining circulation for the notes was itself in contradiction to that of obtaining permanent funds for the government's needs. We now see that the receivability feature, which was designed to contribute to the immediate aim, brought results that could not fail to complicate and make more difficult the task of securing permanent funds.

THE WHIGS ATTEMPT TO FUND THE DEBT

The barrage of criticism which was fired against the Democrats in connection with their policy of resorting to short-term financing would lead one to look to the Whigs for a radical change of policy. One might have expected from them a virtual dependence upon long-term securities. By way of anticipating our later discussions, we may point out that expectations of this nature were partially rewarded soon after the Whigs regained power, by the loan of 1841,[3] and indeed by two subsequent attempts[4] to secure funds on the

1 Knox, *op. cit.*, p. 421.

2 Dewey, *op. cit.*, p. 234.

3 *Act of July 21*, 5 Stat. at Large 438, ch. 3.

4 *Acts of April 15, 1842*, 5 Stat. at Large 473, ch. 26 and *Mar. 3, 1843*, 5 Stat. at Large 614, ch. 81.

basis of long-term obligations. We include an account of these efforts in our discussion because they richly illustrate the manner in which financing devices which might otherwise never have been used, grow out of the clash between political dogma and economic necessity.

The advent of the Whigs as proponents of a loan policy was marked by a proposal for a $12,000,000 loan for funding the debt which, they were careful to point out, already existed.[1] The bill was passed,[2] but not without persistent opposition from the Democrats who, with all the gusto of their former selves, again denied the existence of a debt, and repeated the anti-loan arguments which had supported their policy of short-term borrowing.[3] Some evidence that the arguments pertaining to the desirability of an earlier redemption[4] date took effect is found in the fact that the term was reduced to three years from the longer period which was favored by Secretary Ewing,[5] and first provided for in the bill.[6] The securities were accordingly little more than glorified treasury notes, as far as the period of the loan was concerned.

Finally, and more impressive than all of the weak points of the measure, the loan itself was a failure. As can be seen from the table,[7] less than half of the offering was taken.[8]

Thus, even granting that the loan involved a switch from

[1] *Cong. Globe,* 27th Cong., 1st Sess., vol. x, p. 161, Fillmore, July 7, 1841; p. 165, Seargent, July 8, 1841; p. 175, Salllonstall, July 9, 1841.

[2] *Ibid.*, p. 226.

[3] *Cong. Globe,* 27th Cong., 1st Sess., vol. x, pp. 161 (Gordon), 165 (Pickens), 178 (Hunter), 179 (Holmes), and 180 (Van Buren).

[4] *Ibid.*, p. 178, Mr. McKay; p. 179, Mr. Gilmar.

[5] *Treas. Report,* 1841, p. 443.

[6] *Cong. Globe,* 27th Cong., 1st Sess., vol. x, p. 161.

[7] Loan No. 83.

[8] See *infra,* p. 66 for a discussion of the manner in which the interest factor affected the situation.

a floating to a funded debt we can see from the smallness of the issue that the action represented little more than a flourish. Furthermore, the government was left poorly supplied with funds with which to meet its obligations. Before the end of the year, the Treasury was in a sad plight and by the beginning of 1842 the situation was deplorable. A $14,-000,000 deficit with requirements of $3,500,000 for the current quarter, greeted the Whig congress. Particularly from opponents who favored issuing treasury notes, the administration received the depressing announcement that there was no prospect of obtaining the necessary funds by loans in time to meet the emergency.[1]

Whigs who could swallow their pride accordingly found themselves whipped into line in support of the pet theme of their arch-enemy. Moreover, their feeble attempts to make the bitter dose more palatable did little to improve matters. To be sure, their assurance that the floating debt would soon be funded [2] contrasted with the Democrats' ideal of a liquidated debt; but the promise was little short of an admission that instead of doing what they wanted to do, they had been forced to follow in the footsteps of the Democrats. Moreover the claim that the treasury notes were issued only to meet an emergency, might itself have been a parrot's version of the earlier [3] pleas of the Democrats. Nor was the action of the Whigs in adopting the financial tactics of their opponents entirely overlooked—a fact which may partially explain the strong opposition which developed within the party itself.[4]

[1] *Cong. Globe*, 27th Cong., 2nd Sess., vol. xi, p. 102, Fillmore, Jan. 6, 1842.

[2] *Ibid.*, p. 103.

[3] *Cf. Cong. Globe*, 26th Cong., 2nd Sess., vol. ix, p. 108, Jan. 18, 1841, Mr. Jones.

[4] *Cong. Globe*, 27th Cong., 2nd Sess., vol. xi, p. 103, Mr. Davis and Mr. Wise; p. 113, Mr. Cooper and others; p. 114, Mr. Marshall, Jan., 1841.

Finally, however, the necessity of the hour prevailed on Congress to pass the bill.[1]

Although the original sales plus the re-issues reached an ultimate total of approximately eight million dollars,[2] the proceeds of the sale of treasury notes did not by any means meet the financial needs of the time. Congress accordingly faced the task of filling the gap which was originally left by the failure of the loan of 1841. The problem was clearly one of devising selling features for the purpose of making the stock attractive to the purchasers.

In this connection Secretary Ewing professed to see only one feature which could be depended upon to secure the desired result. He urged an increase in the period of the debt to 12 years.[3]

Before taking up other features in detail, we may cite the reason for Secretary Ewing's stand on the question of terms. The reader will recall that the passage of the loan act of 1841 was the occasion for discussion pertaining to the prospective length of the loan. The period of three years which was finally adopted came as a concession from the administration and as a deviation from the policy as outlined by Secretary Ewing. This episode now stood the Secretary in good stead when, after the failure of the loan, he came back with his recommendations for means of assuring the success of the new offering. He was able to point out that the failure of the loan had come as a result of a step which was opposed both to his own ideas and to those of his political party.[4]

[1] *Ibid.*, p. 146, Mr. Evans; p. 148, Mr. Woodbury; p. 118, Mr. Fessenden, Jan., 1842. *Act of Jan. 31, 1842*, 5 Stat. at Large 469, ch. 2.

[2] Tablt, Loan 84, column E.

[3] *Cong. Globe*, 27th Cong., 2nd Sess., vol. xi, Mar. 16, 1842, pp. 325-326. It would appear that Mr. Filmore did not agree (*ibid.*, p. 114, Jan. 19, 1842).

[4] The resulting implications were later utilized to good advantage. See *Cong. Globe*, 27th Cong., 2nd Sess., vol. xi, p. 329, Mar. 12, 1842, Mr. Filmore.

That facts do not warrant the interpretation which the Secretary's statement invited becomes apparent if one delves into the happenings of the period. This was done more or less accidentally by one of the Secretary's own henchmen, who pointed out that while the authorizing act had permitted an interest payment of 6%, the Secretary had allowed his desire "to save the public money by getting a loan on the best terms he could," to result in an attempt to secure subscriptions as much as one-half point below this figure.[1]

His opponents were quick to attack the wisdom of this action and to place the blame for the failure of the loan upon Mr. Ewing's higgling proclivities [2] and the resulting low rate of interest. The records apparently disclosed some evidence in support of this suggestion that the interest payment was inadequate.[3]

Although there appeared arguments against the higher rate which this experience would have suggested,[4] the loan of 1842 as finally issued carried the highest rate allowed in the authorizing act.[5] Provision was also made for sale below par, a privilege which had been advanced as a necessary expedient.[6]

To the inducements of higher interest, longer terms, and perhaps, the discount, the administration appended yet another provision for the purpose of safeguarding its financial position. An arrangement was made for a continuation of

[1] *Cong. Globe*, 27th Cong., 2nd Sess., vol. xi, Mar. 16, p. 325.

[2] *Ibid.*, Mr. Roosevelt.

[3] *Ibid.*, p. 114, Fillmore, Jan. 10; p. 118, Underwood, Jan. 11, 1842.

[4] *Ibid.*, p. 118, Jan. 11, 1842, Gamble.

[5] *Act of April 15, 1842*, 5 Stat. at Large 473, ch. 26.

[6] *Cong. Globe*, 27th Cong., 2nd Sess., vol. xi, p. 328, Mr. Filmore; p. 329, Mr. Johnson. (The act, however, added the safeguard ". . . . no part thereof shall be disposed of under par until the same has been advertised a reasonable time . . . .")

the payment of interest on treasury notes which were coming due.[1]

In spite of the several arrangements which were designed to facilitate the sale of stock, the subscriptions to the loan were far from satisfactory. Furthermore, on a large part of what was subscribed, the Treasury was forced to resort to the privilege of selling at a discount.[2] Nor is that all: the absence of any authority for the issue of treasury notes left no alternative to the continued sale of stock at a sacrifice.

An attempt to alter both aspects of the undesirable situation was made in a bill which again forbade the sale of stock at less than par, and at the same time authorized the issue of treasury notes to the amount of six million dollars.[3] This was still another step away from the historical policy of the Whigs. After little more than a year in power the party, against its wish, had thus been driven to use the device which its opponents had utilized from choice and for purposes of political strategy.

Subsequent steps indicate that the force of circumstances served to induce the Whigs not only to utilize the type of security employed by their political opponents, but also to resort to the Democrats' plan of attempting to bestow upon the treasury notes that magic power which makes an obligation acceptable as currency. At least one new feature should receive our attention. A note issued under the Act of Mar. 3, 1843[4] contained on its back a novel feature in the form of a promise on the part of the government to purchase

[1] *Act of April 15, op. cit.*, sec. ix.

[2] *Cong. Globe*, 27th Cong., 2nd Sess., vol. xi, p. 964, Aug. 29, 1842, Filmore.

[3] *Act Aug. 31, 1842*, 5 Stat. at Large 581, ch. 287.

[4] 5 Stat. at Large 614, ch. 81. Only $270,000 were issued. (*Treas. Report*, vol. iii, p. 613), Dewey (*op. cit.*, p. 234) points out that the Committee on Ways and Means held that the notes were demand notes and were unconstitutional.

the note at par upon its presentation at either of the Treasury's depositaries in New York City.

This significant action came upon the heels of the realization on the part of the Secretary that non-interest bearing notes would remain in circulation.[1] Irrespective of the origin of the plan, of its purpose, or of the smallness of the amount of notes issued, we may call attention to this contract to buy securities as being one of the most interesting features in American finance. It could hardly have failed to add to the liquidity of the notes.

Argument by the Secretary of the Treasury substantiates the belief that he was in accord with such plans to secure funds by making notes liquid, and by so doing making possible the issue of obligations bearing a low rate of interest. In his opinion, the exigencies of the Treasury demanded that an effort should be made to relieve the government of a high rate of interest.[2]

Having traced the course of short-term financing through the visissitudes of political life from 1837 to 1843, we have covered what is, for our purpose, the most important aspect of the financial history of the years immediately preceding the Civil War. There remains the task of referring to a few independent developments of some significance. We shall take them up in turn.

MEXICAN WAR FINANCING

The Treasury-note fight in all of its political ramifications was carried over into the Mexican War period to furnish what was for that period, one of the few developments of interest.

[1] This fact had impressed itself upon him when notes were not returned after interest payments thereon were stopped. (*Treas. Report*, 1843, vol. iii, p. 613. Bolles, *op. cit.*, pp. 577-8; Knox, *op. cit.*, p. 42.)

[2] *Treas. Report*, vol. iii, p. 613.

By this time the ousted Whigs were in a position to stand aside and criticize the issuing of notes by the Democrats. Opposition to short-term financing was weakened, however, by the fact that any objector was now open to the rejoinder that the status of treasury notes had been established and defended by both parties.[1] But if this situation made the Democrats more free to utilize notes, the experiences leading up to it had apparently made them too wise to exercise their freedom. In any event, the needs of the war period were met in large part by long-term loans.[2]

SECURITY PURCHASES BY THE TREASURY

During the period in question, we find several developments which call to mind circumstances and situations of the previous periods. In this instance as before, poorly arranged maturities failed to provide redeemable notes sufficient to absorb all available funds.[3] The trend of market prices, also repeating its former history, was such that bonds could not be bought at par, and again, the Secretary's request that he be given permission to buy at market prices [4] elicited from Congress the desired authorization.[5]

At least three aspects of the purchasing operation (especially those of the middle fifties) are of interest.

First, we must recognize that the millions of dollars in purchases constituted a permanent reduction in the public

[1] *Cong. Globe*, 29th Cong., 1st Sess., p. 1099, July 15, 1846, McKay. See also, *Cong. Globe*, 35th Cong., 1st Sess., pp. 62, 66, 67, 71, 74, 75, 85 to 89 and 105 to 111.

[2] *Act of July 22, 1846*, 9 Stat. at Large 39, ch. 64; *Act of Jan. 28, 1847*, 9 Stat. at Large 118, ch. 5; *Act of Mar. 31, 1848*, 9 Stat. at Large 217, ch. 26; *Act of Sept. 9, 1850*, 9 Stat. at Large 446, ch. 40.

[3] Dewey, *op. cit.*, p. 256.

[4] *Treas. Report*, 1848, p. 305; 1852, p. 6. For reference to similar experiences during the two previous periods, see *supra*, pp. 30 and 53.

[5] *Act of Mar. 31, 1848*, 9 Stat. at Large 217, ch. 26; *Act of Mar. 3, 1853*, 10 Stat. at Large 189, ch. 97, sec. 9, at p. 212.

debt rather than a mere flourish for political or financial effect.[1]

Second, ideas on the subject of "par" had evolved to the point where purchases were permitted and actually made at premiums which ranged as high as 21%,[2] and under conditions which made it necessary to buy through confidential agents in order not to enhance the price of securities.[3]

Finally, purchases in the middle fifties are significant because of the manner in which the Treasury assumed the role of 'Fairy Godmother' to American business. Purchases were made with the intention of exerting a beneficial effect upon business conditions.[4]

MISCELLANEOUS FEATURES

In addition to the important developments which we have described, a few minor features deserve a comment in passing.

An attempt to combine the ideal of sales at par with that of securing the benefit of competitive bidding, resulted in what may be described as an interesting if not a ludicrous situation in 1857. The Secretary, taking advantage of the discretionary power bestowed upon him by the Authorizing Act,[5] announced that offers would be received at par but

[1] *Treas. Report*, 1855, p. 7. From Mar. 4, 1853 to Nov. 4, 1854, the public debt was reduced from $69,000,000 to $39,000,000.

[2] *Treas. Report*, 1853, p. 5. The wisdom of such purchases was challenged by members of Congress especially when it developed that Secretary Cobb was soon forced to go into the market and borrow money to take the place of what he had disbursed for high-priced bonds. (*Cong. Globe*, vol. 27, pt. ii, p. 110; also *ibid.*, pt. iii, p. 386, Mr. Cameron.

[3] *Treas. Report*, 1848, p. 306.

[4] *Treas. Report*, 1857, p. 11. (For a comprehensive account of similar activities of the Treasury in aiding business, see David Kinley, *The Independent Treasury*, National Monetary Commission, 61st Cong., 2nd Sess., Senate Doc. No. 587, pp. 208-290.)

[5] *Dec. 23, 1857*, 11 Stat. at Large, ch. i.

that the bidders would be allowed to insert the rates of interest at which they would subscribe to the Treasury notes. There resulted a heterogeneous mass of securities with upwards of a dozen rates of interest.[1]

There is observable an almost complete shift over to the plan of placing securities without the payment of commissions. (See table.) Authorizing acts went so far as to stipulate that no commissions were to be paid.[2]

Along with the abandonment of the use of agents, there arose the practice of advertising loans. The action first came as a means of assuring the government that sales would not be made at a discount until the public knew the nature of the issue.[3] Later, as we know, advertising came to be a team mate of direct selling.

Some of the acts of this period made provision for coupon bonds.[4] Since this arrangement facilitates the collection of interest it is especially attractive to holders who reside in foreign countries. Because of the manner in which it operates it may be considered a selling feature of the bonds.[5]

SIGNIFICANT DEVELOPMENTS OF THE PERIOD

In our analysis of the developments of the period we have seen how the course of events forced the government to secure money with which to meet its pressing obligations; how

[1] Knox, *op. cit.*, p. 70.

[2] For example see the *Act of Mar. 3, 1843*, 5 Stat. at Large 614, ch. 91, and the *Act of July 22, 1846*, 9 Stat. at Large 39, ch. 64. The *Act of July 21, 1841*, 5 Stat. at Large 438, ch. 3, on the contrary provided for the employment of agents and for the payment of a commission of 1/10 of one percent.

[3] *Act of April 15, 1842*, 5 Stat. at Large 473, ch. 26.

[4] *Act of Mar. 31, 1848*, 9 Stat. at Large 217, ch. 26; *Act. of June 14, 1858*, 11 Stat. at Large 365, ch. 165; *Act of June 22, 1860*, 12 Stat. at Large 79, ch. 180.

[5] James S. Gibbons, *The Public Debt of the United States* (New York, 1867), p. 31, discusses the feature from this point of view.

the dogmas of a political party prevented it from acknowledging the true state of affairs and caused it to attempt to deny the existence of a funded debt; and, finally, how political strategy caused the administration to turn to short-term financing as a means of meeting the needs of the hour, and at the same time of avoiding the disgrace which would have accompanied an admission that loans were actually necessary.

The period following 1837 may accordingly be remembered for the peculiar manner in which political pressure contrived with finance theory to lead the Treasury into a sole dependence upon short-term financing. This dependence in turn necessitated the adoption of a number of features for the purpose of facilitating the task of placing the resulting treasury notes. The means of making them acceptable involved an attempt to encourage their use as currency. In this connection the principal reliance was placed on the fact that the notes were receivable for all dues to the government. This feature was successful in that it placed the notes in circulation, but it was disastrous in that the loans came to be of a transitory nature, with the result that the treasury was constantly being embarrassed by the necessity of making new issues or re-issues. The history of the period is accordingly useful in supplying illustrations of certain inherent possibilities in the receivability features as well as contrbuting some interesting examples of the use of specific financing devices.

CHAPTER IV

Civil War Financing: Conditioning Facts and Theories

THE HERITAGE FROM PRE-WAR FINANCE

The years from 1857 to 1861 supplied at least two proposals which are, from a narrow point of view, entitled to consideration under the head of selling features. One of these consisted of a plan for improving the security back of the loan by reverting to the policy of appropriating the proceeds of the sale of public lands to the redemption of the bonds. The proposition invited not a little discussion but in the end was abandoned.[1]

The other proposal involved the permission to sell securities at a discount or at an adjusted rate of interest and, it so happened, was accompanied by developments which ultimately forced Congress to grant the requested authority. The story is of some interest. The first offering of $10,000,000 of the $21,000,000 authorized in 1860[2] was subscribed in full at par or better for the 5% stock.

Before payments were met, however, diminished revenue, unusual demands upon the Treasury, poor management on the part of the Secretary, and depressed business conditions,[3]

[1] *Cong. Globe*, 36th Cong., 2nd Sess., pt. i, p. 42; vote 44, House, Dec. 10, 1860; pp. 65-67, Dec. 12, 1860; 68 vote, Senate. Cobb suggested this plan for the treasury notes which were to be issued after the failure of subscriptions. *Treas. Report*, 1860, p. 9.

[2] *Act of June 22*, 12 Stat. at Large 79, ch. 180. The offering had been made on September 8, by circular only. (*Treas. Report*, 1860, p. 480.)

[3] *Cf.* John Sherman, *Recollections of Forty Years* (New York, 1895), pp. 251 *et seq.*

had combined to cast a shadow over the financial world. As a result, payments on $2,978,000 of the subscriptions were not made.[1]

The failure of the subscription to materialize spelled the doom of the unoffered portion ($11,000,000) of the loan: It was at this point that the Treasury accordingly requested [2] and received [3] permission to sell treasury notes on such terms as would make them attractive to purchasers. Taking advantage of his new liberty, the Secretary then invited bids. The resulting small subscriptions at rates as high as 12% proved disappointing to those who had persistently claimed that conditions would permit the issue of securities on customary terms.[4]

While the more advantageous terms of the succeeding offerings [5] gave evidence of some improvement in the status of the Treasury, the situation up to the beginning of hostilities was by no means satisfactory. For our purpose, therefore, several conclusions stand out: In the first place, the financiers of the Civil War were left with a heritage of difficulties which greatly complicated their task. Secondly, even before the war, financial strategy had compelled the Trea-

[1] *Treas. Report*, 1861, p. 11. The inability of the Government to place its obligations was the more noticeable because of the ease with which previous loans were floated. Issues under both the Treasury note authorization of $20,000,000 in 1857 (*Act of Dec. 23*, 11 Stat. at Large 257, ch. xi) and the renewing act of 1859 (*Act of Mar. 3*, 11 Stat. at Large 425, ch. 82, sec. 5, p. 430) as well as the fifteen-year loan of 1838 (*Act of June 14*, 11 Stat. at Large 365, ch. 165) had apparently been placed without difficulty.

[2] *Treas. Report*, 1860, p. 9.

[3] (*Act of Dec. 17, 1860*, 12 Stat. at Large 121, chs. i, iv, p. 122.) The necessary amendment was proposed by the Senate (*Cong. Globe*, 36th Cong., 2nd Sess., pt. i, p. 88).

[4] *Cong. Globe*, pt. i, pp. 66-68, Mr. Simmons, Senate. Wesley C. Mitchell, *A History of the Greenbacks* (Chicago, 1903), p. 7.

[5] *Treas. Report*, 1861, *passim*, Mitchell, *op. cit.*, pp. 8, 9, 12 and 13.

sury to resort to inducements in addition to the usual interest rates in order to place securities. The fact serves as an omen of difficulties which were to be experienced in connection with the task of keeping Treasury operations on a business basis. While the government met the issue squarely in 1860 by allowing sufficient financial remuneration to offset any unwillingness to invest, it was hardly to be expected that such action would continue to withstand war-time political pressure.

To these two conclusions we may add a third of established validity. Chase himself was poorly equipped to solve the difficult problems which arose from the start, and which demanded the wisdom and judgment of an astute financier.[1] Even though we admit his sincerity of purpose and refrain from analyzing his actions in an effort to detect the use of means for furthering his own personal ambitions,[2] we must nevertheless at least recognize that his training was hardly of a nature to enable him to cope with the complicated problems of the day. Only by keeping this fact in mind can we understand the Secretary's actions.

[1] In respect to Chase's financial ability a New York banker with whom he carried on negotiations had this to say:

"Yet, in truth, it may be said, that for a man of his brain-power, his business capacity was comparatively moderate. He undoubtedly was learned in the law; skilled in political combinations; at home in Blackstone's Commentaries and Euclid's problems, but the mysteries of our Clearing House always seemed to surpass his comprehension" (p. 6). J. E. William, *The War Loans of the Associated Banks to the Government in 1861. Letter to Congressman Kelly, Feb. 14, 1867.*

See also the indictment of James Gallatin:

"Shameful incompetency, with all the self-conceit of ignorance distinguished the early efforts of many of the officers of the Government, immediately upon the accession of the administration in 1861. In finances there was a total paralysis . . ."

P. 30, *National Debt, Taxation, Currency, and Banking System* (New York, 1864).

[2] *Cr.* Hugh McCulloch, *Men and Measures of Half a Century* (New York, 1889), p. 186.

On the occasion of his very first attempt to secure money, Chase refused available long-time funds and took a chance on securing the badly needed revenue through the issue of treasury notes. If the Secretary had only observed the needs of the treasury and the uncertainty of the immediate future he would have concluded at least that reliance upon treasury notes was a risky expedient.[1]

Since the step was taken for the purpose of reducing the rate of interest the action supplies proof that from the start Chase was subject to a distinct bias toward saving interest. This attitude apparently prevented him from recognizing the need for operating the Treasury on a business-like basis. Throughout his career, indeed, he was particularly open to plans for saving interest.

In connection with the general topic of interest payments, we shall now study the question of legal limitation upon the rate and of the specification of terms on which the securities can be sold.

RATE AND TERMS

The first of these topics may be disposed of in short order. Every act of the war period either specified the rate of interest or placed a definite maximum above which it could not go. Thanks to the Treasury's success in manipulating matters, however, the restrictions on the rate were at no time such a handicap as to make it necessary for the Secretary to demand a nominal rate of interest in excess of the level to which Congress had become accustomed.

The war measures began with the familiar requirement that bonds could not be sold at less than par.[2] Conditions

[1] James Gallatin criticized the Treasury severely by pointing out that it would be better to pay three or four per cent more than to risk the embarrassment which treasury notes might later bring. *Letters to S. P. Chase*, Mar. 27, 1861 (New York, 1861). *Cf.* Mitchell, *op. cit.*, p. 12.

[2] *Act of July 17, 1861*, 12 Stat. at Large 259, ch. v, sec. iv, p. 260.

preceding the loan of Feb. 25, 1862, however, were such that permission was granted to sell the bonds at "market price".[1]

While Chase's interpretation prevented sale at a discount there is little doubt that the framers of the measure intended to grant to the Secretary the power to sell securities at whatever price they would bring.[2]

Irrespective of whether or not Chase's interpretation was correct, the facts are that, with one exception,[3] no effective permission for selling Civil War bonds at less than par was granted prior to the act of Mar. 3, 1863. This measure,[4] repealing the restriction on the terms of sale, and the succeeding acts,[5] gave the Treasury a free hand in the matter of fixing terms. Even before this time, however, there appears no conclusive evidence that the Treasury was greatly hampered by the legal restriction on the rate of interest. We must accordingly look elsewhere for an explanation of Chase's efforts to maintain interest rates at a low level. The

[1] 12 Stat. at Large 345, ch. 33, sec. ii. *Cong. Globe*, 37th Cong., 2nd Sess., pt. i, pp. 763-766. Senate, Mr. Fessenden.

[2] *Cf.* Mitchell, *op. cit.*, pp. 104 *et seq.*, especially pp. 107-8.

[3] The exception occurred as a result of the provision of the *Act of Aug. 5, 1861*, 12 Stat. at Large 313, ch. 48, sec. 7, p. 314. See *Treas. Report*, 1861, p. 9, "the Secretary under the authority of the seventh section of the act of Aug. 5, 1861, arranged this third loan, also, with the associates, by agreeing to issue to them fifty millions of dollars in six per cent bonds, at a rate equivalent to par for the bonds bearing seven per cent interest authorized by the act of July 17." While technically this represented a sale below par in reality it was merely a means of placing six per cent bonds on a seven per cent basis.

[4] *Act of Mar. 3, 1863*, 12 Stat. at Large 709, ch. 73, sec. 1, p. 10.

[5] *Act of Mar. 3, 1864*, 13 Stat. at Large 13, ch. 17, sec. i; *Act of June 30, 1864*, 13 Stat. at Large 218, ch. 172, sec. 1; *Act of Jan. 28, 1865*, 13 Stat. at Large 425, ch. 22, sec. 1; *Act of Mar. 13, 1865*, 13 Stat. at Large 468, ch. 77, sec. 1; *Act of Apr. 12, 1865*, 14 Stat. at Large 31, ch. 39, sec. 1.

facts already mentioned all point to a conclusion which will be substantiated in the succeeding section.

BIAS AGAINST INTEREST PAYMENTS

From the first, Chase gave evidence of his concern over the task of keeping the cost of the war down to a minimum. The result of his thought on how " to enable the government to obtain the necessary means of prosecuting the war to a successful issue without unnecessary cost, . . ." consisted of transferring to the Government at least a part of the 150 million dollar bank circulation, this circulation, he carefully pointed out, " constitutes a loan without interest, from the people to the banks." [1] This statement followed another in which he declared that the 6½% representing the average interest on the public debt was higher than the United States ought to pay.[2]

From the time when Chase used the legal tender possibility as a threat to force the banks to grant the first loans of the war [3] until 1864 when his resignation became effective, Chase's action continued to exemplify the manner in which this attitude on the part of administration leaders influenced treasury operations. A few arguments advanced in connection with the issues of legal tender will illustrate the point: Mr. Spalding [4] declared the reason for legal tenders to be that bonds and stocks could be sold only at a ruinous dis-

[1] *Treas. Report*, 1861, p. 17.

[2] *Treas. Report*, 1861, p. 16. For a criticism of Chase's early action and an appeal that stock be offered on a business basis, see James Gallatin's *Letters to S. P. Chase* (New York, 1865), especially pp. 15, 17, 20 and 21 of the letter of May 7, 1861.

[3] Albert Bushnell Hart, *American Statesmen, Chase* (New York, 1899), pp. 222-223.

[4] *Cong. Globe*, 37th Cong., 2nd Sess., pt. i, pp. 523-524, Jan. 28, 1862—House. *Ibid.*, pt. iii, p. 2767, June 17, 1862; Mitchell, *op. cit.*, pp. 48-50, 74 and 96.

count. Even after the first issue of legal tenders, Mr. Hooper argued that the benefits of issuing notes for circulation should be given to the government rather than to the banks,[1] and by so doing continue to provide means for carrying on the war without cost. Mr. Collamer put the matter succintly by stating that the only difference between issues of notes and bonds was that the first was a loan without interest while the other was a loan with interest.[2]

Mr. Morrill in opposing the second issue declared that the only argument made for the increase of notes was that of saving interest.[3] Chase himself spoke of the legal tenders as a loan without interest,[4] and was careful, in figuring the cost of financing, to include these non-interest bearing obligations in a manner that brought the average interest payments down below five per cent [5] and later to a level below four per cent.[6]

As late as 1864, Chase's attempt to save one point of interest, it is generally conceded, brought about the practical failure of an important loan.[7] Nor was the Secretary's concern over interest rates confined to immediate outlays. On the contrary, he looked beyond the war period to include post-war financing. As a result, his insistence upon the right to redeem outstanding securities within a short time after the end of hostilities was responsible for attaching the five-year redemption privilege to the five-twenties [8] when, in

[1] *Cong. Globe*, 37th Cong., 2nd Sess., pt. iv, p. 2882—House, June 23, 1862.

[2] *Cong. Globe*, 37th Cong., 3rd Sess., pt. i, p. 871—Senate, Feb. 11, 1863.

[3] *Cong. Globe*, 37th Cong., 2nd Sess., pt. iv, p. 2884—House, June 23, 1862.

[4] *Treas. Report*, 1862, pp. 2-9.

[5] *Treas. Report*, 1862, p. 2.

[6] *Treas. Report*, 1863, p. 13.

[7] *Infra*, p. 105.

[8] *Treas. Report*, 1862, pp. 25-6.

the opinion of many, a twenty-year bond could have been issued to much better advantage.[1]

It is hardly to be expected that such an attitude toward the question of interest payments would result in the placing of loans on a sraight-forward business basis. On the contrary, we would expect the Treasury to resort to measures for the purpose of reducing the rate of interest and of concealing the true cost of obtaining funds.

The course of events—political, military, economic, and financial—served to strengthen rather than to weaken the tendency in this direction. For one thing, the enormous demands occasioned by the war not only far surpassed in amount any sum which the Treasury had even been equipped to supply, but they also far exceeded, both in amount and in duration, any estimates or guesses of Administration leaders.[2] These facts had a two-fold effect. In the first place, the immediate needs of the treasury were always larger as well as more urgent than they would have been had the future been foreseen with greater precision. In the second place, the same events which occasioned the fluctuating but ever urgent and augmented demands of the Treasury apparently served to make the public uneasy as to the probable future course of events. Accordingly, unstable business, prospective trouble with England, or unfavorable news from the front, no doubt exerted an exaggerated influence upon the market for Government securities.

[1] *Cong. Globe*, 37th Cong., 2nd Sess., pt. i, pp. 773-4, Sherman, Feb. 12, 1862—Senate. *Cf.* Mitchell, *op. cit.*, pp. 103, 104, 114, 115 and 123.

[2] One writer has summarized the situation by referring to the following facts: In July, 1861, expenses for the year 1861-1862 were predicted at 318 millions of dollars which must be compared with 475 millions actually spent. Similar comparisons for the following year disclose figures of 475 millions and 715 millions respectively. (Hart, *op. cit.*, p. 235. See also McCulloch, *op. cit.*, pp. 283 *et seq.*

INADEQUATE TAXATION

Nor was confidence in the Government strengthened by the adoption of an adequate tax program. On the contrary, the consensus of opinion seems to be that, especially during the early part of the war, the administration failed to supply taxes sufficiently high to reassure would-be investors of the Government's intentions to meet its obligations.[1]

A possible curb on extravagance was accordingly lacking, and an effective means of strengthening the Treasury's credit remained unused. This lack of an aggressive tax policy combined with the other factors which we have mentioned to force the administration to resort to measures and devices which would otherwise have been unnecessary.

The list of theories and practices which apparently influenced or compelled the resort to special features and devices must now be extended to include a brief treatment of developments in the currency and banking fields. While we might have considered a number of arrangements in the field of banking and currency as separate financing devices, we have chosen in the main to treat the development as a whole and to consider only its general bearing on the more specific problems of financing.

THE CURRENCY SITUATION

We have frequently had occasion to refer to the lack of a stable national currency prior to the Civil War and to the manner in which the currency situation conditioned the activities of the Treasury. The question of the form in which payments were to be made constituted one of the most important problems engendered by the state of the currency. During the incumbency of Hamilton, again in connection

[1] *Cf.* Mitchell, *op. cit.*, pp. 18, 37 and 103. For recommendations on taxation see Gallatin's *Letters, op. cit.*, p. 21 and James Gallatin, *Government Finances and Currency. Letters to Daniel Wilmot.* Hall, Clayton, and Medale, 1862.

with the financing of the War of 1812, and later upon the occasion of the specie circular of 1836, the Treasury's stand upon the question attracted the attention befitting a national issue.

Before the advent of the financing problems of the Civil War, the idea that the payments to the Treasury should be kept on a specie basis had become sufficiently prevalent to establish the practice by law.[1] An act of 1836 [2] forbade the acceptance of bank notes in denominations less than $20, while the sub-Treasury acts attempted to place all payments on a specie basis.[3] These legal actions compelling the Treasury to accept only specie may be considered as the logical outgrowth of the uncertain and unsettled status of the country's media of exchange. Moreover, at the same time that the experience with the currency was encouraging the setting-up of legal safeguards against the receipt of insecure currency, developments were also leaving their imprint upon administration leaders, to the extent that Chase was unwilling to avail himself of an opportunity to be free from the legal restrictions. The situation arose in connection with the Treasury's relations with the banks.

EARLY RELATIONS WITH BANKS

At the outset, Chase looked upon loans from banks as the "safest, surest and most beneficial plan" for raising funds.[4] Three loans of $50,000,000 each were accordingly negoti-

[1] For a brief account of developments prior to the Civil War, see A. McF. Davis, *The Origin of the National Banking System*, National Monetary Commission, 61st Cong., 2nd Sess., Senate Doc. No. 582, pp. 28 *et seq.*

[2] *Act of April 14*, 5 Stat. at Large 9, ch. 52, sec. 1.

[3] *Act of July 4, 1840*, 5 Stat. at Large 385, ch. 41, sec. 19, p. 390; *Act of Aug. 6, 1846*, 9 Stat. at Large 59, ch. 90 secs. 18-19, p. 64; also *Act of Aug. 4, 1846*, 9 Stat. at Large 53, ch. 4.

[4] *Treas. Report*, 1861, p. 8.

ated with banks which were, thanks both to the presence of strong reserves and to the absence of remunerative alternative uses, willing to accommodate the Government.[1] According to custom and legal requirements, specie equivalent to the entire sum borrowed would have to be transferred to the Sub-Treasury. Even at the time of the negotiations, however, the impossibility of such action was clearly seen, not only by an agitated group of bankers,[2] but also by members of Congress. One of the latter (Mr. Spalding) accordingly drew up an amendment looking to the suspension of the Sub-Treasury Act in so far as specie payments for loans were concerned.[3] It was at this point, however, that the psychological background of the administration leaders prevented both the overthrow of the legal restrictions and the admission into Government finance of modern principles and practices of banking. In short, friendly feeling on the part of Chase and his associates toward the Sub-Treasury system was to be blamed, according to Mr. Spaulding, for modifications and subsequent interpretations which practically defeated the intentions of the original amendment. The same critic goes still further to suggest that the Treasury's action in excluding the use of credit in Government financing made the suspension of specie payments inevitable.

[1] *Treas. Report*, 1861, p. 9. Mitchell, *op. cit.*, pp. 20-23.

[2] *Cf.* Gallatin's *Letters to Daniel Wilmot, op. cit.*, pp. 5-6. Even Robert J. Walker, who had been instrumental in starting the sub-treasury system and thereby "divorcing the banks and the Treasury," came around to support a reunion "... to enable the Government to effect loans upon their stock..." *Review of our Finances*, Dec. 19, 1862 (N. Y. pub. Library T. I. F., pp. v, 75, no. 5).

[3] Spaulding to Gibbons, Letter March 29, 1870. Spaulding, *Financial History of the War*, 2nd ed., appendix, pp. 51-4. See *Act of Aug. 5, 1861*, 12 Stat. at Large 313, p. 314, sec. 6.

SUSPENSION AND ITS REACTION ON THE TASK OF FINANCING

Failure to shuffle off the customs and ideas which had come down as a heritage from the past,[1] may accordingly be held more or less responsible for the general use of media other than coin. In other words, the Treasury's attempt to avoid this practice in connection with its own transactions contributed to the suspension of coin payments in both public and private transactions. The general consequences of this development have been so exhaustively treated that we need do no more than appropriate the facts which are pertinent to our own topic. Two points stand out: In the first place, suspension meant that the sphere of usefulness of the banks to the Government was, to say the best, diminished materially.[2] The action meant that the banks could no longer be of service in supplying the specie which would have been necessary had the Government continued the policy and practice to which Chase had so bravely but foolishly announced his adherence. As a result the Government was, of all, the most injured.

To the private bank, suspension of specie payments amounted simply to an announcement that in the future one medium would be used to the exclusion of another. To the Government, on the other hand, suspension by the banks meant in the first instance that this source of specie was now gone and that suspension on the part of the Government was accordingly inevitable. This action in turn involved a complete overthrow of the accepted standard of value. Worst of all, there was no acceptable medium to take the place of the deposed specie.

[1] *Cf.* James Gallatin, *The National Finances, a Reply to a Speech in Congress by Samuel Hooper* (New York, 1864), p. 7.

[2] *Cf.* Mitchell, *op. cit.*, pp. 38-42.

THE TREASURY'S NEED OF A CURRENCY

This absence of a desirable currency accounts for a trend of thought which, together with the actions trailing in its wake, gave rise to some additional circumstances of importance to our subject. In the first place, it was only natural that the Government should have felt itself called upon to supply the much-needed currency. Its action in doing so was the more defensible in view of the fact that numerous private banks were emitting a horde of notes of diverse forms and varied degrees of security. Treasury notes were accordingly advanced as a substitute for bank notes. The pleas for their use amounted to little more than a statement of preference for Government money as against bank notes.[1]

With the issue thus drawn it was to be expected that the imagination of administration leaders would be aroused by the possibility of utilizing the barren currency field as a source of much-needed revenue.

In the attempts to take advantage of the apparent opportunity the Treasury was continually harassed by the presence of competing media of exchange.

ELIMINATION OF COMPETING MEDIA

For this reason a tax on bank notes had appeared as an integral part of the Secretary's plan of 1862 and had been

[1] *Treas. Report*, 1861, p. 17; *ibid.*, 1862, pp. 12-14; *Cong. Globe*, 37th Cong., 2nd Sess., pt. i, pp. 524-6, Jan. 28, 1862, Mr. Spalding; 2nd Sess., pt. iv, p. 2885, Mr. Lovejoy; 2nd Sess., pt. iv, pp. 3072-3 and 3076, Mr. Sherman; 3rd Sess., pt. i, pp. 840 and 842-3, Mr. Sherman; 3rd Sess., pt. ii, p. 1117, Feb. 19, 1863, Mr. Harrison; 3rd Sess., pt. ii, pp. 1142-3, Feb. 20, 1863, Mr. Baker. *Cf.* Mitchell, *op. cit.*, pp. 85, 98, 112.

For a banker's reply to the argument that inflation was caused by the banks, see James Gallatin, *National Debt, Taxation, Currency and Banking System* (New York, 1864). On page 19 the writer points out that the bank-note circulation in May, 1863 exceeded that at the time of the outbreak of the war by only twenty million dollars.

widely approved.[1] In keeping with the ideas of Chase and those of his associates, several steps were taken along the lines of eliminating competing currencies and finally their death knell was sounded.[2]

One final word may be in order. From all indications it appears that the National Banking System itself arose largely as an outgrowth of the confused attempts to make the monetary system subservient to the financing needs of the government.[3]

Having now referred to a number of the facts and ideas which influenced the financial developments of the Civil War period, we are ready to look at some of the points at closer range. In doing so we should remember that the background as given is necessarily grossly inadequate for our purpose. Had we called upon the historians for a full treatment of the various subjects, including the banking and currency situation, the picture would be complete enough to enable us to see much more clearly the justification for subsequent measures. In our own discussions, however, we must forego this interesting and illuminating study and pass along to a consideration of such financing arrangements as

[1] *Treas. Report*, 1862, pp. 15-16; *Cong. Globe*, 37th Cong., 2nd Sess., pt. iv, p. 3076, Senate, July 2, 1862; Hart, *op. cit.*, pp. 281-282.

[2] The postage currency *Act of July 17, 1862* (12 Stat. at Large 592, ch. 196) forbade the issue of small notes by state banks. The act of Mar. 3, 1863 worked in the direction of limiting the amount of circulation of banks by placing a 1% tax on all amounts issued in excess of a certain percentage of the capital stock. (12 Stat. at Large 709, ch. 173, sec. 7, p. 712.) The same act placed a tax of 5% each half year on fractional currency. The final blow was struck with the ten per cent tax on State Bank circulation. (*Act of Mar. 3, 1865*, 13 Stat. at Large 469, ch. 78, sec. 6, p. 484.) This action received the support of Hugh McCulloch, who, as comptroller, recommended its adoption to Fessenden. (*Treas. Report*, 1864, page 54.)

[3] See in general, Davis, *op. cit., passim*, and the Nat'l Bank Act, *Act of Feb. 25, 1863*, 12 Stat. at Large 665, ch. 581.

were adopted for the purpose of securing urgently-needed funds and as a means of avoiding high nominal rates of interest.

The most important of these features had to do with making the government's obligations more or less acceptable as money and thereby encouraging or compelling their acceptance and retention by the public. The attempt to appropriate the characteristics of currency of course, reached its zenith in the legal tender provision.

Our primary interest in this infamous provision, it should be remembered, arises not from its connection with the currency, but rather because of its adoption as an aid to the disposition of government obligations. In this respect, the provision in question was simply one of a series of features each resembling this one in that its utility depended upon its functioning so as to enable government obligations to pass as currency. For this reason the topics which are shortly to be considered shed much light upon the subject of Civil War financing.

CHAPTER V

Civil War: Special Financing Devices

RECEIVABILITY

In the Sub-Treasury laws, treasury notes were placed in a position which would apparently have left the question of their receivability to the discretion of the Secretary of the Treasury. The framers of subsequent authorizing acts, however, seemed to consider it wise to place the notes on a more certain basis. In any event, we find that without an exception, succeeding measures up to the outbreak of the war stipulated that the notes were to be receivable in payment of dues to the government.[1]

On the other hand, when we come to examine the first war act,[2] we find that a provision for the use of treasury notes in payment of dues to the government was notably absent. This omission was later corrected only in so far as the demand notes were concerned.[3] Furthermore, since the latter obligations were redeemable in coin upon demand, the addition of the receivability feature served merely to supplement an existing plan for redemption.

Later issues either of legal tenders or of treasury notes possessing the legal tender feature, were made receivable for all dues with one important exception. The privilege of paying import duties was denied them.

[1] Citations appear throughout Chapter IV and Chapter V.

[2] *Act of July 17, 1861,* 12 Stat. at Large 259, ch. 5.

[3] *Act of Aug. 5, 1861,* 12 Stat. at Large 313, ch. 46, sec. 5.

Regarded from the point of view of financial strategy, the government's refusal to accept its obligations in payment of import duties may be looked upon as one of the shrewdest manoeuvers of the period. As a result of this restriction, the Treasury was guaranteed that the receipts from its major source of revenue would consist of much-needed coin.

The same idea of restriction seems to have prevailed throughout the war. Extension of the receivability feature to apply to all payments to the Treasury was even denied to the fractional currency.[1]

To be sure, receivability for all dues (including import duties) was accorded to postage stamps for payments of less than five dollars,[2] and to coin certificates [3] for payments in any amount. These examples of inclusive receivability are not of great importance, however, for the simple reason that the first applied only to small amounts and the second was virtually equivalent to payment in coin since gold of almost the face value had to be deposited. It thus appears that a policy of limiting receivability prevailed in the finances of the period.

In at least one respect, however, receivability was extended in a comprehensive manner. This was in the arrangement for accepting outstanding obligations in exchange for new issues.

The potentialities of this aspect of receivability entitles it to a reference in passing. It was the policy of the Treasury to require that payments for new issues be made in " coin or lawful money ". Upon virtual disappearance of coin from circulation, holders of securities of the " lawful-money " variety accordingly enjoyed almost an exclusive

[1] *Act of Mar. 3, 1863,* 12 Stat. at Large 709, ch. 75, sec. 4, p. 711. *Act of June 30, 1864,* 13 Stat. at Large 218, ch. 172, sec. 5, p. 220.

[2] *Act of July 17, 1862,* 12 Stat. at Large 592, ch. 196, sec. 1.

[3] *Act of Mar. 3, 1863,* 12 Stat. at Large 709, ch. 73, sec. 5, p. 711.

right to purchase new issues. If emissions of legal tenders had been kept within reason and if the new issues had been put out on an attractive basis it is entirely conceivable that the privelege in question would have come to be of material value.

Even under conditions as they were, it is probable that the receivability feature in its several manifestations placed government obligations in a position to benefit, first, from the convenience enjoyed by holders and, secondly, from the increased usefulness of the notes as a medium of exchange. While in most instances the advantages so gained are not measurable, and while in all instances the desirable results were minimized because of the absence of proper coordination, we may nevertheless be permitted the conjecture that the feature contributed to a certain extent to the public's willingness to purchase and hold the acceptable securities.

We find in the demand note at least one example in which it is possible to approximate a quantitative measure of the addition to the value of the security consequent upon the adoption of the receivability feature.

It will be recalled that these notes were receivable for all dues to the Government, including customs, that they were convertible, and that they were later made legal tender for all debts. We shall first dispose of the other features before attempting to evaluate the effects of the receivability feature.

The legal tender feature would serve only to keep the demand on a par with United States notes. The provision for redemption in gold would operate in the direction of maintaining their parity with gold as long as they were being redeemed. It is logical to assume, however, that with the suspension of specie payments, this feature would diminish in importance. In fact, it is doubtful whether the hope of redemption in gold would have much more effect on their price than it would upon the price of bonds; and yet on a day when 6% twenty-year bonds were quoted barely above par, demand notes were selling at a premium of 71.[1]

This reference to the bonds suggests yet another hypothesis. Since the demand notes were convertible into the attractive 6%, twenty-year bonds, might not this fact have been influential in keeping up the price of the demand notes? The answer is easily found. The fact that the price of the notes was, as we have already indicated, at a level above that of the bonds into which they were convertible dispels any thought that this factor maintained the price.

We must conclude that the legal tender feature, the promise to redeem in coin, the conversion privilege, and even that part of the receivability feature which was applicable to legal tenders as well as to demand notes, were by their very nature incapable of maintaining the price of demand notes. On the other hand, it is easy to see that the feature which permitted an individual to substitute demand notes for gold in making payments to the Government would logically result in maintaining the price of the former at a level approaching that of the precious metal. We may accordingly conclude that the receivability feature together with events which made it of value, may be thanked for the high price of the demand notes. A rough approximation of this value may be had quite readily in the form of figures showing the excess (already stated as being approximately 70 points) of prices for demand notes over the prices of the bonds into which they were convertible.

One can easily see that the receivability feature could not under any conditions have held up the prices of the entire volume of war securities. At the same time, the degree in

[1] Feb. 28, 1863 *Hunts*, vol. 49, p. 471. See also *ibid.*, p. 70, and vol. 48, pp. 542-543 for comparative prices of these and other issues from May, 1862, to May, 1863.

which the receivability clause contributed to the currency of the demand notes illustrates the manner in which the feature works. These facts concerning demand notes suggest that other receivable securities were similarly affected. This would be notably true of the treasury notes, which shared in part the benefits enjoyed by the demand notes.

A significant step was taken in connection with the issue of obligations for the purpose of assisting the railroads.[1] Bonds as well as treasury notes, coupons for services rendered to the Government, and other evidences of debt against the United States, were declared receivable in repayment of the railroad bonds.

Although developed during a period when similar features were being drafted into the service of war-financing, the receivability feature was not extended to war bonds. We may accordingly content ourselves with a bare mention of its use in connection with the subsidy bonds and wait until a later period for an example of its use as an integral part of a financing program.[2]

PAYMENT UPON DEMAND

The promise that notes would be redeemed upon demand[3] included certain novel characteristics[4] which could scarcely fail to make it the most effective feature thus far found for

[1] *Act of July 1, 1862,* 12 Stat. at Large 489, ch. 120, p. 493.

[2] *Infra,* ch. x.

[3] *Act of July 17, 1861,* 12 Stat. at Large 259, ch. 5, sec. 1; *Act of Aug. 5, 1861,* 12 Stat. at Large 313, ch. 46, sec. 5; *Act of Feb. 12, 1862,* 12 Stat. at Large 338, ch. 20, sec. 1.

Later use of the idea is to be found in *Act of Mar. 2, 1867,* 14 Stat. at Large 558, ch. 194, and in the *Act of July 25, 1868,* 15 Stat. at Large 183, ch. 237. The *Act of Feb. 25, 1862,* 12 Stat. at Large 345, ch. 33, sec. 1, substituted legal tenders for $50,000,000 of the previous "demand notes."

[4] See *supra,* p. 68, for an account of an earlier offer to redeem upon demand.

securing the acceptance of the notes at the time of issue.[1] Under careful observation, however, close resemblance to receivability becomes apparent. One can see that the provision differs from receivability only in that the arrangement for accepting securities was extended to apply to any quantity and circumstances and in that the government substituted coin payments for a tax receipt or for a newly issued government security. As long as redemptions were being made the obligation to redeem on demand worked hand in hand with the provision for receiving notes as payments to the government. The government's own obligations came to predominate in its holdings of currency. As a result, the Treasury found itself compelled to arrange for making disbursements in such currency as it received.

PAYMENT TO PUBLIC CREDITORS

The practice of using governmental obligations in meeting the claims of creditors who were willing to accept them was a survival from former periods. Even just prior to the outbreak of hostilities, the Treasury was authorized to issue treasury notes in payment of the Government's debts.[2]

At an early stage of war financing, there was introduced a variation from the plan of allowing creditors to invest in whatever issues happened to be placed before the public. Special securities designed for the purpose of settling the claims, especially of small creditors, were issued at the same time that more remunerative investments were being offered to purchasers who could make payments in coin.[3]

[1] For a criticism of demand notes, see Sherman, *op. cit.*, p. 259.

[2] *Act of Dec. 12, 1860*, 12 Stat. at Large, ch. 1; *Act of Mar. 2, 1861*, 12 Stat. at Large 178, ch. 68.

[3] The *Act of July 17, 1861* (12 Stat. at Large 259, ch. 5, sec. 1), for example, provided for the isuse of non-interest bearing notes in denominations as low as $10.00 in payment of salaries and other debts of the United States, while the same act provided for 3.65% notes and for a maximum of $20,000,000 in notes with an authorized interest rate as high at 6%.

Later an enactment [1] made provision for a special form of security which was correctly described as a certificate of indebtedness. Legally these interest-bearing obligations were to be used only where the creditor was willing to receive them. We find an occasional suggestion, however, that this willingness existed, if at all, merely because of the absence of a satisfactory alternative.[2]

With the suspension of specie payment and the resulting elimination of coin receipts, resort to depreciated bank notes appeared the only alternative [3] to an ever increasing dependence upon governmental obligations. The Secretary made an urgent appeal to all officials for assistance in upholding the requirement that disbursement should be made only in obligations of the United States.[4] Interest on treasury notes and certificates of indebtedness,[5] and even the wages of soldiers,[6] came to be paid in the government's own obligations.

In order that the Treasury should never be without funds, if indeed its own promises to pay may properly be termed such, the Secretary was on one occasion given a " reserve " upon which he could call in an emergency when funds were required for various purposes.[7]

Thus it appears that the Government's use of its own obligations for paying its creditors originally amounted to a mere offer of an investment to creditors. It evolved, however, into a comprehensive scheme to substitute the Govern-

[1] *Act of March 1, 1862,* 12 Stat. at Large 352, ch. 35.

[2] *Cf. Cong. Globe,* 37th Cong., 2nd Sess., pt. 4, p. 2884, June 23, 1862. Mr. Watts-House.

[3] *Treas. Report,* 1863, pp. 7-8.

[4] *Treas. Report,* 1862, p. 14.

[5] *Act of Mar. 3, 1863,* 12 Stat. at Large 709, ch. 73, sec. 2, p. 710.

[6] *Treas. Report,* 1864, p. 21.

[7] *Act of Mar. 3, 1863,* 12 Stat. at Large 709, ch. 73, sec. 3, p. 710.

ment's promise to pay for actual payment. The resulting practice contrived with the several aspects of the receivability feature to complete a security's circuit from the Treasury to the people and back again. Moreover, within the limits of the channel through which the securities flowed while making their way as payments from the government to the people and ultimately back to the Treasury, the obligations, even without the legal tender privilege, enjoyed practically all the power of money.[1] The fact that the flow was limited to a definite channel, and that the current was slackened by numerous obstacles which appeared on the route from the Treasury to the people, could not fail to suggest that the volume of the flow might be increased if the stream were allowed to break the bounds of its confining banks and by so doing allow the dammed-up surplus to circulate over new areas, or to remain wherever circumstances permitted.

The measure which was designed for this purpose of broadening the confines within which the notes would circulate and of removing the hindrances to their free acceptance supplies the material for a separate story, the gist of which will be given in the following section.

LEGAL TENDER

We shall touch lightly upon the familiar subject of legal tender. In the main, the authorizing acts [2] possess little of

[1] An appreciation of the importance of this development can be gained by referring to the magnitude of governmental disbursements. Even in the early part of the war average daily outlays by the Treasury had reached the unthought of level of about two million dollars (Expenditures, *Treas. Report,* 1862, p. 31), while those of later days approximated twice this amount (Expenditures, *Treas. Report,* 1864, p. 32).

[2] The issue of legal tenders was regulated by the following acts: *The Act of Feb. 25, 1862,* 12 Stat. at Large 345, ch. 38, sec. 1; *The Act of July 11, 1862,* 12 Stat. at Large 532, ch. 42, sec. 1; *The Act of March 17, 1862,* 12 Stat. at Large 370, ch. 45, sec. 2, declaring demand notes legal tender; *The Act of Mar. 3, 1863,* 12 Stat. at Large 709, ch. 73, sec. 3, p.

interest other than the legel tender clause itself. The extension of the privilege to obligations bearing interest at 6%,[1] and to securities bearing 6% compound interest, however, constituted an interesting variation from the usual procedure. Since compulsory acceptance was to apply only to their face value, there still would have remained some incentive for holding these notes as investment had not the banks hit upon the scheme of clipping off the coupons and using the fleeced notes as currency. An attempt to prevent this practice was made in the form of a requirement, later modified, that the coupons be removed only by a government officer.[2]

In view of the widespread attention ordinarily accorded to the legal tender arrangement it may be desirable to treat briefly the important facts in connection with its adoption as a financing device.

In the main, it appears, there existed a fair degree of appreciation of the undesirable manner in which the feature operated. Frequent warnings against overissues, pledges that emissions would cease, and actual legal enactment against further issues [3] can be explained only by reference to this anticipation of undesirable consequences.

710; *The Act of June 30, 1864,* 13 Stat. at Large 218, ch. 172, sec. 2; *The Act of Jan 28, 1865,* 13 Stat. at Large 425, ch. 22.

Although fractional currency was not made legal tender for private debts this form of currency may properly be studied in conjunction with the subject of legal tenders. An *Act of July 17, 1862* (12 Stat. at Large 592, ch. 196, sec. 1), provided for the use of postage and other stamps of the United States as currency. The *Act of March 3, 1863* (12 Stat. at Large 709, ch. 73, sec. 4, p. 711) and the *Act of June 30, 1864* (13 Stat. at Large 218, sec. 5, p. 220), authorized the issue of postage and revenue stamps in fractional notes.

[1] *Act of Mar. 3, 1863, op. cit.,* and the *Act of June 30, 1864, op, cit.*

[2] Dewey, *op. cit.,* p. 312; Bolles, *The Financial History of the United States from 1861 to 1885* (New York, 1886), pp. 113-114.

[3] *Treas. Report,* 1863, p. 18. *Cong. Globe, 37th Cong. 3rd Sess.,* pt. 1,

Especially at the time of the first authorization attaching the legal tender provision, a query arose as to why it should be passed. The answer was that it was necessary.[1] In defending this assertion administration leaders began with the accepted fact that the government was in dire need of funds. It was accordingly absolutely necessary to adopt some measue which would enable the government to meet its obligations immediately. The employment of the legal tender feature was the only possible means of attaining the desired results.[2] As a matter of fact, even the statement of administration leaders, including Secretary Chase,[3] supports the contention that the situation was not exactly as they intimated.[4]

At the same time comments of opponents of the measure give more telling evidence that the feature was in reality recognized as merely one of a number of possible means for obtaining funds and that its selection came as a result of the unwillingness on the part of the administration leaders to "pay the price" of any alternative proposal.[5]

p. 840-2. Sherman-Senate, Feb. 10, 1863. For an earlier statement in opposition, see Morrill, *Cong. Globe,* 36th Cong., 2nd Sess., pt. 1, pp. 629-30, February 4, 1862. Mitchell, *op. cit.,* pp. 122, 125 and 128. Also enactment, *Act of June 30, 1864,* 138 Stat. at Large 218, ch. 172, sec. 2, p. 219.

[1] For a criticism of the argument of "necessity" see Samuel J. Spear, *The Legal Tender Acts,* pp. 88 *et seq.,* New York, 1875; also Gallatins *Letters to Daniel Wilmot, op. cit.,* p. 4.

[2] Mr. Fessenden defended the measure as a temporary expedient which was designed to meet an "absolutely overwhelming necessity" (*Cong. Globe,* 37th Cong., 2nd Sess., pt. 1, p. 766, Feb. 12, 1862—Fessenden). Mr. Spaulding told members of the House that it arose from necessity and not from choice (*Cong. Globe,* vol. 32, pt. i, p. 523, Jan. 28, 1862. Spaulding).

[3] *Treas. Report,* 1862, p. 2. See later statements by Mr. McCulloch, *Treas. Report.* 1865, pp. 3 and 1867, p. 10.

[4] See Mitchell, *op. cit.,* pp. 47, 30, 59, 60, 67, 68, 77, 73, 95 and 120 for comments on this aspect of the subject.

[5] See *supra,* p. 79 *et seq.,* for references.

Such an alternative could have been selected from any number of substitute proposals. Thus a plan to replace legal tenders with interest-bearing treasury notes [1] and another, to leave the notes as they were except that they were to be devoid of the legal tender feature,[2] illustrate alternative proposals of one type. Certificates of indebtedness,[3] demand notes,[4] bank notes,[5] the banking system itself, and of course bonds, were all recognized as substitutes for legal tenders.

We are forced to conclude, therefore, that the legal tender feature was deliberately chosen in preference to other financing devices. Why the legal tender provision was chosen from a group of somewhat similar devices as the means of placing the government's obligations in the market becomes evident when we analyze its advantages over the others. No plan involving dependence upon investment funds promised to produce immediate revenue easily. Of the arrangements which tampered with the currency, none rivaled the legal tender feature as a means of appropriating for government obligations the qualities of money.

Even receivability suffered in comparison, for this feature resulted in making notes acceptable as money only in the area in which the government operated as a business enterprise. As a result of the absence, first, of high taxes and, secondly, of attractive securities for which the notes could be exchanged,

[1] Mitchell, *op. cit.*, pp. 65 and 75.

[2] *Cong. Globe,* 37th Cong., 3rd Sess., pt. i, pp. 614-15. Amendment offered by Mr. Vallandigham.

[3] *Cong. Globe,* 37th Cong., 3rd Sess., pt. iv, p. 2884, Mr. Wattes, June 23, 1862.

[4] The *Act of Feb. 12, 1862* (12 Stat. at Large 338, ch. 20) actually authorized the issue of $10,000,000 in demand notes while Congress was debating the legal tender bill. The interchangeability of the two forms of notes is further illustrated by the fact that a plan for substituting legal tenders for the demand notes was incorporated in the legal tender act when it was passed.

[5] *Supra*, p. 79. *Cf.* Spalding, *op. cit.*, p. 13.

the value of the receivability feature was greatly minimized. At best, neither the receivability feature nor any other similar device succeeded in compelling the general acceptance of the notes in private business transactions. It was in this respect that the legal tenders enjoyed an advantage over all the substitute measures. A creditor who received the government's promise to pay might take the securities whither he would and find a market enforced by law. As a result the legal tender feature not only enforced the acceptance of the notes by public creditors and thus supplied a market for the securities, but went still farther to enforce conditions which guaranteed that the first holders would be able to dispose of them at "par". The arrangement accordingly represented a realization to the *nth* degree of the aims of the numerous features which had been used and which have since been employed both to facilitate the sale of securities and to maintain their position in the market. Because of this, legal tenders were repeatedly and successfully used in the task of securing funds for the Treasury.[1] The alleviation of the ills of the time apparently overshadowed the possible evils of the future sufficiently to secure support for the measure as a short cut to financial strength.

CONVERSION

The conversion arrangement was originally the subject of high hopes on the part of administration leaders who expected the conversion notes to be so universal that direct issues of long time obligations would be unnecessary.[2]

[1] The government paid out $188,000,000 in notes and certificates while selling less than $3,000,000 in bonds (*Cong. Globe*, 37th Cong., 2nd Sess., pt. iii and iv, pp. 2880-2881). See Dewey, *op. cit.*, p. 316, for a tabulation of loans for the entire war period.

[2] *Cong. Globe*, 37th Cong., 2nd Sess., pt. iv, p. 2882, Hooper, June 23, 1862. *Cong. Globe*, 37th Cong., 3rd Sess., pt. i, p. 847, Sherman. Mitchell, History, *op. cit.*, pp. 58, 88 and 89.

While their high hopes were not justified, we nevertheless find sufficient use and misuse of the feature to warrant an enumeration of some of the details of its operation.

Looked at from one angle, certain operations of the period appear as adjuncts of a funding program. The means employed were comparable in effect to a revival and amendment of the old acts and the attachment of new features to the outstanding securities. This arrangement, which we have hitherto designated as "post mortem" convertibility, was used extensively during the period.[1]

While the technical make-up of these provisions for the conversion of existing issues into new ones may not differ materially from that of the common funding and refunding measures, they can not be understood so long as one studies only the manner in which they facilitated these operations. On the contrary, these measures must be considered in connection with the financing program itself.

This connection is first suggested by the fact that the feature was attached at the time of issue, and apparently for the purpose of making the securities more attractive. A second common characteristic is to be found in the specification of the security into which the note may be converted.[2]

This form of conversion was prevalent during the entire period. Treasury notes of one type were made exchangeable for stock of the same authorization; the 3.65% notes were convertible into the seven-thirties; legal tenders and certificates of deposit[3] were made convertible into five-twenty

[1] *Act of August 5, 1861,* 12 Stat. at Large 313, ch. 46, sec. 7, p. 314; *Act of Feb. 25, 1862,* 12 Stat. at Large 345, ch. 33, sec. 2; *Act of July 11, 1862,* 12 Stat. at Large 532, ch. 142, sec. 1; *Act of June 30, 1864,* 13 Stat. at Large, 218, ch. 172, sec. 2; *Act of April 12, 1866,* 14 Stat. at Large 31, ch. 39, sec. 1.

[2] *Act of July 17, 1861,* 12 Stat. at Large 259, ch. 5, sec. 1; *Act of Aug. 5, 1861,* 12 Stat. at Large 313, ch. 46, sec. 1.

[3] *Act of Feb. 25, 1862,* 12 Stat. at Large 345, ch. 33, sec. 1; *Act of July 11, 1862,* 12 Stat. at Large 532, ch. 142, sec. 1, 3.

sixes; postage and other stamps [1] as well as fractional currency to the amount of three dollars [2] could be exchanged for United States notes. The list of exchangeable securities was later extended to provide for the redemption of national bank notes in lawful money.

An examination of the operations of this type of conversion accordingly discloses the fact that in its numerous manifestations, the feature served in a very subtle manner virtually to connect all of the governmental issues. The fact that the value of one type of security could not be far out of line with that of another which was convertible into it accordingly operated toward maintaining security prices at a uniform level.

In providing for conversion it was of course intended that the value of the securities should be supported by the attractiveness of those into which they were convertible. On one occasion it became apparent, however, that the reverse was equally true, and that bonds could be degraded to the level of convertible legal tenders. At least this was the excuse Chase offered for not having utilized the remaining authorized but unissued five-twenties to supply much needed revenue. His claims constitute an interesting indictment of the feature in question. The underlying conditions are already known: Legal tenders, we will recall, were made convertible into five twenties. These bonds, in turn, carried a provision which was apparently intended to give the Secretary permission to sell the bonds at a discount but which, according to Mr. Chase's technical interpretation, prohibited sales below par.[3]

[1] *Act of July 17, 1862,* 12 Stat. at Iarge 592, ch. 196, sec. 1.

[2] *Act of Mar. 3, 1863,* 12 Stat. at Large 709, ch. 73, sec. 3, p. 711.

[3] The authorization allowed the Secretary to sell at "market price". It would seem that he stated his position and then refused to admit the possibility of what even his advisers considered as a more common-sense interpretation. His action or inaction on the entire matter, it would seem, demonstrated a lack of executive ability.

According to Chase, the resulting conditions [1] made it impossible for him to dispose of the unissued bonds, because first, he was restrained (according to his own interpretation) from selling bonds below par, and, secondly, the presence of large volumes of notes forced prices of the bonds into which they were convertible down and thereby destroyed the market for additional securities of the same type. As a result, Chase claimed that although he had the right to issue bonds, the technical requirement coupled with the conversion situation made it impossible for him to sell them. In short, two forces were pulling against each other in a way that prevented a satisfactory operation of the Treasury's business and all because financing features had not been properly coordinated.[2]

Chase accordingly requested the repeal of the conversion feature, implying as he did so that the entire difficulty partook of the nature of a legal or technical restriction rather than of an economic or financial barrier. A closer study of the facts, however, discloses that the latter type of barrier was by no means lacking. Furthermore, the discontinuance of a practice of such small proportions as the conversions of greenbacks into bonds,[3] should hardly have been expected to offset both the low rate of interest and the unattractive possibility of having the bonds redeemed within five years.[4]

[1] *Treas. Report,* 1862, p. 25; Spaulding, *op. cit.*, p. 181; Bolles, *op. cit.*, pp. 96-97; Mitchell, *op. cit.*, p. 104.

[2] It may be of interest to observe that Chase's problem was similar to the conversion tangle of 1814 (*supra*, ch. ii) in that in each case the difficulty arose as a result of the fact that all of the authorized securities were not sold at once.

[3] Mitchell, *op. cit.*, p. 89.

[4] *Cong. Globe,* 37th Cong., 2nd Sess., pt. iii, p. 2768, June 17, 1862; Colfax and Sherman. Bolles, *op. cit.*, p. 82. Later (p. 95) Bolles commends the action of Chase.

The Secretary's recommendation that the right to convert legal tenders into bonds be repealed, was put through quietly on March 3, 1863.[1] Supposedly the matter was left to the discretion of the Secretary.[2]

When it is recalled that aside from the receivability feature, the conversion into bonds represented the only definite plan for the redemption of the legal tenders, the action appears serious. Especially would this have been true had there followed no future issues for which outstanding notes were receivable. As it happened, however, holders of legal tenders had ample opportunity to exchange for newly issued bonds. Consequently, Chase's contention that the receivability feature was equivalent to the conversion feature[3] found support at least for a time. The immediate change took place not in the matter of existing practices, but rather in the prospective future of the notes. After the Act of March 3, 1863 had authorized the Secretary to follow his inclinations in the matter of discontinuing conversion, there was little chance that this feature would ever be retained to the point of improving the status of the notes—especially since doing so would depress the five-twenty sixes. Any ideas to the contrary were dispelled on January 21, 1864, when conversion by this means was discontinued.[4]

That the step was taken at this particular time is of special significance. Jay Cooke, following an inflation program, had promoted the sale of the five-twenty sixes until the entire amount authorized had been subscribed. Chase, pleased with his success, was preparing to begin a new and more venturesome enterprise, in which the goal consisted of a

[1] 12 Stat. at Large 709, ch. 73, sec. 3, p. 711.

[2] Spaulding, *Financial History of the War,* 2nd ed., p. 10. Mitchell, *op. cit.*, pp. 115-116.

[3] *Treas. Report,* 1862, p. 25.

[4] Spaulding, *op. cit.*, Introductory, p. 10. Also, pp. 190 and 195.

decrease of one point of interest on the new loan. But if the rate on the forthcoming issue was to be lowered to five per cent, the right to convert legal tender currency into a six per cent bond would have to be discontinued before any purchase of the new bonds would be made. It is not surprising therefore that Chase availed himself of the power to repeal the provision. Nor is it difficult to understand why this step accompanied the close of sales on the five-twenty sixes and featured the beginning of the campaign for the sale of the new issue of five-percent bonds.

The episode brought to light a distinction which Chase had previously ignored when he implied that conversion at will and receivability were synonymous. To be sure there was no difference in the two practices so long as the bonds into which the notes were convertible were being offered to the public. No holder would care whether the transaction by which he exchanged notes for bonds were called conversion or the purchase of a new bond. But when the government ceased to offer such bonds, the distinction became apparent. At this stage, the step appears in its true light as a breach of contract, which, while promising to facilitate the operations of the Treasury, perpetrated an outright injustice on the holders of the legal tenders.[1]

While the Act of March 3, 1865 [2] together with an amendment [3] returned the obligations to their former status by making them convertible into a five to twenty year six per cent bond, it would seem logical to include this development as an aspect of refunding rather than as a phase of the subject of conversion. At least, these steps came too late to

[1] *Cf.* Samuel T. Spear, *The Legal Tender Acts,* New York, 1875, p. 70. Chase himself later admitted that the step should not have been taken. McCulloch, *op. cit.,* p. 186.

[2] 13 Stat. at Large 468, ch. 77, sec. 1.

[3] *Act of April 12, 1866,* 14 Stat. at Large 31, ch. 39, sec. 1.

retrieve the damage done to holders of legal tenders when one of the most valuable features of their notes was taken away.

TEMPORARY DEPOSITS

The arrangement for receiving notes on temporary deposit and for allowing interest on the amounts so received may quite properly be considered a variation of the conversion feature and a device for securing the currency of the notes. The measure called forth not a few arguments, pro and con,[1] and in fact experienced some difficulty in getting started. Once under way, however, it gained momentum and was soon defended as a successful arrangement.[2]

Repeated authorizations including a progressive elevation of the maximum,[3] were necessary in order to keep pace with an ever-increasing volume of notes (including bank notes later) offered for deposit. Even decreasing the rate of interest to 4%,[4] did not prevent a satisfactory response.[5]

The arrangement for converting non-interest-bearing currency into interest-paying investments, and of reconverting investments into cash, affords one of the most interesting of the numerous variations of the conversion privilege. As a device for securing funds, the certificate of deposit operated effectively in obtaining money at a low rate of interest. Al-

[1] *Cong. Globe*, 37th Cong., 2nd Sess., pt. i, p. 764, Fessenden, and p. 772, Sherman, Feb. 12, 1862. Mitchell, *op. cit.*, pp. 85 and 86. Bolles, *op. cit.*, pp. 89-91.

[2] *Cong. Globe*, 37th Cong., 2nd Sess., pts. iii and iv, pp. 2880-2881, Mr. Baker. Pt. iv, p. 2882, Mr. Hooper.

[3] *Act of Feb. 25, 1862*, 12 Stat. at Large 345, ch. 33, sec. 4, p. 346; *Act of Mar. 17, 1862*, 12 Stat. at Large 370, ch. 45, sec. 3; *Act of July 11, 1862*, 12 Stat. at Large 532, ch. 142, sec. 3; *Act of June 30, 1864*, 13 Stat. at Large, 218, ch. 172, sec. 4, p. 219.

[4] The decrease followed the Act of Mar. 17, 1862, in which the Secretary was given permission to offer any rate not greater than 5%.

[5] Mitchell, *op. cit.*, p. 91.

though opponents of the measure saw in the large reserve amounting to one-third of the total deposits [1] a cost item which mitigated against the desirability of the feature,[2] a proper understanding of the nature of this reserve can not fail to dispel any such idea. The sum authorized for this purpose was itself made up of promises to pay, the cost of which amounted to no more than the outlay for printing.

It is at this point, however, that a more valid objection arises. The entire arrangement when scrutinized closely appears simply another scheme supplementing the plan for financing the war by the issue of legal tenders. In the words of James Gallatin, ". . . this proposal to create a deposit system without limit is in fact a proposal to issue more legal tender paper without limit." [3]

In justice to its proponents, however, we must admit that with its round-about method the plan at least provided a satisfactory means of issuing additional legal tenders, and that it even made some progress toward securing investment funds. Although the system was developed in only a rudimentary form and was handicapped by the absence of adequate facilities, it is not difficult to see in the plan the germs of a system of credit extensively utilized in World-War financing. The cynic may even point out that the system resulted to a limited extent in the very sort of accomplishment which Chase's action in retaining the Sub-Treasury had denied to the early financial development.

[1] The *Act of July 11, 1862, op. cit.*, provided for a reserve of $50,000,000 in legal tenders.

[2] *Cong. Globe*, 37th Cong., 2nd Sess., pt. iv, p. 3075, Mr. Collamer, July 2, 1863.

[3] *National Debt, Taxation, Currency* and *Banking System*, New York, 1864, p. 19.

COIN PAYMENTS

Although the provision for the payment of interest and principal in coin would not at present be considered a device for making bonds more attractive, events during the Civil War were of such a nature as to make this feature of no little importance.

We have already mentioned certain actions pertaining to the attempt to obtain coin. In this class may be included the attempt to secure coin payment to the Sub-Treasury, the requirement that custom duties be paid in coin, permission to the Secretary of the Treasury to make direct purchases of gold,[1] and the arrangement for receiving deposits of gold and issuing certificates up to 120% of the value of the gold.[2] All of these actions were occasioned by the fact that in certain payments only gold could be used.[3]

At first the interest payments on both bonds and treasury notes were made in coin. The interest on bonds continued to be paid in coin, but interest on treasury notes, on certificates of indebtedness, and on certificates of deposit came to be paid in lawful money.[4]

Previous to the adoption of lawful money as the currency in which interest on short-time obligations should be paid, the application of the same principle had been made to the thirty-year railroad bonds which were authorized in 1862.[5]

[1] *Act of Mar. 17, 1862,* 12 Stat. at Large 370, ch. 45, sec. 1.

[2] *Act of Mar. 3, 1863,* 12 Stat. at Large 709, ch. 73, sec. 5, p. 711. We may observe that in so far as this act resulted in assembling gold at central points the measure resembled those of a later period when the centralizing of gold in Federal Reserve banks facilitated the attempt of Mr. McAdoo to expand the currency to meet the needs of a program of inflation.

[3] *Cf. Cong.* Globe, 37th Cong., 3rd Sess., pt. i, p. 846, Mr. Powell, Feb. 10, 1863, Mr. Sherman.

[4] *Act of Mar. 3, 1863,* 12 Stat. at Large 709, ch. 73, sec. 2, p. 710; *Act of Mar. 2, 1867,* 14 Stat. at Large 558, ch. 194 and acts between these two acts. *Cf.* Mitchell, *op. cit.*, p. 118.

[5] *Act of July 1,* 12 Stat. at Large 489, ch. 120, sec. 5, p. 492.

This authorization is the more interesting in view of the fact that the contemplated bonds were to be given as a subsidy and were not, therefore, in search of a market. The abandonment of payment in coin only when the promised use of specie was not necessary for placing the securities, may suggest the hypotheses that provision for payment of interest in specie was an important factor when the Treasury was faced with the task of selling its bonds. The hypothesis receives some support in the subsequent recognition of the difference between the rates payable in lawful money and those payable in coin. Secretary Fessenden admitted this difference when, in attempting to avoid anticipated difficulties, he urged that provision be made for paying interest in lawful money even at a higher rate.[1] Later an enactment [2] actually provided that interest could be made payable either in lawful money or coin, but recognized the distinction between the two by raising the limit from 6 per cent where payable in coin to 7.3 per cent if payable in lawful money.

The subject of coin payment must be considered in connection with the repayment of principal as well as with the payment of interest.

A provision for redeeming the ten-forties in coin came after [3] a period of uncertainty in which the exact status of bonds was not definitely known. This uncertainty was occasioned by the peculiar omission from the earlier authorizing act of any specific promise to redeem the five-twenties in coin. As a result, there existed some apprehension that the bonds would be redeemed in legal tenders. The original provision for a sinking fund which was to accumulate coin for the express purpose of retiring the public debt, however, serves as proof of the fact that repayment in gold was

[1] *Treas. Report*, 1864, pp. 23-24.

[2] *Act of Mar. 3, 1865*, 14 Stat. at Large 468, ch. 77, sec. 1.

[3] *Act of Mar. 3, 1864*, 13 Stat. at Large 13, ch. 17, sec. 1.

contemplated.[1] Attempts to dispel concern lest the bonds be redeemed in legal tender appeared in the form of a direct statement from an official of the Treasury Department to the effect that bonds would be paid in coin,[2] in statements from administration leaders and agents for the government,[3] and even in the report of Secretary Fessenden, who in 1864[4] characterized the failure of several of the acts to provide for repayment in coin as "accidental" and proceeded to recommend that proper legislation "remove all doubt on this point."

However, his recommendation failed to result in the desired legislation; nor did any other action on the part of the government prevent a situation which led Secretary McCulloch a year later to urge the legislature to place on record a promise to redeem the five-twenties in coin. By this time, the Secretary pointed out, "the policy of the government in regard to its funded debt is well understood in the United States. . . .", but the measure was still needed to remove the apprehension in Europe that the five-twenty bonds might be called at the expiration of five years and paid in United States notes.[5] Agitation on the subject continued[6] until the efforts to place government securities on a more stable foot-

[1] *Act of Feb. 25, 1862,* 12 Stat. at Large 345, ch. 33, sec. 5, p. 346.

[2] 18 *Bankers Magazine*, p. 10 (cited by Bolles, *op. cit.*, ft. note, p. 316).

[3] *Cf.* Bolles, *op. cit.*, pp. 316-318.

[4] *Treas. Report,* p. 5.

[5] *Treas. Report,* 1865, pp. 25-26. An interesting idea is to be found in President Johnson's contention that holders of the obligations should be paid an amount equivalent to what the government received in real money (McCulloch, *op. cit.*, pp. 220-221).

[6] See for example *Charles Sumner's Speech in the Senate,* July 11, 1868 (published, F. and J. Rives and Geo. A. Baily, Washington, 1868), p. 6 *et seq.*, and a letter of Jay Cooke's under date of March 19, 1868 (appearing in N. Y. Public Library, Volume T.I.E. p.v. 64, No. 10.

ing finally elicited from Congress a definite promise to redeem all obligations of the government in coin.[1]

While this action was taken in time to exert a salutary influence upon a portion of the refunding operations, it came after the day of its greatest possible influence had passed; for in the meantime a large part of the war bonds had been sold without an assurance that they would be redeemed in gold. The resulting uncertainty as to their status could scarcely have failed to increase the speculative character of the investment. The result was that instead of enjoying the benefits of a measure which would have strengthened their price up to the level of par in gold, the bonds suffered from an uncertainty which tended to drag their value down to the level of par in the depreciated currency[2] with which perchance they would be redeemed.

That at least partial confidence in gold redemption could have been secured by a mere inclusion of a promise to this effect no one would deny. It accordingly seems that the government overlooked an opportunity in failing to take this effective means of assuring the public of its intentions.

TAX EXEMPTION

While the problem of exemption as it was known after the appearance of the progressive income tax of 1913 was not present during the Civil War, several developments in connection with the subject of exemption deserve mention.

In the first place, it appears that the states had ever looked with a jealous eye on the federal debt as a possible source of taxes, and that the effort to thwart any such intentions led to the insertion of a section in each of the loan acts declaring bonds to be free from all taxation by or under state authority.[1]

[1] *Act of March 18, 1869,* 16 Stat. at Large 1, ch. 18.

[2] See *Hunts,* vol. 48, pp. 70-71 and vol. 49, pp. 46-47 for prices of bonds.

[1] *Act of Feb. 25, 1862,* 12 Stat. at Large 345, ch. 33, sec. 2, p. 346; *Act*

We should observe that the promise to exempt the securities from taxation by the states did not change the legal status of the bonds, but served merely to clarify their position.

The appearance of the national banks on the scene was the occasion for additional queries concerning the problem of exemption; for here was another source of taxation which was denied to the states. Proposals for the taxation of banks became so insistent as to inspire Mr. Clarke, the comptroller of the currency, to set forth an elaborate argument against such action.[1]

Of special interest is the fact that the Comptroller's suggestion for pacifying those who would allow the states to tax the banks consisted of a plan to issue taxable bonds when the Treasury came to refund the existing debt.

Of equal importance was his argument against state taxation of those government securities which formed the invested capital of national banks.[2]

The entire subject of taxation came up for a full discussion on the part of Secretary McCulloch[3] who contended that the abandonment of exemption (from state taxation) would force the payment of three points additional interest.

In 1869 Secretary Boutwell recommended that exemption be extended over all taxes, unless indeed, it were thought wise to make an exception of the income tax.[4]

of Mar. 3, 1863, 12 Stat. at Large 709, ch. 73, sec. 1, p. 710; *Act of Mar. 3, 1865*, 13 Stat. at Large 468, ch. 77, sec. 2, p. 469; *Act of June 30, 1864*, 13 Stat. at Large 218, ch. 172, sec. 1; *Act of Mar. 3, 1864*, 13 Stat. at Large 13, ch. 17, sec. 1; *Act of Jan. 28, 1865*, 13 Stat. at Large 425, ch. 22, sec. 1. *Cf.* Bolles, *op. cit.*, p. 326 and James Gallatin, *Financial Economy of the U.S.*, p. 16.

[1] *Treas. Report*, 1865, pp. 69-70.

[2] *Treas. Report*, 1865, p. 69.

[3] *Treas. Report*, 1865, p. 26.

[4] *Treas. Report*, 1869, p. 17.

Congress was not long in following the suggestion. The Act of July 14, 1870[1] bestowed upon the authorized bonds a feature which came to be common to American securities. All bonds were made exempt from taxes and duties of the United States as well as from all security taxes levied by or under state, municipal, or local authority.[2]

[1] 16 Stat. at Large 272, ch. 256, sec. 1.

[2] The exact status of exemption of federal securities by the states can be understood only by following court decisions on the subject. The decision by Marshall (McCulloch *v.* Maryland, 4 Wheat. (U. S.) 316, 4 L. Ed. 579, 1819) laid the basis for later decision by enunciating the principle that a state cannot tax instrumentalities of the federal government employed in the exercise of its sovereign powers. A later decision (Weston *v.* City Council of Charleston, 2 Pet. (U. S.) 449, 7 L. Ed. 481, 1829) extended this principle so as to provide that states could not tax property when it is an instrumentality of the federal government. The specified "six and seven per cent stock of the U. S." was accordingly held to be outside the taxing power of the state.

In line with the last decision it was held (in Bank *v.* Supervisors, 7 Wall 26, 19 Law Ed. 60, 1869) in an opinion by Chase, that U. S. notes issued under the acts of 1862-3 were exempt from taxation by or under state authority. A similar decision was rendered on certificates of indebtedness issued for Civil War Supplies. (The Banks *v.* The Mayor, 7 Wall 16.)

These decisions were based on the principle that a general property tax is not permissible insofar as property includes federal instrumentalities.

More subtle reasoning had appeared in a previous ruling (Bank of Commerce *v.* Black, 620, 17 Law Ed. 451 (1862) in which the court held unconstitutional a tax on bank capital where the capital was measured by assets and a part of the latter was invested in government securities. Such a tax, it was held, was a tax on the property which constituted the capital. The doctrine was later applied in the Bank Tax Case (N. Y. *v.* Bank of Commonwealth, 2 Wall 200, 17 Law Ed. 793, 1864) where a tax on paid-in capital plus surplus (less 10%) was held to be void insofar as it was a tax on U. S. stocks.

Attention was directed to another aspect of the question in an 1865 decision (Van Allen *v.* Assessors, 3 Wall 573, 18 Law Ed. 229). The Court held that a tax on shares was not a tax on the capital of the bank,

NATIONAL BANKS AS AN OUTLET FOR BONDS

National banks were compelled to deliver interest-bearing

but on a distinct interest or property held by the shareholder. The Court accordingly held that a tax on bank shares was valid and that the assessment need not be reduced because of the fact that a part of the assets consisted of government stock.

The distinction was again drawn in National Bank *v.* Commonwealth (9 Wall 352) where the Court recognized a distinction between the property or interest of the bank's stockholders and the capital of the bank held and owned by the Corporation. If all of the capital of a bank should be in federal securities, the bank could not be taxed on its capital, but a tax on the shares of the corporation would be permissible. The *Act of June 3, 1864* (13 Stat. at Large 99, ch. 106, sec. 41, p. 112) stipulated that "nothing in this act shall prevent all the shares . . . held by any person or corporation from being included in the valuation of the personal property of such person or corporation in the assessment of taxes."

In Cleveland Trust *v.* Lander (184 U. S. 111, 1902) the Court refused to permit a reduction in the assessment because of investment in U. S. securities.

Still another decision (Home Ins. Co. *v.* N. Y., 134 U. S. 594 1890) established the validity of a states' tax on the privilege of being a corporation and of measuring the amount of the tax by the total capital stock without reduction for any investment in federal securities. In short, therefore, the result of the court decisions has been to legalize certain methods of circumventing the established precedent that states are not to tax federal securities.

This precedent, we gather, was firmly established in McCulloch *v.* Maryland (1819) and Weston *v.* City of Charleston (1829). Consequently, it follows that provisions for exemption appearing in the 1870 act to which we have referred, in the *Act of Feb. 25, 1862* (12 Stat. at Large 345, ch. 33), in sections 3701 and 5219 *Revised Statutes*, and in the various loan acts, in so far as any of them refer to other than federal taxation, amount to nothing more than a mere statement of fact, and did not change the status of federal securities.

On the other hand, the question of whether federal securities were being taxed by states when the latter taxed national banks and the question of the condition under which the state should be permitted to tax these agencies (banks) of the national government has continued to give rise to public discussions and court decisions. Especially during the last few

United States bonds to an amount of not less than one third of the capital stock paid in.[1]

This provision accordingly compelled a national bank to purchase government securities and by so doing realized a purpose which had featured a large part of the arguments for the national bank.[2] Even the arguments of critics of

years (since the end of the last period treated in this monograph), the subject has attracted wide interest as evidenced, for example, by the files of the *Bulletin of the National Tax Association.* For references and interesting discussions see especially R. M. Haig, "Should Banks be Taxed, and How", vol. xv, no. 5, February, 1930, pp. 134-141; Martin Saxe, "The Threatened Discrimination in Banking Taxation," vol. xii, no. 6, March, 1928, pp. 166-175 (quoted from *Bankers' Magazine*, Dec., 1927); H. L. Lutz, "The Evolution of Section 5219, United States Revised Statutes," vol. xiii, no. 7, April, 1928 pp. 205-212.

[1] Against such bonds, the banks might issue circulating notes equal in amount to 90 per cent of the current market value of the bonds, but not exceeding par value if bearing 6 per cent interest. On other government bonds the amount was not to exceed the equivalent of par for 6 per cent securities. (*Act of Feb. 25, 1863*, 12 Stat. at Large 665, ch. 58, sec. 18, p. 669.

[2] Secretary Chase had described the feature as an arrangement which would furnish a market for $250,000,000 in bonds (*Treas. Report,* 1862, p. 5) and perhaps more. "A steady market for the bonds," he said, "would thus be established and the negotiations for them greatly facilitated." Again, "The proposed plan would create a constant demand equaling and often exceeding the supply" (*Treas. Report,* 1862, p. 18). The same idea was advanced by Mr. Sherman, who foresaw an early market for over 330 million dollars of bonds (*Cong. Globe,* 37th Cong., 3rd sess., pt. i, pp. 843-845). Mr. Chandler disclosed hopes equally high when he stated that if the measure accomplished anything it would produce a demand for government securities (*Cong. Globe,* 37th Cong., 3rd Sess., pt. i, p. 877, Feb. 11, 1863). Mr. Wilson worded his opinion slightly differently in declaring that he fought for the measure as a means of sustaining the credit of the government (*Cong. Globe,* 37th Cong. 3rd Sess., pt. i, p. 881), while Mr. Fenton added still another point to the argument by claiming that the plan would not only make a market for the government debt but it would keep up the value of securities (*Cong. Globe,* 37th Cong., 3rd Sess., pt. ii, p. 1118, Feb. 19, 1863).

the measure[1] did not dislodge proponents of the bill from their support of it as a war measure.

We are accordingly justified in the belief that the idea of furnishing a market for government bonds supplied one of the principal reasons for the adoption of the banking system.[2]

THE USE OF FINANCING DEVICES AS A REFLECTION ON CIVIL WAR FINANCING

To find examples of unwise financing, one need do nothing more than study the manner in which financing devices were utilized during the Civil War.

The major difficulties arose as a result of the attempt to appropriate for the government's securities the properties of currency. The issue of demand notes, the adoption of the receivability feature, the establishment of a national banking system, and of course the resort to legal tenders, are to be explained by reference to this attempt and to the confused thinking associated with it. It is especially significant that these actions were the means by which inflation, with all of its evils, was introduced and sustained.

Because of these undesirable results students of finance are almost unanimous in their criticism of the basic theories on which the operations of the period rested. The poor execution of the mere details of financing furnish grounds for further criticism, for examples of blunders and errors in judgment are abundant. An unwise switch to treasury

[1] Mr. Collamer expected the war to be over before the act would get into full swing (*Cong. Globe*, 37th Cong., 3rd Sess., pt. i, p. 869, Feb. 11, 1863). Mr. Baker claimed that the measure could give no immediate relief (*Cong. Globe*, 37th Cong., 3rd Sess., pt. ii, p. 1141, Feb. 20, 1863). Mr. Spaulding admitted that he did not look on the measure as a war act (*Cong. Globe*, 37th Cong., 3rd Sess., pt. ii, p. 1114, Feb. 19, 1863).

[2] *Cf.* Mitchell, *op. cit.*, pp. 37, 103; Bolles, *op. cit.*, p. 212. F. A. Delano, *The Economic World*, Oct 2, 1915, vol. 10, pp. 432-34. *Treas. Report*, 1861, pp. 17-25; *Treas. Report*, 1862, p. 18.

notes, a failure to coordinate the parts of the system of finance so that conversion would take place, an unjust repeal of the conversion privilege, and a failure to add to the attractiveness of bonds by declaring them payable in gold, may be cited as illustrative of the haphazard manner in which the business of the Treasury was carried on.

CHAPTER VI

From the Civil War to 1917

The resumption of specie payment, retirement of legal tender, maintenance of gold reserves and the fight over the silver standard had only an indirect effect upon the task of financing and hence need not receive a full treatment at our hands. It is nevertheless possible to find a few facts which deserve more than a passing mention.

CHANGES IN MARKETING TECHNIQUE

In the first place, we may point out that the technique of disposing of bonds underwent frequent changes. Even in the process of issuing the first bonds of the refunding program, a change was necessary before the bonds were finally sold. In February, 1871, when the bonds were offered as a popular loan the designated agents (national banks and leading bankers) had been allowed one half of one per cent to cover commissions and the expense of printing the bonds. This allowance offered such a small inducement that by August only one third of the loan had been subscribed. It was at this stage that the Treasury introduced a feature which resulted in the entire amount being absorbed by the end of the month. The device which accomplished this astounding result was none other than an agreement to the effect that proceeds of the loan were to be left on deposit with the banks until the funds were needed by the government.[1]

[1] *Treas. Report*, 1871, pp. 17-18; Bolles, *op. cit.*, pp. 326-329.

The same arrangement for disposing of bonds, by means of subscriptions handled in the identical manner, characterized the succeeding bond sales up until the issue of July 2, 1874. At this time, however, the arrangement was again modified to give certain bankers an option on the balance of the 5% bonds authorized by the refunding acts.[1]

On June 9, 1877, a similar contract with the same firms added the important provision that the contractors in turn offer the bonds to the public at par, and accrued interest.[2]

This action is of special interest when viewed as a forerunner of provisions for the popular loans, which later came to characterize American finance. At the time of its adoption the arrangement was regarded an effective means of gaining a wider distribution, and consequently of protecting the market for government securities.[3]

The use of the bond houses during this period was the subject of some interesting comments on the part of Secretary Sherman. He explained that a requirement that the government receive only coin in payment necessitated a resort to these institutions as intermediaries between the Treasury and the bond purchasers. The arrangement simply permitted the receipt of depreciated currency by the bond houses and made possible the sale of bonds. The resumption of specie payments, or rather Sherman's [4] interpretation of this action as wiping out all distinctions between legal tenders and gold, of course removed all necessity for these intermediaries. Consequently, the loan of April 16, 1879, ap-

[1] *Treas. Report*, 1874, pp. 9-10; Bolles, *op. cit.*, pp. 329-330.

[2] *Treas. Report*, 1877, pp. 8 and 9; Bolles, *op. cit.*, p. 331.

[3] *Treas. Report*, 1878, pp. 17 and 18.

[4] *Treas. Report*, 1877, p. 11. See also *Treas. Report*, 1878, pp. 12 and 13, for a similar interpretation of the receivability of notes in payment of customs.

peared as a direct loan to the people.[1] This policy was followed into the nineties but was then abandoned when the failure of subscriptions forced Secretary Carlisle,[2] against both the former policy of his party and his own personal views, to go to the banks with an appeal for funds. His request was granted reluctantly and apparently only when the banks realized that no other means were available for saving the treasury and thereby protecting the business of the country.[3] While the loan of November 1894, was taken by a single bid from a syndicate of banking institutions, it was nevertheless offered for public subscription.[4] Furthermore, notwithstanding the fact that the exigencies of the time required this resort to intermediaries, the principle of direct financing soon reappeared[5] to become so firmly entrenched that not even the major operations of the World War were able to dislodge it.[6]

COIN PAYMENTS

The question of coin payments, which formerly arose in connection with legal tenders, appeared again in a modified form when the bullion value of silver came to be no longer on a par with gold. The situation called forth comments

[1] *Treas. Report*, 1879, p. 15; A. D. Noyes, *Forty Years of American Finance*, New York, 1909, p. 31.

[2] *Treas. Report*, 1894, p. 33; Kinley, *op. cit.*, pp. 311-12.

[3] *Noyes, op. cit.*, p. 214, Kinley, *op. cit.*, pp. 250, 311 and 312. Another exception to the policy of selling by the direct method occurred in 1895, when the Government found it necessary to enter into a contract with a group of international bankers.

[4] *Treas. Report*, 1894, p. 70; Noyes, *op. cit.*, p. 231; Kinley, *op. cit.*, p. 25.

[5] Used in Jan. 1896, Kinley, *op. cit.*, pp. 312-315. This author criticises severely the Treasury's policy of selling direct.

[6] See Noyes, "The Treasury Reserve and the Bond Syndicate Operations," *Pol. Sci. Quart.*, vol. 10, no. 4, p. 573, for an interesting description of events of the period.

from both Secretaries Morrill [1] and Windom.[2] Sherman went so far as to assure the purchasers of the bonds of June 9, 1877 that the securities would be redeemed in coin.[3] As a recognition of the difference in value of gold and silver, he urged the promise that bonds be paid in gold.[4]

During the early nineties, the absence of a definite assurance of redemption in gold caused apprehension that government obligations would be repaid in silver. Nor was the situation improved by an ambiguous statement from the Treasury Department. Only the President's declaration of policy succeeded in quieting the fears of the public.[5]

That the assurance of payment in gold was a feature of no little importance was proven in connection with the loan of 1895, when the bankers who took the 4% security at a rate equivalent to a 3¾% bond at par, offered to take a 3% bond at par provided a gold payment feature was inserted.[6] All questions on the subject of coin payment were finally ended by a notice to the effect that both principal and interest on any bonds and certificates issued thereafter were to be payable in gold coin.[7]

[1] *Treas. Report*, 1876, p. 18. Morrill wrote: "It will not be questioned by anyone conversant with the question at that time (referring to act of 1869) that the popular impression, not to say general conviction, was that the pledge was for payment in gold" (p. 19).

[2] *Treas. Report*, 1881, p. 13.

[3] *Treas. Report*, 1877, pp. 8-10 (Sherman).

[4] *Treas. Report*, 1877, p. 10.

[5] Noyes, *Forty Years, op. cit.*, p. 186.

[6] Noyes, *op. cit.*, p. 235.

[7] *Act of Feb. 4, 1910*, 36 Stat. at Large 192, ch. 25, sec. 1.

BOND PURCHASERS

During the period in question the sinking fund [1] experienced a checkered career. The fact that at first the fund was inoperative led to frequent criticisms and proposals for alternative measures.[2] During the period from 1869, when operations began,[3] until 1892 [4] when operations again ceased, bonds were bought, but in the main only when it was convenient for the Treasury to buy them.[5] From 1892 to 1901 [6] and again during a period prior to 1910,[7] compliance with sinking fund requirements was impossible.

In 1873, extensive bond purchases were made by the Treasury in order to throw its accumulation of funds into the money market for the purpose of relieving the existing financial stringency.[8]

Again between 1886 and 1890, the fact that there was no way of placing the Treasury's surplus money in the market except through bond [9] purchases seemed to be the controlling force back of purchases. A request [10] that Congress authorize purchases above par had been granted. Purchases dur-

[1] Established by the *Act of Feb. 25, 1862*, 12 Stat. at Large 345, ch. 33, sec. 5, p. 346.

[2] *Treas. Report*, 1864, p. 16, and *ibid.*, 1865, pp. 25 and 37; *ibid.*, 1868, pp. 20 *et seq.*

[3] *Treas. Report*, 1869, p. 13.

[4] *Treas. Report*, 1892, pp. 27 *et seq.*

[5] (*Treas. Report*, 1879, p. 8.) In spite of the irregularity of purchase the total purchases of $1,914,000,000 up to 1892 amounted to $990,000,000 more than were required for the sinking fund (*Treas. Report*, 1892, p. 28).

[6] *Treas. Report*, 1901, pp. 8 and 26.

[7] *Treas. Report*, 1910, p. 9.

[8] *Treas. Report*, 1873, pp. 12 and 15; Kinley, *op. cit.*, p. 227 (Oct., 1872), and pp. 230-231 (Sept., 1873).

[9] *Treas. Report*, 1887, p. 26; *Treas. Report*, 1890, pp. 27-28.

[10] *Treas. Report*, 1875, p. 9.

ing the period were made at such high premiums [1] that in the reports from 1886-1890, doubt was thrown on the advisability of continuing such operations.[2]

From this survey we appear justified in drawing two conclusions: First: The experience of the period by no means demonstrated that provision for a sinking fund guarantees the consistent accumulation of funds for debt retirement. Secondly: The excessive purchases by the government undoubtedly strengthened the market for bonds.

RECEIVABILITY

The receivability feature was the subject of extended discussion on but two occasions during the period. The first arose in connection with the problem of coin payments.

During the Civil War, we will recall, a distinction was drawn between United States notes and coin. The former were not receivable for custom duties, nor were they eligible for paying the interest on government bonds. Was this discrimination against the legal tenders to be continued? Did the Treasury have the power to allow the notes to be used for the settlement of custom dues? Secretary Sherman thought it did, and in his report of 1875,[3] he stated that in his opinion a revision of the law to permit the receipt of United States notes for custom duties would be unnecessary. He argued that the resumption act of January 14, 1875, had by implication modified previous laws so as to permit the receipt of United States notes. With resumption accomplished, any doubt on the question was removed and no distinction was made between coin and United States notes,

[1] Kinley, *op. cit.*, pp. 272-273 and 276.

[2] *Treas. Report*, 1886, p. 41; 1887, p. 26; 1888 p. 27; Kinley, *op. cit.*, pp. 272-3.

[3] P. 12.

either in the collection of duties or in the payment of principal and interest on the public debt.[1]

The only other occasion on which receivability was of importance was during the period from 1890-1896. Here it was a combination of receivability together with its complement redeemability, which caused all of the damage. As a result of the inflation and of the foreign trade movements, which followed the passage of the Sherman Silver Act of 1890, legal tender redemptions[2] were rapidly increased for the purpose of securing gold for export. While redemptions of legal tenders were decreasing the Treasury supply of gold, the operation of the receivability feature denied to the Government the opportunity to recoup its depleted reserves from the ordinary sources of revenue; for these sources were themselves productive only of notes.

In spite of efforts of the Treasury to maintain the hundred million dollar reserve, outflowing exceeded incoming specie.[3] Bond issues failed to build up the impaired gold reserves for the simple reason that off-setting redemptions were made in anticipation of coin payments for the bonds. The government consequently found it necessary to enter a special contract whereby a group of international bankers agreed that in exchange for government obligations they would give gold, a part of which was to be[4] obtained from abroad. Only in this manner was the Treasury able to diminish the evil consequences of the broad promises to redeem legal tenders and to accept them as payments to the government.

[1] *Treas. Report*, 1879, p. 9.

[2] Noyes, *Forty Years, op. cit.*, pp. 171-3. Noyes, "*The Treasury Reserve*," *op. cit.*, especially pp. 588-591. *Treas. Report*, 1892, p. 28, 1893, pp. 73 and 77; 1894, p. 69.

[3] Noyes, *Forty Years, op. cit.*, p. 170; *Treas. Report*, 1893, p. 62.

[4] *Treas. Report*, 1895, p. 70; Noyes, *Forty Years, op. cit.*, pp. 234-236. Kinley, *op. cit.*, p. 252.

FOREIGN SITUATION

During the early part of this period, the foreign holdings of American securities were, in the eyes of the secretaries, an ever-present obstacle to orderly funding operations.

On two occasions this apprehension was responsible for the recommendation that bonds be issued with principal and interest payable in Europe.[1] It was hoped that this step would cause securities to be retained in Europe rather than returned at an inopportune time.

Developments in connection with resumption are particularily interesting. On one occasion, the foreign situation was held up as an obstacle to the resumption of specie payments,[2] while later the sale of bonds abroad was undertaken as an integral part of the program for accomplishing resumptions.[3]

With specie resumption an accomplished fact, the bugaboo of large foreign holdings seems to have vanished for a time, only to reappear in 1891 when returning American securities and offsetting exports of gold attracted attention. Liquidation of securities continued intermittently[4] until 1895, when a change in the opposite direction set in and the problem[5] ceased to be of importance.[6].

[1] *Treas. Report,* 1865, pp. 22 and 26. *Ibid.,* 1868, pp. 18, 22 and 25.

[2] *Treas. Report,* 1869, p. 15 (Boutwell).

[3] *Treas. Reports,* 1878, p. 28, 1879, p. 15 (Sherman). For an account of foreign developments just prior to resumption, see *Treas. Reports,* 1871, p. 19; 1874, pp. 9 and 10; 1875, p. 11; 1876, p. 11; 1877, p. 8; 1878, p. 9.

[4] Noyes, *Forty Years, op. cit.,* p. 165.

[5] Noyes, *op. cit.,* pp. 242-4.

[6] A discussion having some bearing on the problem of foreign investments is to be found in a paper by Charles T. Spears, *Annals American Acad. of Pol. and Soc. Science,* no. 540, Sept., 1907.

LEGAL TENDER PROPOSALS AND THE CIRCULATION PRIVILEGE

The Spanish American War was the occasion for some more or less strong but unsuccessful attempts to reintroduce legal tenders into American finance.[1]

The circulation privilege [2] as it was originally projected in the National Banking Act and its subsequent amendment,[3] attracted little attention until the 80's when normal redempions and bond purchases out of surplus forced bond prices to enormous premiums. From this time until 1891, when deficits put an end to redemptions and purchases, this situation continued to lead to the retirement of circulating notes by the banks and of eligible bonds by the government. Accordingly when the Treasury came to finance the Spanish American War the banks had the privilege of issuing an additional $400,000,000 in notes. Moreover, so valuable was the circulation privilege that banks considered even a 3% bond bought at par highly profitable.[4]

Through a round-about but effective method, therefore, financiers of the war followed in the foosteps of predecessors who had met urgent and formidable needs by tampering with

[1] *Cong. Rec.* 55th Cong., 2nd Sess. P. 4341 Ap. 28, 1898; Mr. Butler offered a resolution for the issue of additional legal tenders. P. 4420 Ap. 29, Resolution (memorial) from New York City against the issue of bonds and in favor of issuing legal tenders. P. 4492 May 2, 1898; Mr. Butler argued against bonds and in favor of legal tenders.

[2] By the circulation privilege is meant the privilege of using the bonds as a basis for the issue of bank notes.

[3] The *Act of Mar. 2, 1867*, provided that 3% demand loan certificates were eligible for deposit to secure bank circulation to an amount equal to 60% of the total circulation issued. A $300,000,000 maximum imposed on bank currency (*Revised Statues*, sec. 5177) was removed by the specie Resumption Act of 1875. (*Act of Jan. 14, 1875*, repealing sec. 5177, *Revised Statute.*) For an account of the circulation privilege see A. D. Hoyes, *History of the National Banking System*, National Monetary Commission, 61st Cong., 2nd Sess., Senate, Doc. No. 572.

[4] *Treas. Report*, 1898, p. 79.

the monetary system of the country. In the Spanish-War period there was, from the point of view of financing expediency, no admitted need of altering the monetary structure and no apparent intention of doing other than depend upon investment funds.

Despite the absence of a need therefor, however, the objective for which former secretaries had risked the credit of the government was realized incidentally and without the asking. Moreover, the government continued to reap a harvest of low interest rates from this time until World War financiers began to deny the circulation privilege to bond issues.[1]

In the intervening period, however, the conversion feature was subjected to a critical examination and dissection from which it barely emerged with its life. Having recognized that loans at two percent were not on an economic basis, the Treasury came to consider the moral obligations of protecting the holders against undue declines. Out of this concern over the proposition of maintaining values at an equilibruim arose two corollaries. First, the tax on the circulation privilege should be adjusted so as to absorb the excess of the interest above two per cent. Secondly, the extent of the influence of the circulation feature upon market values should be ascertained.[2]

The latter problem in turn gave rise to a plan for an experiment in issuing a security without the circulation privi-

[1] Thus in 1900, practically all of the 2% bonds of 1930, excepting those exchanged for outstanding securities, were absorbed by the banks. What was evidently a careless omission from the authorizing act left a doubt as to whether the Panama Canal bonds of 1902 were available for circulation. (*Treas. Report,* 1902, p. 25.) The circulation feature was attached to the next issue, however. (*Act of Dec. 21, 1905,* 34 Stat. at Large, pt. i, and pt. v, sec. 1; *Treas. Report*, 1900, p. 15.)

[2] *Treas. Report,* 1909, pp. 5-6; 1910, p. 3.

lege.[1] It was also responsible for declarations, first, against the practice of using the privileges as a means of attaining an artificial level of interest and, secondly, in favor of the policy of making bonds a legitimate investment in the open market.[2]

It might be added that at least a few of the trends of the period materialized in a manner which had a marked influence upon the task of financing the World War. Our next task will be to describe some of the more outstanding developments in this direction.

[1] In 1911, the 3% fifty-year Canal bonds were actually offered without the privilege and were sold at a premium of 2.58. (*Act of Mar. 2, 1911*, 36 Stat. at Large, pt. i, p. 1013, ch. 195.)

[2] *Treas. Report*, 1911, p. 5.

CHAPTER VIII

Adjustment in the Financial Structure

An authority on the Federal Reserve System has said that "the history of the reserve system during the eight years from 1914 to 1923, is a history of war financing and of war banking." [1] We might with equal truth state conversely that the history of World-War financing is a history of the Federal Reserve System and of the financial organization of which it was the center.

While it is impossible to accord a full treatment to all those complex developments in banking and finance which affected the fiscal operations of the Government, it is nevertheless desirable to bring to mind as a background at least a general picture of the financial structure of the time. Our treatment of this phase of the subject will resolve itself in the main into a cataloguing of those changes which altered the task of Government financing.

DEPOSIT OF GOVERNMENT FUNDS IN BANKS

The First Liberty bond act made an important change in the floating of government bond issues. The act [2] permitted the Treasury to deposit until needed the proceeds from the sale of bonds and certificates of indebtedness in state banks and trust companies as well as in National banks previously designated as depositors,[3] thereby avoiding the dis-

[1] H. Parker Willis, *The Federal Reserve System* (New York, 1923), p. 849.

[2] *Act of April 24, 1917,* 40 Stat. at Large, pt. i, p. 38, ch. 4, sec. 7.

[3] *Treas. Report,* 1917, p. 25. *Federal Reserve Bulletin,* May 1, 1917, p 337.

On the subject of the abolition of the Sub-Treasury System, see *Hearings before the Committee on Banking and Currency of the House of Representatives on H. R. 11209,* February 10, 1920, 66th Cong., 2nd Sess.

turbance which would have accompanied the transfer of large sums of money either to the Sub-Treasury or to a small number of selected banks.[1] As the money was disbursed by the Government, it inevitably flowed back into the banking system where it again swelled the accounts of private depositors.

Two proposals looked toward an even more elaborate use of the banks. The first would have removed the requirement that government deposits were not to exceed the amount withdrawn from banks for purchases of Liberty bonds. A second proposed that no interest be charged on the government's deposits.[2]

The contribution of the banking system to the financing program was further augmented by a measure which stipulated that the reserve requirements were not to apply to deposits of government funds.[3] The insignificant clause containing this provision made it possible for the banking system to absorb a bond issue of almost any size whatever. The only prerequisite to an immediate absorption was that the banks, either from choice or under pressure,[4] extend sufficient loans to bond purchasers. The proceeds from the sale of the bonds would then be deposited in the bank. Since these deposits were free from the reserve requirements, there was no legal limitation on the amount that could be financed in this way.

[1] See *Federal Reserve Bulletin*, May 1, 1917, p. 337, and June 1, p. 424. Also William A. Scott, "Bond Issues and the Money Market" appearing in *Financial Mobilization for War* (Chicago, 1917), p. 127 *et seq.*

[2] *Senate Committee on Finance Hearings on H. R. 5901-6511*, pp. 22-28.

[3] *Act of April 24, 1917*, 40 Stat. at Large, pt. i, p. 35, ch. 4, sec. 7; *Act of Sept. 24, 1917*, 40 Stat. at Large, pt. i, p. 288, ch. 56, sec. 8, p. 291; *Act of April 4, 1918*, 40 Stat. at Large, pt. i, p. 502, ch. 44, sec. 8, p. 505; *Revised Stat.*, sec. 5191.

[4] Willis, *op. cit.*, p. 1119, indicates that it was originally the purpose of McAdoo to force the loans on the banks but that these leanings were later abandoned, at least in part.

Moreover a possible strain on the banks was not to be expected at the time when the funds were transferred from private accounts to the Government's credit. Only when Government deposits were being replaced by individual deposits requiring reserves, was there an occasion for worry in respect to the adequacy of reserves.[1]

Another aspect of the subject of government deposits had to do with the security required of banks acting as government depositories. Collateral equivalent, on the terms stipulated to the amount of the government deposits, was required as security from each of the banks acting as a government depository.[2] This requirement in turn gave rise to two arrangements which should be mentioned in connection with our subject.

In the first place, the requirements specifically demanded that twenty-five percent of all securities deposited for this purpose be made up of obligations of the government.[3] In addition to this absolute requirement concerning the use of Government securities, there was another provision which could scarcely do otherwise than encourage the use of government obligations for this purpose: Eligible securities were divided into four classes, each of which was subject to a special regulation in respect to the terms upon which bonds falling in this classification would be accepted. Obligations of the

[1] For this reason, the plan providing for the making of Liberty bond payments on the installment plan (Department Circular No. 78, May 14, 1917, *Treas. Report,* 1917, p. 87), really approached the matter from the wrong point of view in so far as helping the banks maintain reserves was concerned.

[2] See *Revised Statutes,* sec. 5153 and amendments thereto. Also see Liberty Acts. For example the *Act of April 24, 1917,* 40 Stat. at Large, pt. i, p. 35, ch. 4, sec. 7, p. 37, provided that such deposits should be secured in the manner required for other deposits by section 5153, *Revised Statutes,* and amendments thereto.

[3] Sec. 5153, *Revised Statutes,* as amended; *Treas. Report,* 1917, p. 126.

United States were practically the only bonds acceptable at par.[1] As a result of the several regulations a given investment in government obligations was allowed to take the place of a larger investment in other securities. This situation undoubtedly served to strengthen the position of the class of securities so favored.[2]

[1] The classifications were as follows: (*Treas. Report,* 1917, p. 133, Dept. Cir., No. 92.)

1. Securities acceptable at par. This classification included:
   a. Bonds and certificates of indebtedness of the U. S. Gov't.
   b. Bonds issued under the U. S. farm-loan Acts.
   c. Bonds of the Phillipine Islands, Porto Rico and the District of Columbia.
2. Securities acceptable at market value. This class included bonds of any state of the United States.
3. Securities acceptable at 90% of market value. This group included:
   a. The 3½% and other bonds of the Territory of Hawaii.
   b. Approved notes, certificates of indebtedness, and warrants issued by any state of the United States.
   c. Approved bonds of any County, City or political subdivision in the U. S., also approved notes, certificates of indebtedness and warrants which are direct obligations of County, or City as a whole.
   d. Commercial paper and bankers acceptance eligible for rediscount or purchase by Reserve Banks.
4. Securities acceptable at 75% of market value. This list included certain bonds of railroads and obligations of governments engaged in war against Germany.

The discrimination in favor of Liberty bonds (comprising the bulk of the bonds eligible for inclusion in the first classification), is quite evident when one observes that in securing deposits with bonds of the fourth classification, a bank would render inactive an investment one third larger than would be required if its deposits were secured by Liberty bonds. (This difference would be even greater when the Liberties (which were acceptable at par) could be bought at less than par.)

[2] The amounts of public money held by special depositories at the end of the fiscal years included in the war period, were as follows:

A. June 30, 1917—$783,922,760 (*Treas. Report,* 1917, p. 367).
B. June 30, 1918—$1,491,338,825 (*Treas. Report,* 1918, p. 557).
C. June 30, 1919—$905,411,515 (*Treas. Report,* 1919, p. 723).

REMOVAL OF 10% LIMIT

The extent to which the Government went in removing every obstacle to the purchase of Liberty bonds is well illustrated by the changing of the limitation upon the amount which a bank could lend to any one individual. The previous requirement that an institution should not lend more than 10% of its paid-in capital stock plus its unimpaired surplus, was amended so that notes collateraled by war-time obligations of the Government were not included in figuring the 10% limit upon the amount which could be lent. The new and more liberal provision continued to allow ordinary loans to any one person to the extent of 10% of the capital and surplus and then permitted loans to the extent of another 10% on notes collateraled by Liberty bonds and certificates of indebtedness.[1]

PREFERENTIAL RATES ON NOTES SECURED BY GOVERNMENT BONDS

None of the measures thus far described provided directly for financing the purchases of war bonds by the ultimate investor. This objective was left for a series of actions by the Federal Reserve Board and the Federal Reserve banks.

Previous to the beginning of the war, authority for Reserve banks to extend credit on the basis of government bonds was to be found in three sources.[2] With one excep-

[1] *Act of Sept. 4, 1918,* 40 Stat. at Large, pt. i, p. 965, ch. 176.

[2] (*Federal Reserve Bulletin,* March 1, 1917, p. 158.)

1. Section 13 of the Federal Reserve Act, paragraph 2 (*Act of Dec. 23, 1913,* 38 Stat. at Large, pt. i, p. 250, ch. 6, sec. 13, p. 263), provided that eligible notes could be discounted (if endorsed by a member bank). But Federal Reserve banks were not to discount notes drawn for the purpose of trading in stocks and bonds, except bonds and notes of the U. S. Government. Under this provision, Federal Reserve Banks could discount endorsed notes secured by government bonds and with

tion[1] direct discrimination favoring government bonds did not exist in these pre-war provisions. However, several banking measures soon changed the position of government bonds in the banking structure, and by so doing undoubtedly served to alter their position in the market. We refer primarily to the plan of granting preferential rates of discount on notes secured by government bonds. The Federal Reserve Board first adopted the policy of granting a 3% rate on 15-day notes. Some Federal Reserve banks applied this to all notes of this description, while others supplied the rate only to paper collateraled by government obligations.[2]

On May 22, 1917, the Federal Reserve Board announced that it would ratify a rate of 3½% on customers' loans collateraled either by government bonds or by treasury short-term certificates. It will be observed that this rate was the same as that borne by the first Liberty bonds which were being sold at the time of announcement, but it was one-half point below the rate of discount which was common among the Federal Reserve Banks.[3] The adoption by the several

a maturity of not greater than ninety days. This permission did not include a banker's own note.

2. An amendment of Sept. 7, 1916 (*Act of Sept. 7, 1916*, 39 Stat. at Large, pt. i, p. 752, ch. 461, amendment to Sec. 13 of Federal Reserve Act) allowed the Federal Reserve Bank the privilege of advancing funds to member banks on the latter's own notes for a period not exceeding fifteen days provided the note was secured by specified classes of paper or "by a deposit or pledge of bonds or notes of the U. S."

3. A third way for making an advance on government securities was provided by Sec. 14 of the Federal Reserve Act. Federal Reserve banks were allowed to buy and sell government securities.

[1] An exception was made of government securities in the prohibition against discounting notes drawn for the purpose of trading in stocks and bonds.

[2] *Federal Reserve Bulletin*, June 1, 1917, p. 425.

[3] On March 1, 1917 the rates of discount on (commercial) paper maturing 16 to 60 days were 4% at each Federal Reserve bank except Kansas City where a 4½% rate was to be found. The rate continued at this

Reserve banks of this preferential rate of discount on loans collateraled by government bonds constituted a direct invitation to banks to finance the purchase of Liberty bonds to any extent whatever, and to bring the resulting Liberty-bond-secured notes to the Federal Reserve Bank and rediscount them.[1] These accommodations were extended to non-member banks through an arrangement whereby they could discount Liberty-bond-secured paper with the Federal Reserve banks by using a member bank as an intermediary.[2] Thus, every member of the banking community was free to fall back on the Federal Reserve system to any extent whatever. Why the banking system was able to stand the new and increased demands is a familiar story to students of banking. A mere reference to the important developments will be sufficient to indicate their bearing on our own subject.

CHANGES IN RESERVE REQUIREMENTS

The centralizing of reserves facilitated increased extensions of credit without a commensurate increase in danger. Changes in the magnitude of reserves required by law

level until November 26, when Philadelphia raised the rate to 4½%. By the end of the year, a rate of 4½% was to be found at all of the banks except Boston where 5% was charged.

On January 1, 1917, six banks were discounting 61 to 90 day paper at 4% and six at 4½%. Two others adopted the 4½% rate before the month ended. These rates continued until November 7. On January 1, 1918, the rate of 4½% was to be found in nine banks while 5% was being charged by three banks.

As for paper collateraled by Liberty bonds, 16 to 90 day obligations enjoyed at all banks a rate of 3½% from May, 1917, to Sept. 25, when Cleveland went to 4%. After November 25 and before the end of the year, all of the others went to 4%—(*Federal Reserve Board Annual Report*, 1917, p. 38).

[1] *Federal Reserve Bulletin*, p. 425; *cf.* Noyes, *War Period of American Finance* (New York, 1926), p. 202.

[2] *Federal Reserve Bulletin*, June 1, 1917, p. 426. Also, *Cong. Record*, p. 55—for discussion of this measure.

against deposits removed the technical obstacles to the extensions of credit.[1]

BOND-PURCHASE REQUIREMENT REMOVED

Furthermore, the Government removed the requirements that each national bank should buy and keep on deposit a certain amount of government bonds.[2] The Federal Reserve Act itself partly accomplished this relief by stipulating that all banks thereafter need not meet the requirement, except as deposits of bonds were necessary in order to secure bank notes actually issued. Similar relief was later extended to include all banks.[3]

In so far as the banks actually availed themselves of the privilege of getting rid of holdings not represented by currency they not only set free a comparable amount of assets for credit expansion but also, to the extent that they withdrew their bank circulation, left this field open for the government's manipulation of the currency. That such manipulation constituted an integral part of the financing program appears evident from the events of the period.

[1] The reductions were made in the Federal Reserve Act itself (*op. cit.*, sec. 19, p. 270), and by the *Act of June 21, 1917* (40 Stat. at Large, pt. i, p. 232, ch. 32, sec. 10, p. 239, amending Sec. 19 of the Federal Reserve Act), when a figure was set which has been retained until the present.

The requirements were as follows:

For demand deposits	*Central*	*Reserve*	*Others*
Fed. Res. Act	18	15	12
Amendment, June 21, 1917	13	10	7
For time deposits			
Fed. Res. Act	5	5	5
Amendment, June 21, 1917	3	3	3

[2] National Banking Act, *op. cit.*

[3] *Act of June 21, 1917,* 40 Stat. at Large 232, ch. 32, sec. 9, p. 239. Amended Sec. 17 so as to repeal; Sec. 5151, *Revised Statutes;* Sec. 4 of *Act of June 20, 1874,* 18 Stat. at Large 124; Sec. 8 of *Act of July 12, 1882,* 22 Stat. at Large 164.

CURRENCY AND INFLATION

An act of Oct. 5, 1917,[1] gave national banks permission to issue notes to the amount of not more than $25,000 each in denominations of $1 and $2, and authorized them to issue notes of $5 on the same basis that they issued other denominations. This measure, according to the Federal Reserve Bulletin, was intended [2] to provide a larger volume of small bills. The Bulletin further observed that the Treasury Department had been converting large greenbacks and U. S. notes into smaller denominations, "thereby probably finding a permanent field of circulation for them."

As greenbacks and other circulating notes moved out of the larger and into the smaller denominations, the field for Federal Reserve notes was enlarged.

The filling of this field with Federal Reserve notes was of special significance to the subject of government financing because of the provision that this type of currency could be issued on the basis of notes collateraled by government securities. Changes in reserve requirements against such notes permitted a still further extension of the Central Bank's power to increase its discounts and circulating notes.[3]

In order fully to appreciate the situation which was fostered by these provisions we may now review the entire arrangement under which the Liberty bond issues were financed. Banks, whether members of the Reserve system or not, were encouraged to extend to individual investors whatever accommodations were necessary even in excess of the limits formerly placed upon the maximum to be loaned to one person. The resulting notes could then be discounted at the Federal Reserve banks at a preferential rate of dis-

[1] 40 Stat. at Large, pt. i, p. 342, ch. 74—"To amend laws relating to circulating notes—and to permit issuance of notes of small denominations.

[2] *Federal Reserve Bulletin*, 1917, p. 833.

[3] *Cf.* Noyes, *War Period of American Finance*, *op. cit.*, pp. 208-210.

count. The privilege of issuing Federal Reserve notes on the basis of such paper was accordingly perhaps a logical and even necessary adjunct to the financing plan; for where the necessity of success in floating the Liberty loans made it obligatory on the Federal Reserve banks to discount Liberty-bond-secured notes without limit, the privilege of issuing Federal Reserve notes on the basis of such security afforded a guarantee that the Reserve banks would always be in a position to meet the demands. Recognition of the necessity of the arrangement as a team mate of other features of the financing program, however, should not blind the student of finance to the true nature of the practice. Under the plan in use during the war period, the bonds were first issued by the government, then bought either by individuals or by institutions, and later used as security for obligations which were ultimately to be discounted at the Federal Reserve banks. Since these obligations were in turn used as security for federal reserve notes, the actual result was in many respects the same as it would have been had the government resorted to the more disreputable alternative of issuing paper money directly. But while the indirect method resulted in a formidable issue of currency [1] which was in many respects similar to government paper money, the technical position of notes issued under the former plan was obviously stronger than would have been that of direct obligations of the government.

In the first place, we may point out that not all the government securities reached the stage of additional currency.

[1] *The Federal Reserve Bulletin* for Oct. 1, 1918, p. 927, supplies the information for the following comparison in respect to circulation actually outstanding, i. e., Federal Reserve Notes and Federal Reserve Bank Notes held outside the Treasury and the Federal Reserve Banks:

Feb. 1, 1917	$ 261,944,910
Sept. 1, 1918	2,111,896,668
Increase	1,849,951,758

Consequently the market was not flooded to the extent of destroying the value of the notes. In other words the Treasury, in taking the round-about route to the printing press, found by the roadside so many ways of inducing people to be satisfied without the receipt of actual currency that by the time the money was actually printed the amount of necessary currency was only a fraction of what it would have been had the more direct route been taken.[1] But if the time spent on the roadside with creditors was fruitful in the sense that it brought about a curtailment of the amount of notes to be issued, it appears even more justifiable when one views the improved status which came to the notes as a result of the actions of the roadside's inhabitants. Each of the latter, in addition to absorbing some of the obligations, generously assumed responsibility for that portion of the credit which ultimately reached the stage of note issue. In other words, to drop the figure of speech, the reserve notes were in substance guaranteed by the Federal Reserve System, by the bank, or banks, which endorsed the re-discounted paper, and by the original maker of the note. Thus while the Treasury was providing for the indirect issue of an equivalent of government paper money, it was shrewdly setting up the entire banking system as a buffer. In so far as it subjugated the Central Banking System to the will of the Treasury Department, the plan undoubtedly served to contribute not only to the safety of the notes but also to the success of the remainder of the financing program.

Still another advantage of the indirect over the direct method of issue had to do with the psychological effect of

[1] For an argument which decreases the importance of this factor, see A. C. Pigou, *A Study in Public Finance* (London, 1928), ch. iii, pp. 265-266. He contends that as regards the English experience, if notes had been printed and issued direct they would not have "lived", that is to say they would have been returned to the point that no more would have survived than under the round-about process.

having the notes issued by the central banking system of the country instead of by the government itself. The method used appeared entirely different from a direct issue of paper money, and consequently disarmed opponents who would have been quick to criticize any step which promised a repetition of the well-known evils of an issue of legal tenders.

But advantages along this line were of a specialized sort. While the indirect method gave assurance that the notes would always be redeemed in gold dollars, there was nothing in the plan to guarantee that the dollars in question would not decrease in value.[1] That such a decrease actually occurred is generally recognized and easily proved simply by reference to price indexes. While the gold reserve back of the paper in this country would have prevented a tragedy comparable in extent to that experienced abroad, the fact remains that the difference was one of degree only; for there is little reason to believe that the mere matter of issuing authority would bring about any change in the subtle way in which additional currency worked its way into the business economy and affected prices. In other words, the emission of Federal Reserve Notes undoubtedly exerted the same influence upon the price level as would have a similar issue of government paper money.[2] The same line of reasoning, pursued a bit further, serves to classify, along with the emissions of circulating notes, all actions arising as a result of the measures which made additional extension of credit possible. One of the most important of these, namely, the establishment of the War Finance Corporation, remains to be studied.

[1] *Cf.* Seligman, *Currency Inflation and Public Debts* (New York, 1921), p. 10.

[2] *Cf.* Hugh Dalton—*Principles of Public Finance,* 5th edition (London, 1929). "There is no difference in the two methods, except that the indirect method, besides mystifying simple minds, involves the public authority in the additional expense of paying interest on its loans from the banks," pp. 181-182.

WAR FINANCE CORPORATION [1]

Although appearing so late that its maximum possible effect upon the task of financing the war was never felt, the War Finance Corporation is to be considered one of the most elaborate attempts to adjust the financial structure to the needs of the Treasury.

The proposal for its establishment was prefaced with statements by the Secretary and by others who called attention to a situation in which the government had monopolized the credit resources of the nation, to the difficulty which industries were having in obtaining capital, to the undesirable manner in which issues of private concerns were competing with government bonds on the market, and to the necessity of having some central body to regulate financing programs. According to Mr. McAdoo the corporation was organized as such a central body, "to enable the banks, both national and state banks and trust companies, to continue to furnish essential credits for industries and enterprises which are necessary or contributory to prosecution of the war." [2]

A cursory examination of official records leaves the impression that framers of the measure first had in mind an arrangement for discouraging undesirable financing.[3] The realization of this objective would have had the obviously desirable result of eliminating or minimizing the competition which Liberty bonds were meeting from private companies.[4]

[1] *Act of Apr. 5, 1918*, 40 Stat. at Large, pt. i, p. 506. The bond purchasing activities of the War Finance Corporation are treated in Chapter XIII.

[2] *Senate Committee on Finance, Hearings on S. 3714*, Feb. 8, 1918, p. 8.

[3] *Cong. Record*, vol. 56, pt. iii, pp. 2786 and 3050. Also, pt. iv, p. 3608.

[4] Senator Smith (Georgia) referred to this purpose in a statement to the effect that "We are desiring to occupy almost exclusively the bond market with the sale of Liberty bonds. We do not desire these public service companies to have a bond so attractive that they might cause it to interfere in any way with the sale of Liberty bonds" (*Cong. Record*,

A careful analysis of developments leads one to doubt that the sentiment in favor of restriction of financing was an important factor in passing the authorizing act. On the contrary, before the discussion ended there appeared to exist general agreement that the methods previously employed had been adequate as far as regulation was concerned. The compulsory feature was accordingly removed bodily from the final bill, with the result that the measure was stripped of any pretense of being an instrument for the compulsory regulation of competing issues.

The War Finance Corporation's means of controlling undesirable issues were accordingly indirect and were limited solely to the power to withhold the facilities of the Corporation from the unapproved firms.

Since the restrictive aspects of the organization were practically non-existent, it is necessary to look elsewhere for objectives which explain the setting-up of the War Finance Corporation. One need not search long, however, to find that the motivating idea involved primarily an absolute increase in the volume of credit extensions rather than a regulation or redistribution of existing investment funds.

The need for the proposed enlarged credits was alluded to as being obvious. For one thing banks, business firms, and savings banks [1] had increased their holdings of government bonds and according to Mr. McAdoo,[2] needed relief. Al-

vol. 56, pt. iii, p. 2783). Another side of the situation is described by those who foresaw that the securities of the War Finance Corporation would themselves compete with Liberty bonds on the market. (*Comm. on Ways and Means Hearings on H. R. 9499*, 65th Cong., 2nd Sess., p. 50. Also, *Cong. Records*, vol. 56, pt. iv, pp. 3611 and 3622, McFadden and Kitchin.)

[1] *Senate Com. on Finance, Hearings on S 3714*, Feb. 8, 1918, pp. 14, 23. Also, *Cong. Records*, vol. 56, pt. iii, p. 2785, Simmons and Hollis, also p. 2792, Hollis, and vol. 56, pt. iv, p. 3607.

[2] *Com. on Ways and Means: Hearings on H. R. 3499*, 65th cong., 2nd Sess., Feb. 18, 1918, p. 9.

lowing them to dispose of corporate securities was preferable to letting them unload Liberty bonds on the market.

A situation of far more importance than this factor, however, arose in connection with the flotation of new issues of corporate securities. What was desired was an arrangement to finance such issues out of bank credit rather than to have them compete for funds otherwise available for the purchase of government obligations.

To achieve this objective the framers of the measure deliberately devised a means of transforming long-time investments into liquid, rediscountable securities to be absorbed by the banking system of the country. The adoption of the arrangement followed the arguments of congressional leaders who pointed out that private companies had not been granted the credit accommodations which would be possible were their securities eligible for discount at the Federal Reserve Bank.[1] Provision for the exchange of corporate securities for War Finance Corporation bonds would attain the desired ends provided the latter were given the rediscount privilege.[2]

It thus appears that the following argument which was used by an opponent of the bill can be accepted as an accurate description of the manner in which its authors hoped that the measure would operate. The quotation is from a speech by Senator Hollis: " It is nothing in the world but an effort to convert the securities of an industrial corporation, with the indorsement of the Government upon them, into a liquid form so that currency can be issued in their stead." [3] The fact that the basis for the issue of Federal Reserve notes would be broadened to include (indirectly) corporate securi-

[1] *Cong. Globe,* vol. 56, pt. iii, p. 2781, Senator Simmons; p. 3084, Senator Lodge.

[2] *Cong. Record,* vol. 56, pt. iii, p. 3139, Hollis; p. 3132, Reed.

[3] *Cong. Record,* vol. 56, pt. iii, p. 2790.

ties, continued to be used as arguments both for and against the measure.[1]

For our purpose, it is significant that this provision for issuing Federal Reserve notes on the basis of bonds of the War Finance Corporation represented the final step in the arrangement for depending upon current banking funds for financing the long-time needs of industry. Under the arrangement as set up a private company might come to the War Finance Corporation and secure bonds of the latter corporation in exchange for its own securities. It could then take the War Finance Corporation bonds to the bank and use them as collateral on a note which the bank could in turn re-discount with the Federal Reserve bank. As a final step in the arrangement, the central bank was permitted to use these obligations as the basis for Federal Reserve notes. This plan would logically result in throwing the burden of private corporate financing back on the Federal Reserve Bank. In short, the War Finance Corporation planned to do for corporate financing what previous measures had already made possible for government financing. As a result, all future capital needs, both of industry and of the Treasury, could be obtained from current bank resources.[2]

We are not concerned at present with any far-reaching results of the inflation which inevitably follows the practice of securing financial aid from this source. It is sufficient for our purpose to point out that an arrangement existed

[1] *Cong. Record,* vol. 56, pt. iii, p. 2844, Senator Sherman, p. 2921, Senator Hardwick and Senator Norris, p. 3138, Senator Owen; pt. iv, p. 3673, Mr. McFadden; p. 3685, Mr. Platt. See also, *Cong. Record,* vol. 56, pt. iii, p. 3131—for suggestions that the entire proposition be handled by an amendment to the Federal Reserve Act.

[2] Both Senator Simmons and Mr. Kitchin stated with apparent satisfaction that these bonds were on a par with Liberty bonds in so far as action by the Federal Reserve Bank was concerned. (*Cong. Record,* vol. 56, pt. iii, Simmons, p. 3134, and vol. 56, pt. iv, p. 3610, Kitchin.)

which took care of the financing needs of the country by providing means of expanding credits and finally of issuing circulating notes in whatever amounts were necessary to take care of the needs of the hour.

These various arrangements for insuring the success of the Treasury's operations make it more difficult to see why a Liberty loan should fail than to understand why it succeeded. Where the real pressure could be passed along to the Reserve Banks, failure, if it came at all, should come not at the time of the campaign, but at a later date and in the form of a collapse of the entire banking structure.

CHAPTER VIII

The First Liberty Loan

THE APPEAL TO PATRIOTISM

Beginning at the time when a bond issue was first mentioned, definite efforts to augment the demand for the forthcoming securities were clearly in evidence. By far the most important, and evidently the most effective, of these efforts centered around the appeal to patriotism. It is doubtful whether any other means could have secured four million subscribers to one issue alone.[1] It is against a background of patriotic activity that we must accordingly project our treatment of the various features and devices. At least, two of the latter must be considered in the light of their contribution to the floating of the First Liberty Loan on the basis of a patriotic appeal.

SELLING EXPENSES

There was, in the first place, a provision to the effect that one tenth of one per cent of the issue should be allowed the Treasury for the expenses of issuing and selling the bonds.[2]

[1] *Treas. Report*, 1917, p. 7.

[2] *Act of April 24, 1917*, 40 Stat. at Large, pt. i, ch. 4, sec. 8, p. 37. *Cong. Record*, vol. 55, pp. 688-9, arguments on expenses. The original bill provided for one-fifth of 1%. The amendment to the effect that only one-tenth of 1% be allowed was offered by Mr. Fitzgerald (p. 688), and accepted (p. 689). The subject of expenses on the first loan also came up for consideration in connection with the second loan (*Senate Com. on Finance, Hearings on the Second Emergency Bond Issue*, 65th Cong., 1st Sess., pp. 17 and 26).

While the percentage allowance was the same as that made on the Spanish-American War Loan [1] and was even less than was originally requested by the Secretary, the sum available on such a large issue as that of the First Liberty Loan was ample for an effective organization and for extensive advertising. In order to account for the effectiveness of the expenditures, however, we must again refer to the existence of patriotic sentiment, which it was the object of paid advertising to arouse.[2] Once patriotism was aroused, there followed free advertising and contributions of service which were of immeasurable worth to the government.

SMALL DENOMINATIONS

Still another feature of the bond issue which conditioned the patriotic appeal was the arrangement for small denominations. On the floor of the house, argument was presented for low denominations and an amendment was offered for a bond as low as $25.00.[3] Coupon bonds were actually issued in denominations as low as $50.00.[4]

Before taking up the more important characteristics of the loan, we may mention a few minor features as among those affecting the desirability of the bonds. The bonds were in varied and, therefore, in convenient, denominations; they were to be had either in coupon or in registered bonds;

[1] *Act of June 13, 1898,* 30 Stat. at Large, p. 448, ch. 448, sec.33, p. 467.

[2] Some idea of the advertising program can be obtained from the *Plan of the National Advertising Advisory Board,* contained in New York Public Library, vol. BTZS/—N.C.S.. Samples of the advertisements can be found in a second volume (BTZS/—N.C. 22). Still another volume (*Liberty Loan Campaign, Women's Publicity,* vol. BTZO/—pt. i, and pt. ii), discloses the nature of newspaper publicity, which may be described as free advertising.

[3] *Cong. Record,* 55th Cong., p. 679—Mr. Howard offered an amendment providing for a $25 bond, p. 681. Amendment rejected.

[4] *Treas. Report,* 1917, Exhibit B., p. 87.

and the various types were interchangeable.[1] The use of these features was significant not because of their novelty, but because of their importance in connection with the more or less modern attempt to reach an increasing host of small investors.

SALE AT PAR

The First Liberty Bond Act carried the familiar provision that bonds were not to be sold at less than par. Before this point was finally established, however, Congress had aired the entire subject of bond sales at a discount. The original bill had stipulated that the bonds were to be offered at par but had failed to specify that unsold bonds could not be disposed of at a discount. The possibility of such sales at less than par led to an amendment covering the point at issue.[2]

A provision against the payment of commissions [3] supplemented the prohibition against the sale below par to the extent of effecting a virtual guarantee that all bonds would be sold at par.

CIRCULATION PRIVILEGES

The First Liberty Loan Act specifically denied the "circulation privilege " to the Liberty Bonds.[4] This denial was included in the administration's bill and received little more than a casual mention on the floors of Congress.[5] Thus,

[1] *Treas. Report,* 1917, Exhibit B, p. 62.

[2] (*Cong. Rec.,* 65th Cong., 1st Sess., pp 628 and 634.) It is significant that the amendment was defended on the ground that it would add to the attractiveness of the bonds rather than that it would provide a check on the Treasury. (*Cong. Record,* vol. 55, p. 628.)

Act., *op. cit.,* sec. 1.

[4] The Act, *op. cit.,* sec. 1—By "circulation privilege" is meant the privilege of permitting the use of the bond as security for note issues by National Banks.

[5] *Cong. Record,* vol. 55, p. 626. The provision was merely referred to in the enumeration of items. Another reference to the provision occurred

without a stir, a determined policy on the part of the Treasury Department, gained the elimination of a feature which had possibilities of causing serious disturbances in our banking and monetary systems. If the billions in new issues had been allowed to compete with the existing $700,000,000 of 2's for the latter's place as security for a limited bank note circulation, a precipitous decline in the old issues would have been inevitable. On the other hand, if all limits upon the amount of bank notes had been disregarded, there was of course the danger of superfluous issues.

A single sentence avoided these possibilities for the immediate future and also set a precedent to be followed by framers of subsequent bond acts. The Liberties were accordingly issued without the help of the feature which had practically set the price of government bonds for several decades. In connection with the gigantic task of floating the contemplated billions of securities, however, the measure promised to be worse than useless. It was wisely abandoned.

CONVERSION

During the time the first Liberty Loan campaign was being planned, the conversion privilege[1] was probably subjected to a more critical analysis than was any other specific feature of the forthcoming bonds. In no other instance have the latent undesirable possibilities in a feature been presented by its opponents to a degree that would compare with the way in which the dangers of the conversion privilege were foreseen, or at least predicted.[2]

(p. 636) when the wording was questioned. Of much more interest was a later remark to the effect that the circulation privilege was denied to the Liberty bonds in order that the market for the 2's of 1930 would not be depressed (p. 648).

[1] Act, *op. cit.*, sec. 2; *Treas. Report*, 1917, Exhibit B., p. 87.

[2] *Cong. Record*, vol. 55, pp. 686-7, Sloan and others; p. 747, Senator Norris; p. 686, Mr. Sloan.

In the main, statements to the effect that there was a possibility of the war continuing, that there would be future issues, and that the rate of interest might increase, went unchallenged. Proponents of the measure apparently contented themselves with arguing that Congress must insure the success of the first loan by attaching whatever features would add to the sales appeal. Since the conversion feature offered promise along this line, it was adopted.[1]

TAX EXEMPTION

Tax exemption as well as the conversion feature was undoubtedly utilized because of the belief that it would facilitate the sale of the bonds and thus insure the success of the first issue.[2]

Liberty bond speakers were instructed to refer to the fact that the bonds were to be exempt from all taxes except estate and inheritance taxes, and to remind the purchaser that this feature served as an insurance against future tax levies.[3]

The provision for exempting the bonds scarcely received a passing comment as the first Liberty Bond bill was being transformed into law.[4] Indeed a champion for a political fight against the exemption clause would have been hard to find. Exemption from taxes represented the customary pro-

[1] *Cong. Record,* vol. 55, pp. 686-7, Mr. Hill and Mr. Mann; pp. 746-8, Senator Simmons.

[2] Secretary McAdoo later maintained that the feature enabled the Treasury to sell the bonds at from one-half to one per cent lower interest rate than would otherwise have been possible (*Senate Hearings on H. R. 5901*). The volume of the subscriptions has often been ascribed in part to the attractiveness of the exemption feature (Willis, *op. cit.*, p. 1156).

[3] *The Liberty Loan of 1917,* Campaign Text Book. (In N. Y. Pub. Library, volume *Liberty Loan Pamphlets,* BTZO, No. 1.)

[4] Outside of Congress, the feature aroused criticism. See Seligman, "Our Fiscal Policy" in *Financial Mobilization for War* (Chicago, 1917), p. 6.

cedure up until the time of the loan. There had not been enough variation in taxes on income in different brackets, nor had they been high enough,[1] to make exemption an important concession. Moreover, the plans for the campaign included the sale of bonds to rich and to poor; and campaigners described the exemption feature in terms of a universal appeal. While the astute financier was being set to work comparing net yields on taxable as against tax-free bonds, the small back-woods investor was listening to an account of the attractive features of the bonds, and hearing that the holder need have no fear of the tax collector.[2] For all of these reasons, tax exemption was accepted as a matter of course.

THE RATE OF INTEREST AND THE TREASURY'S POLICY

One of the outstanding aspects of the first issue of war bonds is to be found in the low rate of interest.[3] The administration's adoption of conversion and exemption—two measures which have ordinarily been employed for the purpose of lowering the nominal rate of interest—naturally leads one to question the Treasury's policy regarding the payment of interest.

In his annual report, the Secretary of the Treasury stated two reasons for his attempt to maintain a low rate of interest. First, higher rates would result in increasing the

[1] The rates in force at the time were those of the *Act of Sept. 8, 1916* (39 Stat. at Large, pt. i, p. 756, ch. 463), which provided for a 2% normal tax and a maximum surtax of 13%.

[2] A quotation from *The Liberty Loan of 1917, op. cit.*, will disclose the nature of the latter appeal: "State, county and city taxes often amount to as much as three cents on the dollar; the exemption from taxation of these bonds makes them in such cases equivalent to a 6½% investment" (p. 14).

[3] *Cong. Record,* vol. 55, pp. 677 and 759. See in general, Benjamin H. Beckhart, *The Discount Policy of the Federal Reserve Bank* (New York, 1924), and Willis, *op. cit., passim.*

cost of the war, and secondly, they would result in greater "depreciation in all other forms of investment securities." [1] The first of these is of course, a mathematical truth; but it is hardly to be considered that an annual increase of perhaps 20 million dollars (the additional expense involved in a one point increase in the interest rate) was in itself a matter of primary concern to the Treasury. The second reason pertaining to the depreciation in other securities may, for all the proof to the contrary, have influenced the Secretary's opinions. But if Mr. McAdoo intended to protect the capital values of existing investments by maintaining a low rate on government securities, and if he planned the use of the exemption and conversion privileges in order to make the latter issues so attractive that they could be sold at the lower rate, then his economic reasoning may be challenged.

If exemption and conversion were able to attract funds from other fields to low-interest-bearing government securities, would not the practical effects be almost the same as if the necessary inducements had been given in the form of higher interest rates? Whether or not we can muster the support for an affirmative answer, we can at least find reasons to think that the attempt to issue securities at a low nominal rate was prompted by motives of a political rather than of a financial or altruistic nature. This belief can in turn be supported by an analysis of certain political ramifications of the situation.

In the first place it should be pointed out that the best financial judgment of the times would probably have resulted in issuing the bonds at a rate of interest of five or six per cent. If, as Mr. McAdoo put it,[2] there was "much confusion of counsel" it is easily seen that the Treasury in announcing a two billion dollar loan at 3½% was ostensibly

[1] *Treas. Report*, 1917, p. 4.

[2] *Treas. Report*, 1917, p. 6.

disregarding a large portion of the counsel. But strange as it may seem, the Secretary apparently found in the situation an incentive for attempting to place the loan at a low rate of interest. If he could succeed in floating the loan at 3½%, the victory would be the more spectacular because of the admitted odds against him. From three different sources, Mr. McAdoo might expect approbation.

In the first place there were those who actually thought that 3½% would place the bonds on a business basis.

Then there were the members of a second group (not so small, if we are to judge by the extent to which they made themselves heard) who favored the low rate and who were willing to resort to means other than the financial appeal.[1] Vague references had even been made to the possibility of forcing the purchase of bonds,[2] and to a return to an equivalent of the legal tender method of financing.[3] In the second group might also be classified individuals who followed in the footsteps of Mr. McAdoo himself[4] in pleading for a decrease in the cost of the War. Some who contended that

[1] Senator Kenyon, for example, in response to Senator Calder's expression of doubt as to the bonds being taken at 3½% intimated that the "patriotic market" for the bonds would absorb the issue (65th Cong., 1st Sess., p. 759).

[2] Mr. Fitzgerald (65th Cong., 1st Sess., p. 628), "My remedy would be, if they are not sold at popular subscription, then to dispose of them otherwise at not less than par, because I believe we can compel these bonds to be taken . . ."

[3] *Cong. Record,* vol. 55, pp. 752-755, amendment by Senator Thomas; rejected, p. 755. In the light of Senator Thomas' argument for non-interest-bearing obligations and his plea for a scheme which was virtually a return to the "greenback" system, it is rather interesting to observe that his amendment provided merely that the certificates were to bear no interest and were to have the "circulation privilege". Since the term "circulation privilege" in its technical usage means simply that the bonds can be used by banks for the purpose of securing their note circulation, it is clear that the amendment did not, as Senator Thomas intimated, provide for the compulsory acceptance of this paper as money.

[4] *Treas. Report,* 1917, p. 4.

wealth should bear the cost of the War looked upon any payment of interest as going that far in the wrong direction. To those who leaned toward this line of reasoning, success of a loan would appear to vary inversely with the rate of interest.

Members of yet a third group invariably set up the same standard of success. Unconsciously, perhaps, the vast majority of business men and others who are more or less familiar with private financing or with investing, accept the yield from a security as fair criteria both of the strength of the issuing company and of its success in financing its operations. Individuals accustomed to this type of analysis would unconsciously measure the strength of the Government and the efficiency of the Treasury Department by the rate of interest borne by the loans.

Thus, from three different quarters, at least two of which represented, one could almost say, opposing camps, Mr. McAdoo might well have courted approbation by fostering a low rate of interest, just as he might have feared the criticism which probably would have arisen had he felt compelled to grant a higher rate.

The outstanding developments in connection with World-War financing apparently arose as a result of the Secretary's early endeavors to secure this approbation. The facts are that in the very first loan he adopted two features, namely, tax exemption and conversion, which were expected to make the bonds attractive enough to permit their sale at the low rate of 3½%. His subsequent action strengthens the fairly general opinion that this low level was the result of a deliberate attempt to maintain an artificially low rate of interest. Assuming that this was true, we should at least give Mr. McAdoo credit for his shrewdness in having weighed the political consequences of his acts even though we suspect that his readings of the balances were somewhat incorrect.

CHAPTER IX

The Second Liberty Loan

NO SALE BELOW PAR. CIRCULATION PRIVILEGE

We may first dispose of two features, each of which was the subject of debate in connection with the first issue of war bonds, but was of no importance in the second. The provision against selling bonds below par and that denying the circulation privilege were retained in the later Liberty Bond acts.[1]

APPROPRIATION FOR EXPENSES

In the matter of the appropriation for selling the bonds, the developments in connection with the Second Liberty Loan were very similar to those of the first in that a request from the Secretary for a liberal allowance was debated and modified by Congress.[2] As the matter finally stood, the Secretary was given a free hand in spending one-fifth of one percent of the amount of bonds and war-savings certificates, and one-tenth of one percent of the amount of certificates of indebtedness.

[1] Second Liberty Bond Act; *Act of Sept. 24, 1917*, 40 Stat. at Large pt. i, p. 288, ch. 56, sec. 1.

[2] *House Committee on Ways and Means, Hearings on H. R. 5901*, 65th Cong., 1st Sess., p. 24. Also, *Hearings H. R. 5901*, 65th Cong., 1st Sess., Sept. 11, 1917. *Cong. Record*, vol. 55, pp. 6577, 6590, 6695, 6704.

A long harangue in the Senate culminated in the passage of an amendment for an appropriation of one-fourth of one per cent for expenses incurred in the emission of bonds. (Discussion, *Cong. Record*, 65th Cong., 1st Sess., pp. 7124-32.) In the Conference reports to the Senate, and to the House, this figure was changed to one-fifth of one per cent. (*Cong. Record*, vol. 55, pp. 7271 and 7286.)

This arrangement promised the Secretary three times as much to spend on the Second Liberty Loan campaign as he had in prospect on the first.

CONVERSION

The Second Loan granted the conversion privilege [1] but added the important provision that the conversion right would expire upon the failure of a bond holder to take advantage of his first opportunity to convert. The new conversion arrangement may be considered as conforming almost perfectly to the Secretary's altered ideas on the subject.[2] Whether or not the change resulted from discontent with the feature as it was incorporated in the first loan can not be ascertained. What does appear as obvious, however, is that the provision marked a step away from that uncertainty which follows the practice of leaving to all existing bonds the privilege of converting into any new issue, and in the direction of the policy of making each loan stand on its own responsibility.

That a complete abandonment of the conversion privilege was not unthought of is proved by Mr. Sloan's fight against the utilization of conversion in any form. He argued that the privilege added nothing to the sale of the bonds, that it increased the burden upon the people, and that holders of old bonds would continue to depress the market in order to force the government to pay higher rates.[3]

Mr. Kitchin brushed aside these arguments with the statement that Mr. McAdoo thought the feature was necessary as an aid in selling the bonds.[4]

[1] Act, *op. cit.*, sec 4, p. 290.

[2] *Senate Committee on Finance Hearings*, 65th Cong., 1st Sess., pp. 7 and 12.

[3] *Cong. Record*, vol. 55, 65th Cong., 1st Sess., p. 5649.

[4] *House Comm. on Ways and Means, Hearings on H. R. 5901*, 65th Cong., 1st Sess., pp. 4-8.

THE ADMINISTRATION'S CHANGE ON EXEMPTION

The Second Liberty Loan Act provided for exemption from all taxes except (a) estate or inheritance taxes, and, (2) sur-taxes, excess profits taxes, and war profits taxes. Interest on an amount of bonds, the principal of which did not exceed $5,000 was exempt from the latter group of taxes (group b).[1]

The plan of making the bonds subject to surtaxes, excess profits taxes, and war profits, marked a distinct break, outwardly at least, from the policy of full exemption as it appeared in the First Liberty Loan.[2]

But the change by no means represented a decrease in the ability of the Treasury Department to make effective its ideas. On the contrary, the abandonment of full exemption must be credited to the self-same administration whose leaders had championed the cause of exemption only a few months before. Mr. McAdoo gave as his[3] reasons for this change in policy, first, that the plan adopted would not enable the rich, through the purchase of government bonds, to obtain exemption from a graduated income tax.[4] Complete exemption would result in a class of rich enjoying incomes wholly free from tax burdens.

A second reason, according to the Secretary, was to be found in the fact that the people who subscribed to the first

[1] Act, *op. cit.*, sec. 7, p. 291.

[2] First Liberty Act, *op. cit.*, sec. 1.

[3] *House Comm. on Ways and Means, Hearings on H. R. 5901*, 65th Cong., 1st Sess., pp. 20-21.

[4] For a public statement on this point, see, W. G. McAdoo. *The Second Liberty Loan*, an address delivered at the annual convention of the American Bankers' Association. Government Printing Office, 1917. He said in part: "The position of the government must always be to offer a bond upon terms fair and equitable to all alike and which will make the widest possible appeal to all the people without regard to the extraneous fact that a man may be poor or rich," p. 13.

issue of liberty bonds were little influenced by the exemption feature and would have been equally satisfied with only an exemption from the normal income tax. A 4% bond, exempt from normal taxes but subject, nevertheless, to surtaxes, should appeal to members of the middle classes who, Mr. McAdoo concluded, had hardly been touched by the first loan.

A critical reader may find in these statements an interesting mixture of reasoning. Taken separately, either of the two may appear logical enough; considered together, they seem to conflict; while if they are studied in conjunction with the previous actions of the Treasury Department, they force one to search elsewhere for the true cause for the abandonment of the tax-exemption feature.

Let us examine all possible combinations of circumstances which would have furnished the basis for the two statements. Logically speaking, there are possible four such combinations, as follows: First: Previous bonds were not bought by the rich whereas the second issue would be absorbed by this class. Second: First Liberties had not been bought by the rich and there was no chance of their group buying Second Liberties. Third: The rich had bought the first and would buy the second. Fourth: The rich had bought the first but would not buy the second.

The first situation would justify both the contention that the feature would lead to a class of exempt rich and that it was of little use in the first loan. However, a study of the facts leads one to question the basic assumptions. In spite of the Secretary's apparent attempts to leave the impression that the Treasury depended upon small investors, the size of subscriptions suggest that the major portion of the volume of sales was to subscribers of means.[1]

[1] "The great bulk of that loan," Mr. McAdoo said in reference to the first issue, "was subscribed by men of small means in this country, and

The established fact that the bonds actually were bought by the rich supports the first part of the second assumption. But if the remainder of the assumption, namely, that the forthcoming bonds would not be bought by the rich, were also true, then the Secretary's ostensible concern over a class of exempt rich was uncalled for.

The third set of assumptions appears logical enough until we come to the assertion that full exemption would not make the bonds any more attractive than would the proposed partial exemption.[1]

Finally, the fourth and most logical combination suggests that the Secretary believed that the bonds of the first issue had been sold to the rich with the result that exemption had been instrumental in placing the securities, but that the fea-

we had to make that loan appeal to them in a very large part on the score of patriotism, because the rate of interest was too low and the exemption did not benefit them enough to make it attractive to them as an investment per se." (*Hearings H. R. 5901*, 66th Cong., 1st Sess., p. 30.) Another instance in which one is left to draw an inference of the same nature is found in the Secretary's annual report (*Treas. Report*, 1917, p. 7), where Mr. McAdoo points out that of the total number of people who subscribed to the loan, 99% were in the class of small subscriptions of from $50 to $10,000. The error of this inference, which the casual reader logically draws, is obvious when we observe that the high percentage refers to the number of subscribers and not to the amount subscribed. As a matter of fact, the remaining one per cent of subscribers representing the larger subscription actually accounted for approximately one and three-quarter billions, or 57% of the loan. Of this amount, over two-thirds came in individual subscriptions which were in excess of $100,000. (*Treas. Report*, 1917, p. 7.) The amount of subscriptions in each of the respective classes was as follows:

Size of subscription	*Amount subscribed*	
$ 50 to $ 10,000		$1,296,684,850
10,050 to 100,000	$ 560,103,050	
over $100,000	1,178,438,950	
		1,738,542,000
		$3,035,226,850

[1] *House Comm. on Ways and Means, Hearings on H. R. 5901*, p. 35.

ture would not be effective in the second because rich purchasers would be lacking. But if this was his belief, his public statements are as misleading as they are contradictory. In order to eliminate the mistaken impression, we would be forced to revise Mr. McAdoo's statements. His remarks depreciating the part played by the exemption feature in the first loan, and the one disclosing his concern over the effects of exempting future issues of bonds, should be reversed so as to change the loans to which the statements are to apply.

The result of this analysis is to make the student of finance look upon these and other [1] public statements of the Treasury head as mere rationalizations designed to satisfy the people concering a matter of public interest rather than as factual statements which would give an idea of the basis upon which government policies were projected.

Having disposed of the Secretary's own statements by showing that they fail to supply a dependable explanation of the Treasury's change of front on the exemption question, we are compelled to search elsewhere for an account of the circumstances affecting the decision. By so doing we are able to detect no less than four different factors.

In the first place, Mr. McAdoo, although adopting the feature in order to insure the success of the First Liberty loan, had never been an ardent advocate of tax exemption.[2]

[1] For example. "The change in the tax-exemption feature was deemed essential in order that the bonds might be of the same value, as far as taxation is concerned in the hands of all investors." (*Treas. Report*, 1917, p. 9, a statement to the same effect appears in *House Hearings on H. R. 5901*, 65th Cong., 1st Sess., p. 86.

[2] See *H. R. Comm. on Ways and Means, Hearings on First Liberty Loan*, 65th Cong., 1st Sess. *Hearings on H. R. 5901*, pp. 20 and 35, and especially, p. 69. His most emphatic statements came in response to questions concerning his stand on the subject. "Personally, I do not favor exemption of any bonds from taxation. I think it altogether a mistake . . ." "I favor no exemption so far as I am concerned. I mean my own views are very emphatic about that. I think it is altogether a mistake to exempt bonds from taxation."

No doubt he accordingly welcomed any step in the direction of abandoning the practice.

A second reason for turning away from tax exemption is doubtless to be found in a loss of confidence in the feature's ability to aid in placing the securities. With the ink scarcely dry on an issue of two billion dollars of exempt securities it was hardly to be expected that exemption would facilitate the sale of the Second Liberties as it had that of the first bond issue.

A third factor evidently found its origin in Mr. McAdoo's increased dependence upon his ability to sell bonds on the basis of a patriotic appeal. This appeal he was planning to direct toward the great middle class.[1] A large appropriation for expenses made possible a campaign which would reach these masses. A defense of normal taxes [2] but not a provision for full exemption fitted in with this program.

Finally, the abandonment of full exemption rendered a real service to the administration by supplying the Secretary an excuse for adding one-half of a point to the interest rate. As a result the Treasury was accordingly able to offer a 4% bond and at the same time leave the impression that the bonds were being issued on terms as advantageous to the government as were those of the first loan.[3]

It was apparently due to all of these circumstances that Mr. McAdoo advocated the plan of subjecting the bonds to surtaxes as ardently as he had championed the cause of exemption only a few months earlier.[4]

[1] *House Comm. on Ways and Means, Hearings H. R. 5901*, 65th Cong., 1st Sess., p. 21.

[2] *House Comm. on Ways and Means, Hearings H. R. 5901*, 65th Cong., 1st Sess., pp. 22 and 69-70.

[3] *Cong. Record*, vol. 55, pp. 6580-81, Fordney, p. 6590, Moore, pp. 6640-1, Morgan.

[4] *House Hearings on H. R. 5901*, p. 42. His lead was followed by Kitchin. *Cong. Record*, vol. 55, pp. 6572-3, 6538 and 6650. For opposing arguments, see, *ibid.*, p. 6579, Fordney; pp. 6640-1 and p. 6649, Sloan.

It is significant that one of the proposals appearing in the course of the discussion involved the issuance of two types of bonds—one taxable and the other tax-free. Mr. McAdoo opposed this scheme (which was later adopted in connection with the Victory Loan) on the grounds that it would be difficult to explain the difference to new investors.[1]

EXEMPTION OF SPECIFIED AMOUNT

The Secretary also opposed the plan of granting exemption on the income from a specified amount of bonds. This exemption, he thought, was of no value, would be difficult to interpret, and would merely result in confusion.[2] In spite of the Secretary's original objection, however, this measure was included in the law.[3] At the time of its passage, the plan was probably considered too insignificant in its scope to bring forth much argument. From the vantage point of one looking back on the development of the entire period, the appearance of the measure is significant because it discloses the legislators' unwillingness to give up completely a device (exemption) which they still believed would add something to the selling value of the bonds. Of even greater importance is the fact that the use of this novel device served as an entering wedge for a practice which was subsequently utilized to such an extent that the status of liberty bonds underwent a revolutionary change.

Quite the opposite of the proposal to revert to total exemption and the one to exempt $5,000 of bonds from the

[1] *House Comm. on Ways and Means, Hearings H. R. 5901*, p 46.

[2] *Senate Comm. on Fin., Hearing on H. R. 5901*, Sept. 11, 1917, pp. 15-17.

[3] (Act, *op. cit.*, sec. 7, p. 291.) The amount affected by the exemption was decreased from $10,000 as proposed in Mr. Cannon's amendment covering the matter, to $5,000. In its final form, the amendment received the endorsement of Mr. Kitchin, who declared that it would have a salutary effect in popularizing the loan. (*Cong. Record*, 65th Cong., 1st Sess., vol. 55, p. 6692.)

surtax was advanced in an unsuccessful amendment introduced by Senator LaFollette making the income from the bonds subject to the normal tax.[1]

The amendment was opposed on the ground that such a step would interfere with the sale of the bonds.[2]

A subtle point lay concealed in a proposal of Secretary McAdoo to the effect that the law be worded so that exemptions would be listed and the bonds remain subject to all forms of taxation not specified in the list of exemptions. The new statement was to replace one which declared that the bonds were to be subject to certain specified taxes only and were to remain exempt from all other taxes.[3] Under Secretary McAdoo's plan, subsequent war taxes on the bonds could be levied in any form except those which were itemized in the list of exemptions. On the other hand, the old plan of granting exemption from all taxes except those specified precluded the possibility of collecting revenue by levying new forms of taxes on the bonds. The proposed plan left the Treasury's hands free and was obviously advantageous to the government. At the same time, the Secretary contended that the possibility of future taxation would not cause the purchaser to hesitate to buy the bonds. In spite of these arguments, however, the proposal of the Secretary on the matter was not followed.[4]

Mr. McAdoo's plea for this proposal stands as an interesting contrast to his argument against the plan of reserving the right of subjecting the bonds to normal taxes after the war.

[1] *Cong. Record*, 65th Cong., 1st Sess., vol. 55, p. 7180.

[2] *Ibid.*, p. 7160, Senator Stone; *House Comm. on Ways and Means, Hearings on H. R. 5901*, 65th Cong., 1st Sess., pp. 22 and 69, Mr. McAdoo.

[3] *Senate Committee on Finance, Hearings on H. R. 5901*, Sept. 11, 1917, pp. 12-15.

[4] The wording of the act followed the former plan of exempting the bond from all taxes except those specified.

It is clear that the actual results of the two arrangements would be identical in that they would each make the future net yield of the bonds uncertain. The reason that Mr. McAdoo condemned the one [1] and favored the other, therefore, is undoubtedly to be found in his belief that the possible effects of the one would be recognized by the prospective purchasers, and would, accordingly, discount the bonds in their eyes, whereas the other would not interfere with the sale of the bonds in any such way.

MATURITIES AND THE RATE OF INTEREST

Previous discussion has already brought to light pertinent material on the subject of the rate of interest. The certificates of indebtedness supplied the topic for a verbal fight on an entirely new aspect of this question.

Secretary McAdoo had requested that the interest on the certificates be left to his discretion. He contended that in fixing the rate Congress would tie the hands of the Secretary of the Treasury and prevent his meeting temporary conditions in the money market, with the possible result of embarrassment to the government.[2] In spite of objections,[3] including an amendment to the effect that interest on the certificates should be limited to that borne by long-time obligations,[4] the Secretary secured the desired discretion.

A fight very similar to the one in which an effort was made to limit the Secretary of the Treasury in the matter of

[1] *House Comm. on Ways and Means, Hearings H. R. 5901*, p. 45.

[2] *House Comm. on Ways and Means, Hearings H. R. 5901*, 65th Cong., 1st Sess., pp. 17-18, 44, 65-7.

[3] *Cong. Record*, vol. 55, p. 6579, Mr. Fordney.

[4] The amendment was introduced by Senator LaFollette, opposed by Senator Stone, and finally rejected by the Senate. (*Cong. Record*, 65th Cong., 1st Sess., p. 7179; Stone's opposition, p. 7180. Rejection of amendment, p. 7180.)

the interest rate on the certificates of indebtedness was waged against the plan of leaving this executive free to arrange the maturities of the bonds. Senator LaFollette was again the author of an amendment covering the point at issue. He proposed to specify that the bonds would be redeemable five years, and payable twenty years, after issue.[1] Mr. McAdoo had committed himself to the principle of prior redemption, but contended that maturities should be left to the discretion of the Secretary of the Treasury, presumably with the idea that he could and would adjust the maturities so as to meet market needs and in a manner which would facilitate refundings. These arguments [2] of the Secretary were used by Senator Stone [3] in combating Senator LaFollette's proposal. The amendment was defeated and the Secretary was given a free hand in arranging maturities.

SUMMARY

Viewed in its entirety, the Second Liberty Bond Act, together with the discussions incident to its passage, discloses some interesting developments in government financing. Described in dogmatic and summary fashion, these developments were as follows:

The requirement for sale at par and the denial of the circulation privilege to the bonds apparently came to be considered as fixtures in government finance.

The conversion privilege suffered its first set-back in the form of a provision for limiting the right to the first opportunity to arise. This was a step in the direction of making each loan stand on its own responsibility and of relieving

[1] *Cong. Record,* vol. 55, pp. 7169-7179. Discussion by LaFollette and others.

[2] *House Comm. on Ways and Means, Hearings H. R. 5901,* 65th Cong., 1st Sess., p. 28.

[3] *Cong. Record,* vol. 55, 65th Cong., 1st Sess., pp. 7174-5.

the government of that permanent burden of uncertain and unknown weight which it was liable to be called upon to bear as long as holders of the old bonds had the privilege of converting into any subsequent issue.

With the coming of the Second Liberty Bond Act, the administration reversed its policy in regard to exemption and advocated that the bonds be subjected to surtaxes, excess profits and war profits taxes. In brief, the explanation of this action simply was that the exemption feature was not expected to add much to the sales appeal of the bonds, whereas, its abandonment facilitated the Treasury's task of securing permission from the legislature to name a higher rate of interest. At the same time the step furnished a reason for the higher rate, so that confidence in the government would not be shaken. Mr. McAdoo, for his own reasons, chose to state other causes for the change in policy.

While the discussion was principally on the question of exempting the bond incomes from the surtaxes, debates on numerous minor points also took place. The question of subjecting the bonds to the normal tax came up for consideration. A measure exempting the income from $5,000 bonds came as the initial use of what later came to be a popular device. There was raised, too, the involved and complicated question whether exemptions should be specified. While the discussions do not display the degree of knowledge on the part of the legislature that might be desired, there is at least evidence that the financing devices were receiving some attention.

CHAPTER X

The Third Liberty Loan

POLITICAL TECHNIQUE EMPLOYED IN PASSING THE ACT

Efforts toward eliminating discussion[1] on the Third Liberty loan were apparently facilitated by the feeling that the proposed law was merely an amendment to the Second Liberty Bond Act[2] and that consequently it was not necessary to discuss the details of the measure. As a result, neither the statements of Treasury officials nor the debates of members of Congress afford much material of interest. On the other hand, the very fact that a number of new features were introduced with little if any attention, constitutes an interesting reflection on the legislative bodies and at the same time furnishes implications which will afford the basis for our discussions of the Third Liberty Loan Act.

Before turning to a consideration of the salient features of the new Act, we may observe that for the first, and indeed for the only time, the question of tax exemption took a back seat, and remained unnoticed during the passage of a Liberty Bond Bill. The provisions of the Second Liberty Bond Act, were simply retained in the Third.

THE ABANDONMENT OF CONVERSION

The conversion feature, on the other hand, was brought into the lime light, and subjected to the criticism of its op-

[1] *Cong. Record*, vol. 56, 4322, 65th Cong., 2nd Sess.

[2] The full title of the bill read: "An Act To Amend an Act approved Sept. 24, 1917, entitled", etc. (*Act of April 4, 1917*, 40 Stat. at Large, pt. i, p. 502, sec. 44.)

ponents, among whom might now be found the administration leaders.

Mr. Kitchin in his report on the bill, included a reference to the provision that the bonds were not to be convertible.[1] Since this leader had formerly contended that the government should give the bonds the conversion privilege, his present action against the feature, it was argued, was an evidence of inconsistency. In answer to this charge, Mr. Kitchin justified his action by referring to the large amount of bonds outstanding and to the fear that holders of these bonds would attempt to force a high rate of interest on subsequent issues.[2] Since this reason had formerly been used by the administration's opponents in the course of discussions on the First Liberty Loan, Mr. Kitchin's defense may be interpreted as a virtual admission that his opponents had been right, and that the plan of granting the privilege of conversion had been a mistake, or at least that it had, or would in the future have, undesirable results.

Among the succeeding arguments for doing away with conversion[3] one stressed the claim that the removal of the feature would eliminate the incentive for refraining from purchasing. This claim was especially significant in view of the fact that it was almost a word-for-word repetition of the administration's former plea for the conversion feature.

THE INTEREST RATE AND THE TREASURY'S POLICY

The Third Liberty Bond Act made still another important change by increasing the yield to 4½%. This rate represented an increase of one-fourth point over that of the bonds of the second issue.

[1] *Cong. Record*, vol. 56, pp. 4315 and 4322.

[2] *Cong. Record*, vol. 56, p. 4323.

[3] *Cong. Record*, vol. 56, pp. 4323, 4331 and 4342.

A justification for this increase was not hard to find since the price of bonds in the market apparently gave the Secretary sufficient grounds for asking the legislators to grant a higher rate of interest. Accordingly, he was not forced to resort to the practice of bartering for an increase in the rate as he had done in the previous issue when he gave up the exemption feature.[1] Instead, Mr. McAdoo, according to his own testimony,[2] placed himself in the position of fighting for a lower rate of interest than would otherwise have been established. This fight was especially significant in view of the complexity of the problem ahead. The market was such that outstanding government securities were more attractive at existing prices than were the forthcoming bonds at par. Part of Mr. McAdoo's method of solving this problem can be learned from his own statement:

" The treasury," he said, " stood firm in the belief that the rate of interest would not of itself maintain Liberty bonds, at par in the financial markets; that the price of Liberty bonds, even though quoted at less than par on the exchanges, would not deter the American people from buying at par the same bonds when offered by their government to secure the necessary funds to carry on the war; that the patriotism of the American people was not measured by interest rates nor de-

[1] Although Senator Simmons pointed out that the Third Liberties would lack a feature (conversion) which was an important incentive in floating the first two issues (*Cong. Record,* vol. 56, p. 4529), Mr. McAdoo's statement to the effect that the conversion privilege . . . "had become no longer necessary for the sale of the bonds . . . ," (*Treas. Report,* 1918, p. 6), shifted attention to another aspect of the subject. As a result the abandonment of conversion was not utilized, as was the giving up of the exemption feature, for the purpose of justifying an increase in the rate. On the other hand, possibilities of utilizing the step were not entirely overlooked. Mr. McAdoo contended that the absence of the conversion feature would lead to the stabilization of interest at his selected level.

[2] *Treas. Report,* 1918, p. 6.

termined by the fluctuations in the market price of government bonds on the stock exchange." [1]

In form, a bouquet to the American people, but in substance a demand that purchasers look not at the financial aspects of their dealings in Liberty Bonds, this statement is in truth a frank denial that the Treasury purports to give an obligation equal in value to the money exacted from purchasers of Liberty Bonds. One would hardly look for a more definite avowal of the plan to resort to an appeal to patriotic rather than to financial motives. But, if the administration intended to trust in the patriotism of the American people, it was also, to paraphrase a familiar expression, determined to keep its powder dry, by taking certain steps in the direction of improving the status of the bonds on the market. The first action along this line involved the small increase in rate. Three other measures must be considered as being in the same class. They are, first, the plan of making the bonds acceptable at par in payment of estate taxes, secondly, the arrangement for buying bonds on the market, and finally the effort to free banks from state taxation on their holdings of government bonds.

THE RECEIVABILITY FEATURE

The Third Liberty Bond Act provided that any bonds bearing interest at a higher rate than four per cent per annum, and owned by any person continuously for at least six months prior to the date of his death, should be receivable by the United States at par plus accrued interest in payment of estate or inheritance taxes.[2] The Committee on Ways and Means, according to its chairman, Mr. Kitchin, believed that this feature would add to the attractiveness of the bonds, and thus increase purchases and also that it would have a

[1] *Treas. Report*, 1918, p. 6.

[2] Act, *op. cit.*, sec. 6 (sec. 14 of Act as amended), p. 505.

salutary effect upon the market price of the bonds. Mr. Kitchin later added [1] his own definite comment to the effect that the feature would induce the rich to buy these bonds rather than to convert their assets into money with which to meet estate taxes. With this slight [2] attention, the provision was inserted in the act.

In so far as the measure was intended for the purpose of maintaining the par value of government obligations, it marks an important milestone in World War financing. Up until this time, the Treasury Department had busied itself with plans for floating large issues of bonds. Its worries had centered on the problem of appealing to the patriotism of the people in an attempt to induce them to purchase the bonds. From this time on through the post-war period public interest as well as the activities of the Treasury officials, will be found to be concerned to an ever-increasing extent with the task of maintaining the bonds' position in the market. The topic to be discussed next, covers another scheme which was launched with the avowed purpose of bettering the position of government bonds on the market.

THE PURCHASE OF BONDS BY THE GOVERNMENT

The Third Liberty Bond Act,[3] gave the Secretary of the Treasury authority to use five per cent of the proceeds of the bond sale in purchasing Liberty Bonds on the market. Bonds could be bought at par plus accrued interest. The stated purpose of the section was that of stabilizing the price of bonds and it was implied that the direction of the resulting price stabilization would be upward. Belief that such action was necessary was fostered by the low prices of Liberties on the Market. This market situation was in turn said

[1] *Cong. Record*, vol. 56, p. 4316.

[2] *Cong. Record*, vol. 56, p. 4328.

[3] Act, *op. cit.*, sec. 6 (sec. 15 as amended).

to be the result of manipulation which had been used by certain factions in their efforts to force the government to pay a higher rate of interest.

PROPOSAL TO EXEMPT BANK-HOLDINGS OF GOVERNMENT BONDS

One of the most interesting of the several measures which were advocated for the purpose of improving the status of Liberty Bonds, was the one looking to the exemption of bank holdings of Liberty Bonds from state taxation.[1] The states, it was contended, were really taxing government bonds indirectly by including such bonds in the appraisal of capital stock and surplus for taxation purposes. Section 5 of the original Third Liberty Bond Bill, proposed to alter this situation by providing that in assessing capital stock of banks for purposes of taxation by any state, the amount of government bonds was to be subtracted from the total capital assets.[2]

As the issue was finally put, arguments that the measure represented a just compensation to the banks for their service in holding government obligations,[3] as well as a means of securing their continued cooperation,[4] were met by the claim that the measure was not needed,[5] that it was a violation of the rights of states and would diminish their revenue,[6] and that the right of the Federal Government to take such action was questionable.[7]

The action of Congress on similar measures leaves little doubt that if the measure had ever been presented for a vote

[1] See *supra*, p. 113, footnote.

[2] *Cong. Record*, vol. 56, p. 43; 4, Bill reported by Kitchin.

[3] *Cong. Record*, vol. 56, p. 4348, Phelan.

[4] *Ibid.*, p. 4327, Kitchin.

[5] *Ibid.*, p. 4336, Mr. McFadden, p. 4345, Mr. Dominick.

[6] *Ibid.*, p. 4345, Dominick.

[7] *Ibid.*, p. 4345-6.

the majority of both houses would have voted in the way that would have promised to facilitate the forthcoming bond issue. However, as a result of confusion in the minds of members of Congress as to what interpretation was to be placed upon the measure as it was worded, the bill failed to come to a vote.

Two interpretations were made. One group, apparently including the framers of the provision, contended that the measure was intended to permit the subtraction of holdings of Liberty Bonds from taxable capital,—an interpretation which could conceivably allow a bank to escape taxation altogether. Another group were of the opinion that the amount of Liberty Bonds held by a bank was to be related to its gross assets and the resulting ratio used in determining the proportion of net capital which was to be taxed. This confusion over the interpretation proved fatal largely because it arose within the ranks. The tragedy appears the greater because of the innocence of the offender.

Kitchin, without knowing the intention of the framers of the measure, and apparently without a careful study of its contents, launched blindly into a defense of the plan, or rather of his interpretation of it. Entirely against his wishes and without his knowing it, however, his interpretation had unfortunately run counter to that of other administration leaders. Even an amendment, designed to clear up the point at issue, was accordingly too late to patch up the difficulty. In the Senate Committee, the entire provision was scrapped on the grounds that its inclusion would lead to confusion and to delay.[1] Consequently one of the administration's plans for influencing bond prices failed to materialize.

[1] See *Cong. Record,* 65th Cong., 2nd Sess., p. 4443-51, Mr. Kitchin, Mr. Sterling and Mr. Sloan; p. 4530, amendment in Senate striking out Sections; p. 4616, House agrees.

ACCEPTANCE OF LIBERTY BONDS AS SECURITY

The proposal for inducing banks to hold Liberty Bonds by exempting such holdings from state taxes calls to mind a device of another nature, but one with a similar function. Mr. McAdoo made an effort to encourage the use of Liberty Bonds in lieu of other security wherever a bond was required by law or regulation. The government paved the way by permitting certain bidders and contractors to deposit Liberty Bonds, acceptable at par, for guaranteeing proposals or securing the performance of contracts.[1]

SUMMARY

While the Third Liberty Bond Act was hurried through Congress on the ground that it was merely an amendment to the Second, a number of circumstances in connection with its passage as well as several features of the act itself, make it distinctive.

The exemption feature, which was in its principal manifestation discarded in the second act, was not restored. The conversion privilege was also omitted. Consequently, these two aides of war finance now found themselves excluded from the field in which the administration had formerly claimed that they were indispensable.

The Third Liberty Loan is important also because of the fact that by the time it was being framed, the situation in respect to Liberty Bonds on the market had become acute. Following, and it might be said as a result of, the financial methods employed in the first two issues, the price of Liberties had dropped to such an extent that the task of placing new bonds was a difficult one. The plan for meeting the situation included primarily a forceful appeal to the patriot-

[1] *Treas. Report*, 1918, pp. 73-74. Liberty bonds were also accepted as security for payment of excise taxes, etc., at face value, whereas other bonds were accepted at 50% of their value only.

ism of the people and included a request that purchasers ignore financial motives in their dealings with the government. Then, as though appreciating the fact that this suggestion would not be followed by everyone, officials devised several measures for the purpose of increasing the attractiveness of the bonds. The interest rate was increased to 4½%; the bonds were made acceptable in payment of estate taxes; an arrangement was made whereby the government entered the market and bought bonds on its own account for the purpose of "stabilizing the price of bonds"; and, finally, there was an unsuccessful attempt to exempt from state taxation bank holdings of Liberty Bonds. All of these measures may be seen to have had the two-fold purpose of giving additional "sales talk" and of improving the status of the bonds in the market. The last of these two general aims had become increasingly important as the forces of the market depressed bond prices from a height which had been made possible by an appeal to non-financial motives.

CHAPTER XI

FOURTH LIBERTY LOAN

MARKET CONDITIONS

In floating the Fourth Liberty Loan, the Treasury Department was faced with the task of selling an amount of bonds which was approximately equivalent to the sum of the first two issues. Sales had to be made in a market in which three enormous issues had already been absorbed. Furthermore, outstanding bonds were at the time selling below par. There was accordingly a factual basis for the worries of Secretary McAdoo, who, in a letter to Mr. Kitchin,[1] lamented the state of affairs and admitted that while the bond-purchase fund had been very useful it had not been effective in sustaining the price of bonds.

It accordingly appeared that either an increase in the rate of interest or the addition of some other inducement would have to be adopted.

In connection with this matter the fact that the exempt 3½'s were outstripping higher rate taxable bonds could hardly fail to attract the attention of administration leaders. Nor was the development considered a mere passing flurry on the market. On this point, a second basic trend had not a little bearing on the subject. We refer to the growth of incomes in the higher tax brackets. Moreover, thanks to a deliberate attempt to boost bond prices, income taxes had been raised for the deliberate purpose, we are led to believe, of enhancing the value of the exemption privilege. As a result of both of these developments, an increasing number of owners of war fortunes were in a position which made it

[1] *Treas. Report*, 1916, pp. 14-17.

worthwhile to seek refuge from the augmented and excessive income taxes. It was to these individuals, presumably, that tax exemption would continue to appeal sufficiently to make it desirable to utilize the feature in connection with the forthcoming issue. Unfortunately, however, the stage was not altogether clear for such an action. To attach the feature to the new issue, and disregard the status of the old, could hardly have failed to work in the direction of creating a discrepancy between the prices of the new and those of outstanding securities. To apply complete exemption to the new issues would accordingly have invited the conversion of all outstanding 3½'s with the result that the Treasury would lose an amount equal to three quarters of one percent annually on the face of the bonds so converted.

While the danger of such loss did not exist in so far as 4's and 4½'s were concerned,[1] a more formidible obstacle stood in the way of increasing the relative attractiveness of the new bonds. In the absence of the conversion privilege there was nothing to prevent attractive new securities from selling at a higher price than were those already outstanding. Consequently, there was a danger that the entire policy of the administration would be thrown into political disrepute as a result of objections from holders of the low-priced bonds. For this reason the administration could not afford to strengthen new issues by resorting to any measure which would have lowered the relative price levels of outstanding securities.

How far these considerations influenced the actions of Treasury officials is largely a matter of conjecture. We do

[1] In the Second Liberty Loan, it will be remembered, the section on conversion had specified that the privilege was to be limited to the first time it was offered. The third loan, by supplying this first opportunity, accordingly removed the right to convert Second Liberties into subsequent issues. Consequently, neither of these issues was convertible into the Fourth Liberty Bonds.

know, however, that there was inserted an Argus-eyed feature which apparently looked at each aspect of the problem.

CONTINGENT EXEMPTION [1]

The plan for meeting the complex situation was advanced by Mr. McAdoo and supported by Mr. Leffingwell.[2]

In brief it involved simply an arrangement whereby the exemption of bonds of former issues was made contingent upon the purchase of Fourth Liberty bonds.[3] The purchaser of the new bonds could secure exemption from surtaxes on an amount of $30,000 (principal) of the Fourth Loan, and, by buying this amount, he could secure exemption on a maximum of $45,000 of former issues.[4]

In the main, arguments for the measure centered around

[1] This term has been introduced to cover an arrangement in which the enjoyment of the exemption privilege was made contingent upon the holding of securities of previous issues.

[2] Letter of Sec. McAdoo to Congressman Kitchin, appearing in *House Comm. on Ways and Means Hearing on "Supplementary Bond Legislation"*—Sept. 12, 1918, pp. 3-6 and 24-27.

[3] Mr. McAdoo had previously opposed a similar plan.

[4] Since exemption was limited to 1½ times the amount of the holder's subscriptions to the fourth issue, $45,000 represented the maximum exemption. (*Act of Sept. 24, 1918*, 40 Stat. at Large, pt. i, p. 965, ch. 176, sec. x.) After the Fourth Liberty Bonds were issued, therefore, it was possible for an investor to secure exemptions on $30,000 of four Liberties, $45,000 on previous issues other than first 3½'s (provided he had bought $30,000 of the Fourth Liberty Bonds) and $5,000 on any outstanding 4's or 4¼'s except the fourth liberty bonds. This permitted an aggregate of $80,000 in exempt bonds in addition to holdings of First 3½'s in any amounts. First 3½'s converted into the Fourth 4¼'s partook of the exemption features of the fourth issue, and the amount accordingly had to be subtracted from the $30,000 of Fourth 4¼'s on which exemption was allowed. Incidentally, it may be observed that since first 3½'s so converted lost the permanent exemption and acquired instead the exemption of a limited period terminating two years after the expiration of the war, any conversion of these bonds into Fourth 4¼'s, even though continuing to be exempt for the time, would serve ultimately to decrease the amount of exempt bonds in existence.

the purpose of supplying "sales talk" for use in disposing of the new issue.[1]

While the measure undoubtedly strengthened the demand for the Fourth Liberties, the new issue was forced to share some of the benefits of the Treasury's concessions with the other affected issues. Some compensation for foregone benefit appeared, however, in the form of a smoother operation of the financing machinery. Since it was the policy of the administration to depend upon oiling up the machinery rather than upon supplying the motive power, this measure fitted admirably into its plans. Indeed, when considered separately, and from the standpoint of expediency, this ingenious scheme for meeting the rather baffling and complicated problem of the hour appears as one of the most shrewd as well as one of the most original examples of financing tactics to be found during the period. Unfortunately, however, if the student of finance looks either backwards to the conditions which gave rise to the measure or forward to the results, his feeling of admiration may quickly disappear.

Previous to the measure, there had been consistent efforts to place bonds without supplying a sufficient appeal to assure them of a resting place among investors.[2] Even a clever arrangement to support the market for these over-priced bonds in a way that was not recognized as a direct bounty to the holders must now be looked upon virtually as an admission that the Treasury had been wrong. Such an admission, alas, encompassed not merely the decision in respect to the selection of a single feature, but the entire operations of the Treasury. The finger of criticism is accordingly to be leveled at the basic financial policies of the administration.

[1] *Cong. Record*, 65th Cong., 2nd Sess., vol. 56, p. 10259, Mr. Kitchin; p. 10301, Mr. Fordney and Mr. Longworth; pp. 10436-37, Simmons.

[2] Although the rate had been raised from 3½% to 4% and then to 4¼%, it can hardly be thought that any one of these rates was adequate at the time the bonds were issued.

If we follow up the results of the arrangement in question, we find little to change the opinion gained from looking back at the conditions and circumstances which preceded its adoption. The provision supposedly granted only limited exemption. A study of actual holdings, however, has given not a little support to the general understanding that during the period of exemption the bonds were ordinarily held in such proportions as to result in complete exemption.[1] We can accordingly not look upon the provision for contingent exemption with unmixed admiration.

Another phase of the exemption problem came up for consideration in the form of a proposal to exempt bonds payable in foreign monies. Section 3 of the Fourth Liberty Loan Act provided that such bonds, if owned by non-resident alien individuals or by foreign corporations not engaged in business in the United States, should be exempt from all taxes, state and federal. Administration leaders apparently looked upon the provision as being necessary if the Treasury was to be able to sell bonds abroad and thereby carry out the purpose of stabilizing foreign exchange.[2] The measure was passed.[3]

[1] The results appear in an unpublished manuscript by the writer. Liberty Bond holdings of people who had died during and immediately following the war were found by an examination of appraisals for the inheritance tax (transfer tax) in New York, Kings and Nassau Counties, New York. Data were assembled on a sample of estates aggregating some three hundred million dollars. The results showed that the Liberty Bonds were almost invariably held in amounts which would assure their exemption. Major exceptions to the rule were found only in those cases where the unexempt portion was available for use in paying federal estate taxes at a gain even greater than was to be derived from the exemption feature.

[2] Letter from McAdoo to Kitchin dated June 12, 1918 appearing in *Hearings, House Comm. Ways and Means*, June 27, 1916, 65th Cong., 2nd Sess., p. 4. *Cong. Record*, vol. 56, p. 8431, Kitchin; p. 8691, Simmons; pp. 8692 and 8698, Smoot, Simmons and Kellogg.

[3] *Ibid.*, p. 8698. Act, *op. cit.*, sec. iii, p. 845.

CONTROL OF MARKET TRANSACTIONS

One of the most interesting of the various plans for bringing other than market forces to bear on the price of Liberties was contained in Section 5 of the Act of Sept. 24, 1918, as originally proposed.[1]

The provision had for its purpose the regulation of transactions in Liberty Bonds and, in its original form, went so far as to give the President power to prohibit the transfer of bonds on the market. The proposal came as one of a series of events and expressions of opinion.

Previous to the framing of the Fourth Liberty Loan Act, Mr. McAdoo had lamented the fact that owners of Liberties were being induced to trade their bonds for other securities and for merchandise. Deploring[2] the fact that the individuals who originally owned the Liberties often got the poor end of the bargain, he also accused as unpatriotic those who parted with government bonds. He then proceeded to warn all concerned in these unpatriotic and otherwise undesirable transactions that suitable legislation would be advocated in the event such action did not cease.

The arrangement for control of the market may be considered as the fulfillment of this threat. Mr. Leffingwell declared that the provision was for the purpose of protecting the bondholder, especially against the practice of exchanging Liberty Bonds for worthless securities, and that it was not intended to deprive him of any valuable right.[3]

After a considerable amount of argument,[4] the provision

[1] Appears in *Cong. Record*, 6th Cong., 2nd Sess., p. 10272, as H. R. 12923.

[2] *Treas. Report*, 1918, p. 15.

[3] *House Comm. on Ways and Means, Hearings on Supplementary Bond Legis.*, 65th Cong., 2nd Sess., Sept. 12, 1918, pp. 33-34.

[4] *Cong. Record*, vol. 56, p. 10272, Report on the bill; 10289, Kitchin; pp. 10297-300, Smith, Young and Hayes.

was first eliminated by the Senate,[1] but then restored.[2] Its wording was tempered, however, by the elimination of the provision that the President could prohibit sales. As the measure finally passed, therefore, the President was given authority to investigate and regulate transactions in government bonds and certificates of indebtedness.

In the face of the support which was accorded to the control measure just described, the fact that Mr. Leffingwell raised a vehement protest against the suggestion that people be compelled to subscribe for a specified pro-rata of Liberty Bonds is worthy of note.[4]

In concluding the discussion of the Fourth Liberty Bond Act, we should recall that the privilege of paying estate taxes with Liberty Bonds acceptable at par, and the arrangement for buying bonds in the market for the account of the government, applied to this issue.[5]

The privilege of conversion, discontinued in the Third Liberty Loan Act, remained unused in floating the Fourth Loan. Refusal to grant the circulation privilege to the bonds also again characterized a Liberty Bond Act. The act itself left the question of maturity and of redemption entirely with the Secretary of the Treasury, who issued twenty-year bonds redeemable any time after fifteen years.[6]

[1] *Cong. Record, op. cit.*, p. 10444.

[2] *Ibid.*, p. 10660.

[3] *Ibid.*

[4] H. R. House Comm. on Ways and Means, *Hearings on Fourth Liberty Bond Bill*, 65th Cong., 2nd Sess., p. 18, June 27, 1918.

[5] The Fourth Liberty Bond Act was merely an amendment of the Second Act as amended by the Third.

[6] *Treas. Report*, 1918, p. 178. Dept. Cir. 121.

SUMMARY

By the time of the Fourth Liberty Loan, financial conditions were anything but satisfactory. Expressions of doubt as to the success of a new loan, echoes of dissatisfaction and discontent because government bonds were selling at a discount, pleas for price-maintenance measures, as well as criticisms of the actions of people who were disposing of their bonds, were heard on all sides. The Treasury and its henchmen responded with the familiar appeal to patriotism. In spite of the bold declaration of dependence upon patriotism, however, there is evidence of an almost feverish search for features which would either add to the attractiveness of the bonds, or improve their status in the market. Indeed, according to Senator Simmons, it was the purpose of the Treasury Department to use every promising means that might occur to it as likely to affect the value of the bonds and maintain them at something like their par value.[1] The difficulty lay in the fact that similar attempts had characterized each of the three previous loans with the result that the supply of effective features had been exhausted.

It is not surprising, therefore, to find a number of proposals which apparently came as the result of the more or less random thoughts on the part of officials who wanted to improve an undesirable situation but who experienced difficulty in finding the means of accomplishing the desired ends. As an example, we may cite the unsuccessful attempt to regulate transactions in Liberty Bonds. Even when looked at from our present vantage point it is difficult to discover any effective steps which could have been taken along this line.

The novel provision for contingent exemption, on the other hand, undoubtedly possessed some merit as an expediency measure for meeting the immediate needs of the hour.

[1] *Cong. Record*, vol. 56, p. 10435.

At the same time, the conditions which demanded that the advantages of exemption be shared with previously sold bonds were identical with those which gave rise to other measures. In each instance action was taken as a means of covering up the undesirable conditions which had followed in the wake of the administration's policy of placing bonds on a non-business basis. The fact that such conditions, with their resulting difficulties, had become increasingly important with every succeeding issue, furnishes the basis for a query as to how far matters would have continued had a prolonged war made additional issues necessary. Even as it was, the difficulties after less than one and one-half years of hostility had reached such staggering proportions as to make of the fourth loan an interesting subject for the application of financial strategy.

CHAPTER XII

The Victory (Fifth) Loan

PATRIOTISM AND THE RATE OF INTEREST

The cessation of fighting by no means ended the disbursements of funds. On the contrary, the floating debt, according to Secretary Glass, was increasing at the rate of $1,400,000,000 per month.[1] Recognition of the necessity of a fifth loan soon resulted in the request for an authorization to sell five billion dollars in securities, to allot an equivalent amount in the case of over-subscription, and to increase the amount of treasury certificates by two billion dollars.[2]

One of the most interesting phases of the discussion on the proposed loan had for its theme the question of the extent to which patriotism could be relied upon in floating the issue. Secretary Glass followed in the footsteps of his predecessor by appealing to the patriotism of the people. There was not, according to Administration leaders, a sufficient demand for bonds at a rational rate of interest to make it possible to place them solely on an investment basis.[3] It is probable, however, that these statements may be taken as a combination of an attempt to maintain the enthusiasm of

[1] *House Comm. on Ways and Means, Hearings on 5th Liberty Bond Bill*, 65th Cong., 3rd Sess., Feb. 13, 1919, p. 8.

[2] *Ibid.* Four and one-half billion dollars in notes were actually issued. Dept. Circular 138, *Treas. Report*, 1919, p. 241. An over-subscription of $749,908,300 was rejected. *Treas. Report*, 1919, p. 52.

[3] *House Comm. on Ways and Means, Hearings on H. R. 16136*, 65th Cong., 3rd Sess., Feb. 13, 1919, p. 29. *Cong. Record*, vol. 57, p. 4285, Mr. Mann; p. 4287, Mr. Treadway.

the public with a form of lip service to an established institution. As a matter of fact, comments made and steps taken, at least those appearing in connection with the task of securing the authorization from Congress, leave the impression that there was a general consensus of opinion that patriotism could no longer be depended upon to guarantee the reception of a post-war issue.[1]

Not a few statements referred to the inadequacy of the old interest rate,[2] while others included proposals for rates ranging from 4½% to whatever the bonds would bring on the market.[3] Evidence accordingly points to the conclusion that the condition of the market for government securities was causing no little worry. Prevalent belief apparently crystalized on the point that added inducements were required if the issue was to be a success.

OBSTACLES TO A REMUNERATIVE RATE OF INTEREST

That the Secretary of the Treasury concurred in this belief was evident from the fact that he was unwilling to resort to the unused portions of amounts of bonds authorized under previous acts.[4]

But if a proposed act had increased the rate of interest sufficiently to make it attractive to the public, it would certainly have been attacked, first, on the grounds that existing 3½'s would be converted into the higher rate bond, and thus increase the cost of the War,[5] and secondly, on the basis

[1] *H. R. House Comm. on Ways and Means, Hearings*, 65th Cong., 3rd Sess., Feb. 13, 1919, p. 20-1, Secretary Glass. *Cong. Record*, vol. 57, pp. 4720-1, Simmons; p. 4732, Smoot.

[2] *Cong. Record*, vol. 57, pp. 4728 and 4284, Longworth.

[3] *Ibid.*, p. 4718, Smith, p. 4728, Lodge.

[4] Glass, p. 8 of *Hearings* pointed out that over $5,000,000 remained authorized under existing acts. Kitchin, *Cong. Record*, vol. 57, p. 4267 quoted the same amount.

[5] *Cong. Record*, vol. 57, p. 4270, Kitchin.

that the higher rate discriminated against the holders of unconvertible former issues.[1]

The political dangers were especially important in view of the fact that Secretary McAdoo had virtually promised that 4½% would represent the maximum rate of the war. Mr. Kitchin went so far as to hint that this cry of discrimination would have been effective in forcing Congress to allow holders of all former issues to convert into the more attractive bonds.[2]

These possible objections were effectively stopped, however, by a method which was so simple that it amounted to little more than a substitution of words. The securities were termed "notes" instead of "bonds". The change was accordingly heralded by its sponsors as an effective means of avoiding the undesirable consequences of an increase in the rate of interest on bonds.[3]

SECURING DISCRETIONARY POWER

Aside from the belief that the plan of issuing notes would evade the danger of conversion and avoid a charge of discrimination, the change from bonds to notes had an even more subtle justification. Resort to notes would play an important part, according to certain speakers in the Senate,[4] in enabling the Secretary to secure freedom in the matter of fixing the interest rates, and other terms of the issue. Secretary McAdoo had previously waged and won a battle for the right to decide the terms on notes (certificates of indebtedness) at the time of issue, rather than at the date of authorization.

[1] *Cong. Record*, p. 4270.

[2] The extension of time in which unconverted 4's could be exchanged for 4½'s may be considered as a step in this direction. (*Infra*, p. 189.)

[3] *Cong. Record*, vol. 57, p. 4728, Lodge; p. 4732, Penrose; p. 4730, Smoot.

[4] *Cong. Record*, vol. 57, p. 4728, Lodge; and p. 4732, Senator Penrose.

It would accordingly be much easier to secure the desired discretion on notes where a precedent was already established than it would be to secure it on bonds where precedents and traditions of Congress would oppose delegating this power to the Secretary of the Treasury.

Just why the terms should be left to the discretion of the Secretary of the Treasury was made clear by Mr. Glass, who told [1] the Ways and Means Committee that it was impossible to decide upon the proper terms to be applied to these notes, since two months or more would elapse before they would be issued. The proposition was ably defended by Mr. Leffingwell before the same committee.[2]

POLITICAL REASONS FOR RUSHING THE MEASURE

The very fact that it was to be so long before the notes were to be issued might very properly have raised a question as to the propriety of rushing this important measure through Congress instead of carrying it over to an extra session, or even to the next regular session, and thereby bringing the date of authorization and the time of issue somewhat nearer together. To the student of politics, however, reason for the action is easily found. The Treasury, backed by a majority in both houses, could not afford to run the risk of having its plans upset by a changed and unfavorable membership. The safe way of avoiding such an unwelcome development was to do what Senator Penrose declared the administration was doing, namely, put the bill through at the point of a bayonet, and avoid an extra session.[3] Support

[1] *Hearings on Fifth Lib. Loan Bill*, 65th Cong., 3rd Sess., Feb. 13, 1919, p. 8.

[2] *House Comm. on Ways and Means, Hearings on H. R. 16136*, 65th Cong., 3rd Sess., Feb. 13, 1919, pp. 66-67.

[3] *Cong. Record*, vol. 57, p. 4732, Penrose.

from speakers in both houses assisted in overcoming objections to the plan.[1]

MEASURES HAVING TO DO WITH PRICE MAINTENANCE

By the time of the fifth loan the Treasury's responsibility in maintaining prices after sale had come to be the subject of frequent comment.

In connection with the Treasury's attempt to assume this responsibility several measures which had already done yeoman service were carried over and made to apply to the Victory Notes. In this class are to be included the practice of accepting bonds at par in payment of estate taxes, and the plan which we have labeled "Contingent Exemption". The latter arrangement, whereby holdings of former issues were made exempt provided the holder invested in the new issues, was again included to the extent of exempting an amount of old bonds equivalent to three times the amount of Victory Notes purchased. The total exempt was not to exceed $20,000, however.[2]

Still another plan looking toward price maintenance was included in the provision for purchasing an annual maximum of five per cent of this issue.[3]

An equally direct move along the line of bettering the status of outstanding securities came in the form of an extension of time in which to convert 4's into 4¼'s.[4]

[1] *Cong. Record*, vol. 57, pp. 4267. P. 4718, Kitchin; p. 4284, Mr. Longworth; p. 4286, Mr. Treadway; p. 4728, Senator Lodge; p. 4729, Senator Smoot and p. 4741, Senator LaFollette.

[2] *Treas. Report*, 1919, p. 244, *Act of Mar. 3, 1919*, 40 Stat. at Large, pt. i, p. 1309, sec. ii (b) p. 1310. Mr. Glass, *House Comm. on Ways and Means, Hearings on 5th Loan Bill*, Feb. 13, 1919, 65th Cong., 3rd Sess., p. 13.

[3] *Treas. Report*, 1919, p. 241.

[4] *Treas. Report*, 1919, p. 77. Act, sec. v, p. 1311.

MAKING THE NEW BONDS ATTRACTIVE

We have already mentioned the fact that the receivability feature, an arrangement for the repurchase of notes, and a form of contingent exemption, were pressed into service as means of stabilizing prices. While the measures arose out of an interest in price maintenance, their attachment to the securities was undoubtedly made as a result of the belief that their presence would exert a salutary, although indirect, influence upon the task of marketing the bonds. The administration was not content to depend upon these indirect means of making the notes attractive, however. In addition there were accordingly urged more direct and forceful steps, one of which even involved the plan of compelling the purchase of the securities. Fortunately, Secretary Glass refused to consider this extreme measure on the grounds that there had been considerable complaint in regard to coercion already employed.[1] Other means, he implied, should be devised.

The issuance of two types of securities, each of which was supposed to appeal to its own group of purchasers, represented an interesting and novel attempt to make the obligations attractive. Variations in both the interest rate and the degree of exemption served to differentiate the two types. One kind bore 3¾% interest and enjoyed full exemption, while the other variety bore interest at the rate of 4¾% and was only partially exempt.

Pertinent facts suggest that there were valid reasons for the step taken. In the first place, recently-made war fortunes supplied the basis for a belief that there would be a demand for exempt securities. In the second place, the size of the loan made it appear that the Treasury would be compelled to

[1] *House Comm. on Ways and Means*, Feb. 13, 1919, 65th Cong., 3rd Sess., pp. 23-4.

seek purchasers from among tax payers in the lower income brackets where exemption would have little effect. The plan as adopted supplied an inducement in the form of exemption in so far as the feature would be effective, and then supplied a high yield to attract those not reached by this inducement.

A new application of the principle of conversion grew directly from the fact that the issue was divided into two types. Each of these types was made convertible into the other. The provision is distinctive in that it guaranteed to a purchaser the maximum advantages to be had from the features of either of the two types. Since this loan was to be the last of the war period, and since the exempt and (practically) non-exempt securities each bore the highest rate yet affixed to a government obligation in its respective class, the provision for the interchange of the two varieties of securities undoubtedly represented the only effective means whereby the conversion feature could be impressed into service.

THE LOAN AS A WHOLE

With a market glutted with below-par government securities and with patriotism waning as the returning war flags passed by, it is not surprising that treasury officials were taking every possible step to make the new notes attractive. Their trouble was due in the main to the same factor that had given rise to a similar difficulty upon the occasion of the fourth issue. The most effective features had already become exhausted in the service of the earlier loans. Notwithstanding this fact, an ever resourceful department proceeded to revive the features, with the result that the fifth loan provided the setting and the stage upon which practically all of the actors in the drama of war finance came out for a final bow. For the first time since the first issue of war bonds, full exemption was introduced. Even conversion was given a part.

We might continue the figure of speech by pointing out that there were not a few examples of actors who played double roles. The receivability privilege, an arrangement for repurchasing the securities, and a form of contingent exemption rendered a service in connection with the task of marketing by their prospective contribution along the line of maintaining prices. Back of the curtain there occurred a clever and profitable shifting so that what had formerly been considered as bonds now appeared as notes.

As regards the results of the measures, we may say that the fifth, as well as the fourth issue, included some ingenious attempts to meet the rather unfortunate conditions which prevailed as a result of the previous actions and underlying policies of the Treasury Department. In other words, from the standpoint of expediency, the success of the attempts appear laudable; whereas from the point of view of a long-time financing policy, the very fact that the steps were necessary affords condemning evidence of the failure of the program at certain strategic points.

CHAPTER XIII

Significant Post-War Developments

Our discussions of World War financing have thus far had to do with policies pertaining largely to the attempt to sell government bonds at attractive prices and only incidentally with the endeavor to maintain the prices of bonds in the market. In the post-war period this aspect of financing received so much attention that the present chapter will be devoted largely to this subject.

MAINTAINING THE PRICE OF BONDS

The attempts to maintain market prices were justified on various occasions on the ground that people who subscribed for bonds were entitled to some consideration, and that this consideration should express itself in the form of measures to prevent prices from dropping below par. While this superficial reason no doubt sounded plausible enough to those who heard it advanced in public statements and addresses, a more deep-seated cause for action on the part of the Treasury frequently came to the surface when it was admitted that the government responded to the demand of bond holders in order to maintain a market for issues which the government was periodically placing on the market.

The entire situation was faced rather frankly in the statement of the Secretary to the Committee on Ways and Means [1] on March 27, 1918. By this time two issues had already been thrown on the market and the back-wash from the tide

[1] Quoted and commented upon, *Treas. Report*, 1920, p. 110.

of patriotic buying was already making itself felt to such an extent that the Secretary was convinced "that the United States . . . must prepare itself to support the market for its bonds." The policy which the Secretary defended consisted of a plan whereby the government was simply to buy enough bonds in the market to maintain prices at or near par. In the words of the Secretary, "It only means that we should have to sell a few more bonds and then buy them back . . .," a plan which he declared "will be much cheaper for the government than to increase the rate of interest; at least we ought to try it." [1]

The policy advocated on this occasion was put into concrete form by the insertion of a purchase provision in the third loan act, by the adoption of a sinking fund arrangement in connection with the fifth loan, and by the establishment of the War Finance Corporation. We shall next turn to a consideration of developments in connection with each of these provisions.

THE WAR FINANCE CORPORATION AND PRICE MAINTENANCE

At this time we are interested in the War Finance Corporation in its capacity as an agency for maintaining prices of government securities. Administration leaders left little doubt that the desire to influence market prices constituted one of the most important reasons for establishing the Corporation.[2]

Most of the provisions in the Act can be interpreted in terms of a contemplated effect upon the market for government securities. The power to carry on market operations [3] was of course the most direct provision for action to main-

[1] Quoted and commented upon, *Treas. Report*, 1920, p. 110.

[2] *Senate Comm. on Finance, Hearings on S. 3714*, especially pp. 29 and 30; *Cong. Record*, vol. 56, pt. iv, pp. 3610 and 3629.

[3] *Act of April 5, 1918*, 40 Stat. at Large, pt. i, p. 506.

tain satisfactory prices. As a result of this provision any part, or all, of the available resources of this gigantic organization, with power to marshal four billion dollars of capital, could at the request of the Secretary be used for buying back bonds which had failed to find a permanent resting place among investors.

The authorizing act also provided that surplus earnings not required for operation of the corporation were to be accumulated in a reserve fund to be invested in bonds, notes, or certificates of indebtedness of the United States.[1] Even the plan for assisting banks to hold Liberty Bonds may be looked upon as an arrangement of value in maintaining market prices.

In evaluating the activities of the War Finance Corporation, in this connection, we should not lose sight of the fact that the war period during which it was in operation was too short to give us a fair idea of its possibilities had the war continued.

THE 5% PURCHASE PROVISION

The Third Liberty Loan gave the Secretary of the Treasury authority to purchase bonds from time to time until one year after the war. Second Liberties and First Converted were to be bought on the market at an average cost not to exceed par plus interest. Purchases could be made up to 5% annually of the par amount of bonds of such series originally issued. This measure[2] was a most direct recognition of the Government's responsibility to accomplish what Mr. Kitchin had described as the policy of supporting the market for its bonds.[3]

In its simplest operation, the bond purchase fund would

[1] *Act, op. cit.*, sec. 15, p. 510.

[2] *Act of April 4, 1918*, 40 Stat. at Large, pt. i, p. 502, ch. 44, sec. 6 (amended sec. 15) at p. 505.

[3] *Cong. Record*, vol. 56, pt. v, p. 4316.

work as follows: bonds would be issued and subscribed and then some of them would be thrown back on the market. The government would undertake to buy these bonds. Since obligations so purchased would force the Treasury to put out more securities on the occasion of the next issue, the step would be the same as if the bonds were reissued. It will be seen, therefore, that the bond purchase fund was not really a plan for reducing the public debt, but merely an arrangement for taking existing bonds off the market and thereby bolstering up prices. Secretary Houston admitted this purpose on April 10, 1920, when he declared that activities of the bond purchase fund had been made "for the sole purpose of stabilizing the market". A subsequent statement [1] refers to one of the undesirable consequences of such action. "It (the Treasury) has been obliged to borrow at higher rates of interest the money to make the purchases which have been forced on it for the protection of the holders of Liberty Bonds and of the Government's credit." [2] The purchase of $1,746,944,468.11 of securities made on behalf of the fund prior to the suspension of activities on June 30, 1920,[3] may accordingly be considered as having been made solely for the purpose of maintaining the prices on government securities.

After buying on behalf of the bond purchase act was resumed on June 7,[4] 1921, however, purchases were apparently made for other reasons. During the fiscal year ending June 30, 1922, approximately two billion dollars in Victory 4¾'s and 3¾'s were bought in connection with the

[1] *Treas. Report*, 1920, p. 118.

[2] *Ibid.*

[3] *House Doc. 137*, Dec. 5, 1921. Activities were discontinued April 18, 1920 with the exception of bonds taken over from the War Finance Corporation. (*Treas. Report*, 1920, p. 109.)

[4] *House Doc. 137*.

Treasury refunding operations.[1] In these operations the Treasury resorted to the authorization accorded it in the bond purchase provision solely as a means of facilitating its refunding operations and not in accordance with the original aims of the measures. For our purposes, therefore, we need not consider these operations which took place just previous to the provision's expiration on July 2, 1922. Even after eliminating these purchases, however, the activities were by no means insignificant. In its legitimate operations on behalf of market stabilization, the bond purchase fund removed from the market an amount almost equivalent to the first Liberty Loan. The costs of making these purchases should include the difficulties which were experienced in again forcing on the market these bonds, under a new name as it were, but basically under conditions which made the operation one of reissue. During the war and immediately thereafter these "costs" were apparently accepted as being incidental to the operation of the financial machinery, and as means of attaining success for the program as a whole. Later, the attitude of the Treasury Department underwent such a change that, with the exception of the purchases to which we have already referred as being a part of the refunding program, no use was made of the authority to purchase.

The unwillingness on the part of Secretaries Glass and Houston to resort to the authority to purchase evidently grew in the first instance out of an appreciation of the nature of the arrangement. Mr. Houston, for example, referred to the fact that purchases had to be financed by the issue of additional certificates of indebtedness, thus decreasing the funded debt at the expense of the floating debt. Furthermore, circumstances and conditions were different from those of the war period. Waning patriotism and declining prosperity were everywhere resulting in large quantities of

[1] *House Doc. 477*, Dec. 4, 1922.

bonds being thrown on the market at low prices. With some fifteen billion dollars of securities quoted in the 80's, purchases on the part of the Treasury Department would be futile. Still another explanation might perhaps suggest itself to one who attempts to read between the lines. Every indication points to the fact that Secretary Houston desired to leave behind the various methods which had been employed for the purpose of pegging the market for Liberty Bonds. His justification for bond purchases comes not from his own mouth but rather from the pen of a predecessor in office. Appeals that something should be done to give relief [1] to present bond holders were answered by reference to what had already been done and by tactful and thoughtful discussions as to why the proposed measures would be either impractical or ineffective.[2] In the meantime he was setting in motion the machinery of a sinking fund for the permanent retirement of the debt. These activities were carried on in the name of the 2½% sinking fund.

THE 2½% SINKING FUND

The sinking fund under discussion was radically different from the measure which we have been considering in that it was designed as a means of retiring the debt and not primarily for the purpose of affecting the prices of securities. Incorporated as it was in the last war loan [3] this permanent sinking fund marks the turning point in war finance. Previous to this change, every measure was apparently viewed in the light of its possible effects upon subsequent additions to the public debt. With the voting of a specific annual appropriation for debt retirement, Congress definitely began the reduction of the war debt. Nevertheless the arrangement

[1] *Treas. Report*, 1920, p. 110.

[2] *Treas. Report*, 1920, pp. 110, 131.

[3] *Act of Mar. 3, 1919*, 40 Stat. at Large, pt. i, sec. 6 at p. 1311.

doubtless exerted a salutary influence upon the price of government securities.[1]

PURCHASES FROM THE PROCEEDS OF THE FRANCHISE TAX OF THE RESERVE BANKS AND FROM THE REPAYMENT OF FOREIGN LOANS

The sinking fund discussed above made definite provision for annual appropriations to be used in buying government bonds. The two provisions now under consideration appropriated the income from two special sources for a similar purpose.[2] The amounts retired from the franchise tax of the Federal Reserve Banks from 1918 to 1922 totalled $125,114,184.[3]

[1] The activities of the Cumulative Sinking Fund may be tabulated as follows:

Fiscal Year	*Available Appropriation*	*Expenditures*	*Par Amount Retired*
1921	256,230,010.66	254,844,576.50	261,250,250
1922	273,131,331.73	274,481,902.16	275,896,000
1923	284,121,375.46	284,149,754.16	284,018,800
1924	294,920,338.23	294,927,019.57	295,987,350
1925	306,666,755.83	306,666,736.01	306,308,400
1926	321,184,553.71	321,184,468.20	317,091,750
Totals	1,736,254,365.62	1,736,254,456.60	1,640,552,550

Quotations are from *House Doc. 99*, Dec. 6, 1923; *Doc. 469*, Dec 3, 1924; *Doc. 110*, Dec. 8, 1925; *Doc. 556*, Dec. 6, 1926.

[2] *Act of Dec. 23, 1913*, 38 Stat. at Large 251, ch. 6 (Federal Reserve Act) provided in sec. 7 (p. 258) for use of franchise tax in this way. After reciting that earnings above certain dividend claims, etc. be paid to U. S. as a franchise tax, sec. 7 went on as follows: "The net earnings derived by the U. S. from Federal Reserve banks shall, in the discretion of the Secretary, be used to supplement the gold reserve held against outstanding U. S. notes, or shall be applied to the reduction of the outstanding bonded indebtedness of the U. S. under regulations to be prescribed by the Secretary of the Treasury."

[3] *Treas. Report*, 1922, p. 46.

The Liberty bond acts [1] authorized any repayments of the principal of loans to foreign governments to be applied to the redemption or purchase of any bonds issued under the authority of such acts. Prior to 1925, this arrangement was responsible for aggregate purchases of almost three hundred million dollars.[2] These activities are similar to those of the sinking fund in that they belong more properly under the heading of debt retirement. Since the resulting purchases undoubtedly affected bond prices, however, they accordingly deserve consideration in this section.

ACCEPTANCE OF LIBERTY BONDS IN PAYMENT OF ESTATE TAXES, AND FROM FOREIGN GOVERNMENTS

Since the acceptance of Liberty bonds at par in payment of estate taxes constitutes one of the most clear-cut examples of a measure which was designed to fulfill the double duty of facilitating financing and of influencing the status of the bonds subsequent to sale, it may well be singled out for special study.[3]

In the first place, we should call attention to the fact that the provision in question and the one concerned with the acceptance of bonds from foreign debtors, constitutes the only

[1] *Act of April 24, 1917*, 40 Stat. at Large, ch. 4, pt. i, p. 35, sec. 3, and *Act of Sept. 24, 1917*, 40 Stat. at Large, pt. i, ch. 56, sec. 3, p. 284 as amended.

[2] Purchases by years were as follows:

Fiscal year, 1919	$7,921,700
Fiscal year, 1920	72,669,900
Fiscal year, 1921	73,939,300
Fiscal year, 1922	64,837,900
Fiscal year, 1923	32,140,000
Fiscal year, 1924	38,509,150

(*Treas. Report*, 1922, pp. 46-47; 1923, p. 49; 1924, p. 200.)

[3] The results of the writer's study of this subject first appeared in an article on "The Use of Liberty Bonds in Payment of Estate Taxes", *American Economic Review*, vol. xv, no. 2, June, 1925, pp. 275-283.

arrangement whereby the government was forced to pay par for redeemed bonds. It is for this reason that these two measures deserve special attention as instruments of price maintenance. Such an arrangement by its very nature works automatically up to the limits set by the total amount of payments to be made. Other minor requirements, such as the provision that the bonds must have been held for six months, prevented the greatest use of the feature during the time of its maximum value; but these requirements would cease to interfere, if conditions were such as to make it worth while to use the bonds for the purpose in question for a long period. Utilization of the privilege is, of course, expected to occur when it is advantageous to the holder, which means that the Government stands to lose.

It is because of the peculiar nature of the operations of the measure that we look to the post-war period in the effort to discover how the arrangement worked out. Our search is rewarded by a rather interesting account of developments. Narrowing attention down to the one feature of receivability for estate taxes, we find that in two years alone (1921 and 1922) over 47 millions of dollars in estate taxes were paid in Liberty bonds. By figuring the value of the bonds (at market prices) we learn that the value of the government's receipts was diminished by more than four million dollars as a result of its promise to accept bonds at par.[1]

This undesirable consequence may be charged against the arrangement as one of the " costs " of its operation.

The widespread use of the privilege is attested to by another aspect of the study:

An examination of appraisals of seventy-two large estates which were filed for tax purposes during the post-war years discloses that fifty-four owned Liberty bonds and that fifty of these were in a position to profit from the privilege in

[1] *American Economic Review, op. cit.*, p. 476.

question.[1] One estate alone was in a position to profit to the extent of an amount well over one hundred thousand dollars.

The events of the period are peculiarly significant not so much because they demonstrate evil effects actually experienced, but rather because they declare possibilities which would have developed had subsequent affairs (particularly, the trend of interest) been so as to aggravate rather than remedy the situation. The possibilities of undesirable consequences may be described briefly as follows:

First, the "costs," as previously described, could easily have reached undesirable proportions. This possibility appears especially significant in view of the doubtful nature of the contribution made by the feature either in floating the original issues to which the privilege was attached or in strengthening the bonds in the market.

Aside from the inadequacy of the measure to contribute materially to the attractiveness of the original issue and its inability to keep government bonds at par (its ostensible objective, there is to be leveled at the measure another criticism. Instead of setting up a flexible program which would admit purchases at prices at or even barely above market levels, the government had to give certain individuals more than would be necessary to induce them to turn over their bonds. Since the chance of the resulting discrimination increases with the length of the life of the securities receivable, bonds appear more objectionable than do receivable treasury notes.

[1] Receivable bonds included:

First Converted 4¼'s 1932-47 dated May 9, 1918.
First Converted 4¼'s 1932-47 dated Oct. 24, 1918.
Second Converted 4¼'s 1927-49 dated May 9, 1918.
Third Converted 4¼'s 1928- dated May 9, 1918.
Fourth Converted 4¼'s 1933-38 dated Oct. 24, 1917.
Victory Converted 4¾'s 1922-23.

Since the use of notes was of negligible importance they were not listed.

While the objections to the manner in which receivability operates apply to the arrangement with foreign governments as well as to that with tax payers, the question of inadequacy hardly applies. On the contrary there existed the possibility of such wide use of below-par bonds in making payments that the United States was in a position to suffer a great diminution in the value of its revenue.[1]

Again, as in the case of the use of bonds for the payment of estate taxes, we may thank the course of interest rates and bond prices, together with the added fact of a late start, that the privilege was scarcely utilized by the foreign governments. Again, we may suggest, however, that the more or less narrow escapes from undesirable consequences should serve as a lesson to future financiers.

The existence of these several plans for the purpose of bettering the market condition in respect to Liberty bonds by no means satisfied the public. On the contrary, the post-war sentiment in favor of price maintenance was responsible for innumerable proposals for bolstering up the prices of government securities. These proposals may be separated into a number of different groups, each of which we shall now describe.

OTHER PROPOSALS

In May, 1919, Senator LaFollette presented a resolution from the Wisconsin Legislature memorializing Congress to prohibit the purchase of Liberty bonds by scalpers and providing a penalty therefor.[2] A more comprehensive plan,

[1] The whole subject is closely connected with the question of the nature of the original arrangement and the purpose of later agreements. The consensus of opinion seems to be that originally the intention was to consider the debt as a bona-fide obligation (*cf.* R. M. Haig, *The Public Finances of Post-War France* (New York, 1929), pp. 114-115, and Noyes, *War Period in American Finance*, *op. cit.*, p. 176). Any undesirable consequences of the provision in question must accordingly be charged to price maintenance.

[2] 66th Cong., 1st Sess., vol. 58, p. 52.

worked out with the same end in view, was later advocated in conjunction with a proposal to create an antidepreciation fund which was to be used in buying below-par bonds. Brokers were to be prevented from selling or buying at less than par.[1]

As we have already intimated, the central aim of the last mentioned bills consisted of furnishing a market for government bonds by having the Treasury purchase below-par bonds. The same idea was responsible for the proposal of a large number of measures which differed somewhat in the technique of operation but which were invariably designed with the hope that they would exert a favorable influence upon the market by increasing its scope. In other words, their aim was "to furnish a market for government bonds".[2]

One manifestation of the attempt to improve the market for bonds is to be found in the proposals for accepting the bonds for payments to the government. One bill[3] for example would have authorized the use of bonds in making payments for war materials and other property which had been bought from the government. Another of even more significance proposed to accept Liberty bonds in payment of income and excess profit taxes. This proposal was rejected by the Secretary.[4]

1 *H. R., 8540*, Aug. 19, 1919, 66th Cong., 1st Sess., vol. 58, pt. iv, p. 4006; also *H. R. 2419*, April 11, 1921, 67th Cong., 1st (Special) Sess., vol. 61, pt. i, p. 99.

2 *H. R. 6371*, 66th Cong., 1st Sess., vol. 58, pt. ii, June 20, 1920, p. 1542, "to authorize the Secretary of the Treasury to use at his discretion surplus moneys in the Treasury in the purchase or redemption of the outstanding interest bearing obligations of the U. S." *H. R. 8262*, 67th Cong., 1st Sess., vol. 61, pt. v, p. 5901, Aug. 16, 1921.

3 *H. R. 8780*, Aug. 26, 1919, 66th Cong., 1st Sess., vol. 58, pt. v, p. 4400.

4 *H. R. 13869*, 66th Cong., 2nd Sess., vol. 59, pt. vi, April 30, 1920, p. 6386. The Secretary's communication contained an interesting distinction be-

As might have been expected, the exemption feature was proposed as a means of improving the status of the Liberty bonds. The attempt to press the feature into service appeared in a number of forms. First of all, we might mention the endeavor to apply exemptions directly to outstanding Liberty bonds and Victory notes.[1] Later there was revived the move "to exempt from taxation Liberty Bonds now taxed in the guise of capital stock".[2]

Action looking toward the consolidation of the Liberty Loans into one exempt issue and moves to refund by issuing bonds with more attractive exemption features were apparently even more prevalent.[3] Requests for increases in the interest rate likewise characterized the proposals for refunding.[4] To the overtures along this line the Treasury turned a deaf ear. A higher rate of interest, it was claimed, would represent an unnecessary bonus to holders of government bonds. Furthermore, the step would not only prove inef-

tween accepting bonds in payment of income taxes and the practice of receiving them in payment of estate taxes. Bonds should not be accepted in payment of current taxes, he thought, because such action would be a step toward further undoing the work of the Liberty Loan organization in seeking out funds for permanent investment from savings. This objection, in his opinion, did not hold against the acceptance of Liberty Bonds in the payment of income taxes because of the possible effect of the action upon the government's finances. It may be pointed out that if he had carried this argument a step further, it would also have resulted in a condemnation of the acceptance of bonds in payment of estate taxes.

Treas. Report, 1920, p. 125. See *Act of Nov. 23, 1921*, ch. 136, 42 Stat. at Large 227, p. 316, sec. 1325. Acceptance of notes and certificates of indebtedness in payment of internal revenue other than stamp taxes.

[1] *H. R. 14468*, 66th Cong., 3rd Sess., vol. 60, pt. i, Dec. 6, 1920, p. 10.

[2] *H. R. 10875*, 67th Cong., 2nd Sess., vol. 62, pt. iv, Mar. 13, 1922, p. 3835. Note: This was to amend No. 1000 of Title K of Public Act No. 98, approved Nov. 23, 1921.

[3] *H. R. 13355*, 66th Cong., 2nd Sess., vol. 59, pt. v, Mar. 30, 1920, p. 5029.

[4] See also *S. 741*, 67th Cong., 1st Sess., vol. 61, pt. i, April 13, 1921, p. 188; *H. R. 5574*, *ibid.*, pt. i, April 30, 1921, p. 894.

fective in increasing the attractiveness of such a vast quantity of bonds,[1] but would also exert an undesirable influence upon the value of existing exempt securities.

In the minds of one group of individuals, the remedy for the situation was to be found in further action toward altering banking practices. The alteration which was most strongly advanced involved a decrease in the rediscount rate on paper collateraled by Liberty bonds.[2]

At least one proposal involved the direct use of Liberty bonds and Victory notes as the base for Federal Reserve notes,[3] while still another advocated that all Liberty bonds be made eligible for use as security for bank notes.[4]

The plans already described, as well as others involving the drawing of Liberty bonds by lot, direct loans from the government to holders, and the conversion of bonds into interest-bearing currency failed to receive a sympathetic reception.[5]

In addition to whatever benefit would have accrued to the Liberty bonds had any or all of these proposals materialized, the securities were also in line to receive incidental benefit as a result of their part in a number of plans which were primarily concerned with other questions. Three more or less distinct plans for improving agriculture and three for bettering the livestock industry, as well as others having to do with

[1] *Treas. Report*, 1920, pp. 115, 116 and 117.

[2] *Cong. Record*, 66th Cong., 2nd Sess., vol. 61, pt. vi, p. 5966. Letter of Gov. Harding to Senator Sheppard, dated Aug. 26, 1921; *Cong. Record*, 67th Cong., 1st Sess., vol. 61, pt. v, p. 4980, Concurrent Res. 27, of Aug. 13, 1921; *ibid.*, p. 5040, S. J. Res. 101, of Aug. 16, 1921.

[3] *H. R. 6503*, 67th Cong., 1st Sess., vol. 61, pt. ii, p. 1660.

[4] "Plan submitted by Pennsylvania Banker," appearing in the *Philadelphia Public Ledger*, and submitted by Representative Focht of Pennsylvania. 66th Cong., 2nd Sess., vol. 59, p. 9046, May 7, 1920.

[5] *Treas. Report*, 1920, pp. 115-117 and pp. 126-132.

the problems of home buying, had a secondary or incidental purpose relating to the prices of Liberty Bonds.[1]

We find numerous post-war plans for minimizing the bad effects of a financing policy which had not been organized with due regard for its results. In the main, the proposed plans themselves involved the use of undesirable expedients. All in all, the period studied as an aftermath of the financing policies of the war, presents an interesting spectacle of a country paying for the service of its war-time financing devices, even as it repays the loans themselves. Since the story itself is beyond the scope of this study, we have confined ourselves to a mere reference to some of those more important developments which were at the same time closely associated with topics already treated.[2]

[1] For examples. *S. 3563*, May 6, 1922, 67th Cong., 2nd Sess., vol. 62, pt. vi, p. 6437; *S. 3639*, May 23, 1922, *ibid.*, pt. vii, p. 7435; *H. R. 6371*, June 20, 1920, 66th Cong., 1st Sess., vol. 53, p. 1489.

[2] Post-War developments in respect to tax exemption have been avoided entirely. This topic received the writer's attention in an unpublished manuscript (*Tax Exempt Bonds*, 1925, on file in the Columbia University Library) and has been the subject of numerous articles and several books. See references in the concluding chapter.

CHAPTER XIV

SUMMARY AND CONCLUSION

HAVING completed an analysis of federal financing by periods we shall now proceed to summarize our findings by presenting a topical treatment of the principal financing devices. In approaching this task, we find it possible to classify the various measures under the following heads which in reality represent six major steps or stages in the placing of government securities:

I. Problems of Policy and Theory.
II. Preparation of the Field.
III. Arrangement for Selling.
IV. Specific Features Attached to the Securities.
V. Assuring Solvency of the Loan.
VI. Price Maintenance.

These points are discussed in order below.[1]

I. POLICY AND THEORY

A consideration of two topics will illustrate the manner in which certain set policies and theories have influenced the Treasury's choice of financing methods or have conditioned its action in other respects.

Rate of Interest

The limitation upon the rate of interest has apparently arisen in the main out of political pressure (or the fear of it)

[1] Since a full treatment of any topic referred to in this chapter is readily found in the text, we shall refrain from giving specific references except where new material is introduced.

aimed toward keeping the rate down to a level which would appeal to the populace as reasonable and economical. In connection with this aim practically every authorizing act has limited the rate which the Treasury could pay. Freedom from such restrictions is indeed to be found, as for example in 1813 when the usual limitation was omitted, and during the World War when Mr. McAdoo induced Congress to leave the rate of interest to his discretion. By and large, however, we may consider that Congress has ever considered it a duty either to specify the rate of interest or to limit the maximum to be paid.

A factor which has been far more effective than this legal restriction, however, is to be found in the bias which political pressure has instilled into Treasury Officials, which succeeded in restraining them from adopting a nominal rate high enough to encourage the purchase of bonds. Illustrations of such an influence appear repeatedly throughout our history. During the period following the Revolutionary War, objection to high rates led to interesting compensations in the form of premiums, commissions, and discounts in order to keep the nominal rate of interest down. This procedure was repeated in 1812, when such sentiment was also partially responsible for resort to Treasury notes as a means of securing funds at low rates. During the Civil War, the desire to secure loans at low cost was a predominant reason for the legal tenders and the resulting financial chaos. In the modern period, the same reason again accounted for a series of features and for organized efforts to revise the entire financial and monetary structure to contribute to the purpose at hand.

Significance of Sale at Par

The common attempts to prevent sales of securities at prices below par, like efforts to control the rate of interest, ordinarily find their origin in political pressure. Our survey of American financial history has disclosed that two reasons may in turn be found for such pressure.

In the first place, anyone who aspires to measure the success of a financing program is justified in attaching importance to sale at " par " provided he also introduces the subject of the rate of interest borne by the securities.

Looking at the reverse of this proposition we can see that a knowledge of the rate of interest is of no use unless one also knows the price at which a security is to be quoted. In other words, the price is readily and easily recognized as one of three factors (the other two being the nominal rate of interest and the length of time before maturity, respectively) used in calculating net yield—that ultimate criterion of the value of all investments. We are accordingly justified in thinking that the ever-present restriction against sale below par is in reality a logical team-mate of the restriction on the nominal rate of interest, and that it was only by combining the two that the public's wishes in respect to limiting the net yield on securities were carried out. However, entirely too much importance has been attached to " par " for us to agree that legislators and the public were directing their attention to this point in a bond price merely as a convenient figure to use in wording laws in which price specifications were needed. What our financial history suggests on the other hand is that to legislators and to the public the significance of " par " was all out of proportion to its actual importance as a selling figure which could in turn be used in calculating the net yield of the bond. Instead of being considered merely one of any number of prices which are in turn significant only as related to the rate of interest and the term of the bond, " par " was held up as a standard of value and, in and of itself, was looked upon as an independent objective. This situation has been found to have more than a passing interest. With their own more or less fixed ideas as to the proper rate of interest for government loans, and with a misconception of the true significance of par as a mathematical factor in arriving at net yields, legislators have as a rule been handicapped from the start in devising a sound financial policy. Furthermore, their justifications to the masses were received in the main by people whose ideas on finances were even more crude than were those of the legislators. Moreover, Treasury officials themselves may be charged with having ordinarily displayed on this subject either a deplorable lack of financial wisdom, or a political insight which is beyond the comprehension of an ordinary layman. Whether we look to the public as the source of the political pressure or consider that the politically-minded legislator was responsible for his opportunity to acclaim himself a defender of "time-honored principles" (of sales at par and at low interest), or whether, indeed, we place the blame at the foot of Treasury officials, the results are the same. Popular ideas regarding the rate of interest and the sale at par have persisted in exerting an influence upon the financing tactics employed.

Thus, the ideas to which we have referred in a sense furnish the cornerstone for our discussions of special features, many of which followed directly as a result of the ideas.

II. PREPARATION OF THE FIELD

Appeal to Patriotism

Not a little of the work of the government has had to do with an attempt to prepare the market for forthcoming issues. One very important effort along this line may be subsumed under the heading of appeal to patriotism. Not until the Civil War, when the government cooperated with Jay Cooke in the popular loans, did this aspect of finance receive important consideration, largely because previous to this time loans had been placed through banking institutions, and these were in turn left in the main to their own resources.

During the Civil War, however, the financiers supplemented the endeavors of their agents with direct appeals to the public, while during the World War this procedure was utilized as the very cornerstone of the entire sales structure. Paid advertisements constituted only a meagre proportion of the mass of literature and the volume of statements which contributed to the development of public opinion in favor of bond purchase. This public opinion in turn amounted to virtual coercion or compulsion to such an extent that few individuals with funds at their disposal could long resist the pressure to buy bonds.

It is against the resulting back-ground of patriotic endeavor that the financial operations of the Treasury must be projected.

Manipulating the Currency—Inflation

The subject of inflation has received so much attention that it is necessary for us to do little more than refer to the extent of its use and to the manner in which it is connected with financing.

War-time activities invariably act as a spur to business activity and furnish the basis of credit extension. The resulting situation is itself a form of inflation which has conditioned the financing operations of every war period in our history. Aside from these inevitable by-products of war-time activities, however, price levels have not infrequently been altered as a result of more or less deliberate attempts to facilitate the Treasury's operations. In both the 1812 and the 1837 periods, tampering with the currency resulted from the attempt to facilitate the sale of treasury notes by giving them the qualities of money.

During the Civil War direct issues of paper money precipitated an era of inflation.

As a result of the "circulation privilege" financiers of the Spanish American War, entirely without their asking, reaped the benefit of former actions connecting money and government financing.

In World-War financing we find what appears to be the maximum use of inflation as a means of disposing of securities of a supposed investment value. An indirect issue of currency and the maintenance of an artificially low rate of interest, with their effects on the price structure, were apparently depended on to keep the field prepared for bond issues.

Considering the way manipulations of the currency have been utilized, therefore, we do not hesitate to describe this set of actions as one of the most important means of insuring a reception for government securities.

Banking Changes

Especially in modern times inflation has been effected through the banking system. The outstanding example is of course the World War experience.

The fact that the Federal Reserve System was already in existence undoubtedly served to increase its usefulness; on the other hand its youth and the consequent absence of traditions meant that it was sufficiently plastic to permit alterations which would greatly facilitate the task of financing the war. An enumeration of certain measures pertaining to banks will call to mind the nature of the contribution made by these institutions during the World War.

Proceeds of bond sales were deposited in banks and withdrawals were then made in such a manner as practically to eliminate the use of cash in the government's transactions.

Removal of the limitation on loans to one person, adjustment as to the issuing of Federal Reserve Notes, granting preferential rates on notes collateraled by government securities, and other changes in banking practice, invited bankers to throw the entire weight of government financing back on the Federal Reserve System. The War Finance Corporation was designed to perform a similar task in respect to corporate financing.

The developments of former periods appear insignificant when compared with this elaborate use of an extensive banking system as a servant to the Treasury. True, Hamilton's ambitious plan for a bank had materialized to the extent that the First Bank contributed to subsequent financing; but the contribution was distinctly limited to the bank's meagre assets.

The assistance of the bank in the 1812 period was of somewhat more doubtful value, while that of the banks in the 1837 period is hardly worth mentioning. Chase's early attitude toward coin payments precluded the use of private banks, and the elaborate plans for the National Banking System failed to materialize in time for the new system to make itself felt at a crucial point. As a result, Civil War financiers actually suffered from a lack of even the common accomodations of banks. It appears, therefore, that Mr. McAdoo's manipulation of the banking system in preparing the field for government financing must, in view of the extent of the utilization, be considered unique in our financial history.

III. ARRANGEMENTS FOR DISPOSING OF SECURITIES

Use of Banks

Banks were first directly used under a plan in which they subscribed all of a given loan and later they were used to act merely as agents for the government. One or the other of these methods was employed in floating all the loans previous to the War of 1812, with the exception of the 8% loans of 1798 and 1890.

Even the first war loan of the 1812 period was bought directly by the banks. On short-time loans subsequent use of the banks was made possible by the authorizations which substituted borrowing on the treasury notes for outright sale. The long-time loans were ostensibly open for public subscription and were actually subscribed by individuals. Since the bulk of such subscriptions were for the account of banks, however, banks were nevertheless making their contributions to government financing.

Only the unwillingness of Chase to give up the sub-treasury system and the plan of maintaining payments in coin accounts for the failure to utilize the banks during the early part of the Civil War.

Although, as may be seen, the banks during these periods contributed in a great measure to the sale of government securities, it was not until the World War that the fullest use was made of the banking facilities.

Agents versus Direct Sales

Determining whether securities will be sold directly in a popular loan, or through agents, is an important aspect of the subject of bond selling. During our early history the use of agents was very common. Following the Revolutionary War, the arrangement gave an opportunity for the payment of high commissions amounting virtually to discounts on bonds sold.

During the 1812 period, agents were commonly designated and allowed a commission. The lowering of minimum bids from $100,000 to $25,000 supplies some evidence of an attempt to place the loans on a more popular basis.

The use of agents was discontinued entirely in 1843 and in its place was substituted an arrangement for direct sale and for advertising the loan. The difficulty of securing funds during the Civil War, however, brought about a revival of the practice of utilizing intermediaries. Jay Cooke, with a host of assistants, achieved a phenomenal success. During the period following the Civil War, the policy was not consistent. Subscription loans were replaced by arrangements involving contracts with bond houses, modified later to insure the offering of the bonds to the public by the contractors. In 1894 an effort was made to obtain funds by resorting to loans, as in 1879. The Treasury was finally compelled to resort to banks, however, and not until 1896 did the government return to the policy which it later pursued during the World War. This policy involved direct sales, or popular loans, and in a sense represened the evolution of measures of former periods.

With the adoption of direct sales, the use of agents and the provision for their commissions disappeared, to be replaced by advertising and appropriations for selling expenses.

Compulsory Loans

Although not described as such in public statements, a number of actions on the part of the government may, with fair accuracy, be described as forced loans. These have taken a number of forms. First, we may refer to the practice of paying creditors with treasury obligations. This custom had an early antecedent in the bills of credit of the Revolutionary period. Each period prior to the Civil War witnessed the practice of using treasury notes in paying creditors who were willing to receive them. In times of stress when no other means were available, this procedure itself virtually amounted to a forced loan. During the Civil War, the principle involved took a number of interesting forms. First came the practice of issuing, for the purpose of paying creditors, securities which were less attractive than others simultaneously issued. The second variation came as a result of the practice of issuing new obligations designed solely to settle government debts. Finally came the provision for legal tenders, a step which gave rise to a forced loan in the strict sense of the word. Even the modern period was not entirely free from such practices. The manner in which Liberty Bonds were disposed of to soldiers whose pay was docked for the amount of the installments, falls little short of the older practices in which obligations were used to pay government creditors. The resemblance becomes more striking when one recalls that the individual could scarcely be said to have been free to exercise his own choice in the matter.

Even loans from private citizens can not be considered entirely free from the element of compulsion, if one chooses thus to describe the pressure of public opinion and the fear of social ostracism. Although a distinction can be made between this type of compulsion and the kind originating in official or legal sources, it may possibly be agreed that the difference is merely one of degree and not of kind, and that in their effect the two are very similar.

Still another example of the use of compulsion in obtaining loans is to be found in the relations between the Treasury and the banks. It will be recalled that the First Bank was forced by law to lend certain amounts to the government and that after the formation of the bank frequent acts authorized loans which, for all practical purposes, may be considered forced loans. Although the compulsion appearing in the first loans of the Civil War was without legal sanction, it is generally understood that the banks were practically forced to take the loans. Later the provision that National Banks should buy government bonds amounting to one-third of their capital ultimately resulted in furnishing a market for securities to a value of three-fourths of a billion dollars. Even this assistance from the banks did not cause the government to hesitate to use these institutions again when it failed to find other sources to supply its urgent needs during the crisis of 1894. The extent to which the Federal Reserve banks were forced to accede to the wishes of the Treasury, constitutes an interesting phase of World War financing but one which is, however, too controversial for us to summarize here. Finally, we might suggest that the general idea of a ready-made market also found expression during the modern period in a provision for accepting government obligations as penal and contractor's bonds, and in another declaring United States obligations eligible on advantageous terms for reserve against government deposits.

IV. SECURITY FEATURES

An examination of any security discloses that it possesses a number of specific features, aimed toward making the bond attractive to purchasers. In the present section we shall pay special attention to those which, according to our survey, have been used extensively in government financing and which, in a sense, distinguish government securities from other forms of investments.

Tax Exemption

With the exception of a lone provision for tax exemption, authorizing acts previous to the Civil War omitted all reference to taxation. This omission doubtless came because no possibility was seen that the securities would be taxed. During the Civil War period, when there was considerable agitation for taxation by states, authorizing acts began to specify that the securities were to be exempt from all taxes including those levied by the Federal government. This action is important not because of the effect at the time, but because the precedent paved the way for the adoption of exemption on the First Liberty loan. The Second loan and the two succeeding loans carried exemption only on limited holdings.

The Victory 3¾ notes, however, were made exempt in unlimited amounts.

An interesting variation of the exemption feature appeared in what we have termed "contingent exemption" which consists of a plan to exempt former holdings, providing purchases of a given amount of specified new issue were made. A two-fold effect may be claimed for the arrangement. First, it facilitates the sale of the new issue, and secondly, it improves the status of securities on which the exemption is granted.

Of the numerous aspects of the problem of tax exemption, we are largely interested in only one, namely the effect of the provision upon the task of selling the bonds. While this influence has doubtless been over-estimated, we can at least admit the probability that the exemption may, at least at the beginning of the war, remove obstacles to purchasing by acting as an insurance against future taxes of unknown proportions. In this event, increased sales of securities serve to compensate the government for its loss in taxes.[1]

[1] The loss from uncollected taxes is justified, however, only when the purchaser's ideas of future tax possibilities are such that he is willing to pay more for the insurance against taxes than the Treasury contemplates losing from foregoing the revenue from this source.

That the entire problem does not lend itself to a dependable solution becomes evident when one attempts to secure quantitative data on prospective losses or on gains either from additional sales or from a lower rate of interest. When graduated or progressive taxes are introduced into the situation, a difficult problem becomes an impossible one because of the fact that tax losses vary according to the status of the holder. In short there are too many aspects of the subject on which data are lacking for any official to claim that he has a scientific justification for exemption. Deductions from accepted premises give us some basis for an opinion, however. The fact that purchasers in the upper income brackets enjoy the maximum benefits while those in the lower brackets receive no benefits at all would logically give rise to a situation typical of that described in the classical demand curve. Since the bonds are sold on a one-price basis, it appears that this situation would logically result

On the other hand, it is at the beginning of the war that the government can least afford to grant exemptions from future taxes. For this reason, and more especially because of the complicated nature of the entire problem,[1] the desirability of exempting bond yields from progressive income taxes appears questionable.

Receivability

One of the most interesting features yet attached to government securities consists in permitting their use in making payments to the government. One manifestation of the principle is to be found in the plan of allowing treasury notes to be received for the payment of taxes. From the 1812 period to the Civil War, this privilege was extended to apply to all dues to the government. During the Civil War, however, when it became necessary to provide for some receipts in gold, receivability for customs was excepted.

Turning now to receivability as applied to bonds, we find that as early as 1797 evidences of the public debt were made receivable in payments for lands.[2]

The arrangement was repealed April 18, 1806. The way in which low-valued securities were used at par value in paying for land gave rise to an action to compensate those who

in a portion of the purchasers enjoying a surplus over and above the necessary inducement. For this reason all of the government's loss is not effective in producing desired results. Accordingly, tax exemption and progressive taxation are decidedly not to be considered as team-mates.

There exists such a wealth of literature on the question of tax exemption that we shall content ourselves with giving only a selected list.

Hardy, *Tax Exempt Securities and the Surtax*, Macmillan, 1926; *Hearings on Tax Exempt Securities*, U. S. Ways and Means Committee, House, 67th Cong., 2nd Sess., Jan. 16, 18, 19 and March 7, 1922; *Hearings on Tax Exempt Securities*, U. S. Judiciary Committee, Senate, 67th Cong., 2nd Sess; Edwin R. A. Seligman, *Studies in Public Finance* (New York, 1925), ch. vii, "The Problem of Tax-Exemption."

[1] See preceding note.

[2] *Act of Mar. 3*, 1 Stat. at Large 507, ch. xiv.

had paid in coin, to the amount of the difference between the actual price paid and the value of an amount of eligible security sufficient to have made the payment.

In 1861, the provision for repayment of the railroad bonds granted the privilege of receivability to bonds as well as to treasury notes. During the World War, we find an interesting provision to the effect that payment of estate taxes could be made in Liberty Bonds, acceptable at par, and a similar arrangement covering the repayment of the foreign debt to the American government.

The acceptance of Liberty Bonds in payment of estate taxes and in repayment of foreign debts promised to be of considerable importance during the post-war period when government bonds were below par, but its continued use was interfered with by the rise in price of the eligible bonds. It thus appears that the course of events prevented any extensive use of the two modern examples of receivability as applied to bonds. The earlier measures providing for the use of short-term obligations supplied more spectacular examples of the uses of receivability.

Before considering the acceptance of short-term obligations however, it may be well to point out that the feature as applied to these securities had as its apparent objective the making of notes current. In this respect it has apparently been fairly successful. The influence of the feature in this connection was undoubtedly responsible in part for the extent to which treasury notes predominated in financing the War of 1812. Again, in the 1837 period, the receivability feature was depended upon to add to the currency of notes. These in turn constituted the principal source of funds. At this time the attempts to make the notes current were overdone to the extent that a large number of the obligations were returned to the Treasury before the entire issue had been taken by the public. Constant embarrassment and the necessity of frequent issues and re-issues accordingly resulted. The experience during the 1837 period therefore serves as an example of the way in which the receivability feature may, while contributing to the aim of securing currency for the note, defeat the more basic purpose of obtaining revenue for the government. The episode also suggests that the practice of receiving government promises to pay in place of the usual forms of currency may completely eliminate revenue from the sources affected by the arrangement.

If we include the provision for the redemption in gold as an aspect of receivability, we find in the experience of the nineties another example to support these statements. Notes were continually brought to the Treasury for redemption with the result that gold was paid out of the Treasury. When efforts were made to replace these funds by the sale of more securities, the proceeds of the sales were offset by new redemption demands on the treasury. In this instance, as well as in that of 1837, the government was embarrassed because of its inability to make investors retain its obligations. Both of these experiences, as well as the potentialities in connection with the later measures for receiving bonds suggest the possibility of undesirable consequences.

Convertibility

Before it is possible to do anything by way of describing and evaluating the operation of the conversion feature, it is necessary to distinguish among several types.[1] 1. The most simple form of the conversion feature may be accurately described as the privilege of exchangeability. An example of this form is to be found in the 1815 provision for exchanging treasury notes into 6% and 7% bonds, and in the

[1] The term is ordinarily used, as for example by Henry Adams, *Public Debt*, p. 217, merely to describe that particular aspect of refunding which involves an exchange of securities.

Civil War arrangements for converting legal tenders into five-twenties and seven-thirties, treasury notes into 20-year 6% bonds, and treasury notes of June 30, 1864, into bonds of the same act. A distinctive feature of all these measures may be seen in the fact that the exchangeability operated in only one direction. It is also notable that the direction invariably was from short-term into long-term obligations.

An important extension of the principle of exchangeability was made in the Victory Loan Act when full exchangeability in both directions was granted on the two types of notes issued.[1]

The principal advantages of exchangeability are to be found in the manner in which it facilitates the funding operations. On the other hand, the feature has at times proved itself to be rather unwieldy and incapable of manipulation in the desired way. During the period of 1812, conversion took place so rapidly that the Treasury's purpose, namely that of having the notes utilized as currency, was defeated. In the Civil War period, the exact opposite occurred when the hope that the legal tenders would be converted into bonds was not realized. The period also furnished on one occasion a basis for another criticism of this form of conversion: Chase claimed that the privilege of converting the mass of outstanding legal tenders into five-twenties made the sale of the additional issues of the latter impossible. The difficulty arose because not all of the bonds into which the short-term obligations were converted were issued.

This criticism did not apply in the case of conversion as exemplified in the Victory Loans. It would appear, however, that two-way conversion should be resorted to only when very unusual circumstances demand that the public be

[1] For an interesting argument for "two way" conversion during the Civil War see the correspondence of one Pliny Freeman (N. Y. Public Library, T. I. F., p. 22).

given assurance against future developments, or when, as for example at the end of a war, the future is probably foreseen more clearly by the Treasury than it is by the public. Ordinarily, the procedure is objectionable in that it places the Treasury in the position of taking all the risk. Under all circumstances the application of the idea should be made only after careful consideration.

2. The type of conversion thus far considered is, in reality, as was indicated, merely a provision for the exchange of one security for another specified security, and on definite terms. The certainty and definiteness of this form do not appear in a second type of conversion in which we find an arrangement to convert into future issues of unknown terms. A few illustrations will show the varied forms in which this principle expresses itself. The simplest example is to be found in an arrangement whereby Mr. Barker and other subscribers to the ten million dollar loan of 1814, drew from the Treasury a promise that they would be given an option on any more advantageous terms granted to the subsequent subscribers of the same issue.

Previous to this, Mr. Smith and other subscribers to the loan of 1813, had struck exactly the same bargain except that the conversion privilege extended to any loan issued during the same year. Although this application of the conversion feature appears much more complex than was the one involving only the one issue, in practice the 1813 deal caused little difficulty, while the other got the Treasury into all sorts of trouble.

3. The privilege of accepting legal tenders in payment for any subsequent loan is an example of complete conversion. It is significant, however, that this arrangement applied to non-interest bearing notes, and that the privilege had the two-fold purpose of making the legal tenders current and of facilitating the sale of bonds subsequently issued. This sit-

uation meant that Civil War conversion was far less inclusive than was the World War offer to exchange long-term obligations for any bonds subsequently issued. In truth the latter arrangement represented the maximum utilization of the conversion privilege in American financing.

Our financial history has furnished some basis for a criticism of the conversion feature as applied to bonds.

At an early stage in the war of 1812, the existence of outstanding convertible securities forced Gallatin to switch from bonds to treasury notes when he would otherwise have preferred the former. Again in 1813, the payment of a bonus was barely averted. An 1814 transaction was followed by subsequent issues at a much more attractive figure and actually necessitated the payment of a bonus to original subscribers. As a result the gross cost of additional funds was ridiculously high.

If such difficulties could appear as a result of the existence of only limited conversion it is even more apparent that complete conversion would hold potential dangers of importance. While payment of large bonuses to holders of convertible World-War securities was averted, the experiences of the modern period leave us no more ready to condone the privilege. In spite of the fact that the conversion privilege was utilized only in the first two Liberty loans, the feature was attached to a large enough volume of securities to exert a considerable influence on later actions of the Treasury. By the time the use of the feature was discontinued the maximum rate of interest had been reached, so that the step was comparable to locking the stable after the horse was gone. As it was, discontinuing the conversion privilege was an added precaution, and one which would have been very much in place had the Treasury not manipulated matters in a way to avoid higher interest rates. It need hardly be added that the very existence of several billion dollars in convertible securities played no small part in encouraging the adoption of those measures aimed toward maintaining interest rates at the low level set in the first loans. Consequently, the conversion feature is entitled to a large part of the credit or discredit for many of the financing manoeuvers of the period. In fact, it is apparent that a desire to avoid the payment of bonuses to holders of convertible securities constituted a primary motive for a policy of low interest payments. Even considering all the measures engendered by this policy it is doubtful whether the payment of bonuses could have been averted but for the introduction of an interesting and perhaps questionable alternative.

The alternative was a step exactly comparable to the one Gallatin had resorted to under similar circumstances over a century before. The securities were called " notes " rather than " bonds ", thereby avoiding the claim that holders of old securities were entitled to the right to exchange them for the new loan. The questionable aspect of the problem becomes apparent when we observe that the loan actually ran for five years. Although the switch to notes prevented a direct monetary loss from conversion, the general situation was undesirable and must be considered as among the " costs " of conversion.

In order to justify the conversion feature we must find advantages to offset undesirale consequences of the sort described. Administration leaders of both the 1812 and the World-War periods professed to see such advantages in the manner in which conversion facilitated the sale of securities. It was even intimated that funds would not be available unless the feature was attached. An examination of the pertinent facts, however, leaves little doubt that in each instance loans could have been placed merely by meeting the demands of purchasers for a remunerative investment. Moreover, from our present vantage point it appears that in each instance conversion ultimately represented the more costly of the two alternatives. This fact, rather than any generalization pertaining to the use of conversion in the future, should be given weight if the Treasury is again tempted to use the conversion privilege.

4. The conversion principle takes still another form—one in which the provision is not attached to the convertible security at the time of its issue. Instead the right to convert is given to the holder of the obligation in connection with the authorization of a subsequent issue into which it is declared to be convertible. Such action has been common from the Revolutionary period down to the present in connection with the funding and refunding of obligations.

One purpose of such action appears in connection with the attempt to secure permanent funds from temporary obligations. This form finds abundant illustration in every cycle of finance from the 1812 period down. Developments during the 1837 period, may be cited as especially interesting. At first, new authorizations provided for the redemption of outstanding notes. This practice was later modified to provide for reissues, and the law was changed to permit issues up to a certain amount outstanding. The distinguishing mark of the operations during this period was that a definite time limit was placed upon the authorization, whereas, during the World War, no such restrictions were placed upon the issues.

A second example of making existing obligations convertible into the new issue is to be found in connection with the provision for changing temporary into funded debts. For this purpose, outstanding notes are declared to be receivable in payment for bonds. The principle is exemplified in the arrangement for receiving treasury notes for stock in 1815, 1843, and 1857. A similar arrangement provided for the use of certificates of deposit and certificates of indebtedness in paying for the bonds of July 11, 1862, and for the conversions of seven-thirty notes into the 6% bonds of June 30, 1864. During the World War, the authorities resorted extensively to the plan of allowing certificates of indebtedness to be exchanged for any issues of the same type, as well as for Liberty Bonds.

Finally, this type of conversion appears when new issues of bonds are exchanged for outstanding issues. This form is invariably utilized in all refunding programs. and is ordinarily to be associated with this aspect of financing. But while the arrangement may be resorted to primarily for the purpose of facilitating refunding operations, post-mortem conversion may at the same time exert an important influence upon the status of the securities declared convertible. However, attention should be called to the fact that its actual use as a financing device is to be related not to the convertible security, but to those into which the outstanding issue is convertible.

Duration of the Loan

While theories and policies concerning the duration of loans have by no means been as constant as have those concerning the two topics (interest rate and par) discussed at the beginning of this chapter, the subject has nevertheless frequently come up for disposition.

In each major period (including the 90's) the practical financiers assumed the roles of debaters on the academic question of funded versus floating debt. In every instance, those who argued for the funded debt, would doubtless have been given the decision if they had been judged on the basis of logic—and especially if bankers sat in the judges' seat. However, without an exception, short terms were attached [1]

[1] For a modern example of such use of short-term obligations by a foreign country, see Haig, *Public Finances*, *op. cit.*, pt. ii.

to a sufficient proportion of government obligations to enable the resulting notes to make an important contribution to the Treasury in the form of what was, for all practical purposes, a permanent fund.

A glance at our history serves at once to leave a rather definite impression as to the importance which this type of financing has played in Treasury operations and at the same time explains why a mere shortness of time before maturity was resorted to as one of the most important features to be attached to securities to make them attractive.

Especially during the 1812, the 1837, the Civil War, and the 1890 periods, resort to short-time obligations grew out of what was ordinarily thought to be dire necessity. During the first of these periods, Gallatin deliberately went against his own ideas in respect to the desirability of a funded debt only after he had experienced difficulty and actual failure in obtaining funds on long-term obligations. The 1837 period supplies an even more interesting example of the power of economic necessity. Especially does this apply to the actions of the Whigs, who were forced to resort to the very practice (the issue of Treasury notes) which they had criticized and ridiculed when it was carried on by their political opponents.

With the exception of the 1890 period, when the situation was remarkably similar to the 1837 period, the later periods present slightly different situations. During the World War, the resort to short-term obligations could hardly be explained in terms of dire necessity unless, indeed, one cares to claim that the motive of necessity is back of the attempt to secure low nominal interest rates by means of resorting to an inflation which in turn is attained through supplying currency equivalents. Despite all the claims that "necessity" prompted the issue of obligations of the "current" variety during the Civil War financing, the choice of temporary obligations as against a funded debt was made largely as a result of a desire to find a short cut to financial strength, or as a consequence of the unwillingness to " pay the price " of permanent funds.

Having suggested the importance of the role played by short-term obligations, we come now to our second point, which concerns the reason for their extensive use. Why should government officials invariably have turned to the practice of making their war-time obligations payable within a short time? The answer is undoubtedly to be found in the fact that the promise of early maturity lends an element of currency to the government obligations. Equipped with this feature, the government's promise to pay need no longer depend upon the investment appeal. Instead, they could rely upon their liquidity, upon their close resemblance to currency, if you please, to make them attractive to the public. It is apparently for this reason that the Treasury, in its search for a short-cut to financial strength, has so often resorted to the use of notes.

As regards the characteristic of currency as affected by the duration of a loan, the use of additional features is of significance. Making notes receivable in payment of dues to the government, making them payable upon demand, and of course making them legal tender for all debts, simply constitute what is from our present point of view merely a means of minimizing, or of eliminating entirely, that factor —the time element involved in maturity—which stands in the way of the acceptance of government obligations as currency.[1]

[1] *Cf.* Jens P. Jensen, *Problems of Public Finance* (New York, 1921), p. 474.

V. ASSURING SOLVENCY OF THE LOAN

One of the most important steps to be taken for the purpose of adding to the attractiveness of the bond is to assure the holder that the interest and principal will be paid. A number of arrangements have contributed toward the development of this confidence.

Sinking Fund

The sinking fund has a place in our discussion in so far as it affects the situation at two points. In the first place, the most direct manner in which the sinking fund can exert an influence upon the attractiveness of the securities arises when arrangements for it are completed in time to influence the public's confidence before the bonds are sold. The second contribution to the task of financing arises from purchases or retirements actually made. Action which probably exerted an influence of the first type is exemplified in the one per cent sinking fund of February 1862, and to a certain extent, in the operations of the sinking fund during the war of 1812. In this connection, however, the sinking fund is limited by the fact that just at the time when it would be most effective the authorities are unable to buy bonds in accordance with provisions. This was true of the Civil War fund, which failed to operate until 1869. The desirable effects which might have been expected from the sinking fund of 1812, were in part vitiated by the fact that increased demands on the sinking fund were not offset by additional grants of money. As a matter of fact there is little in our country's experience with sinking funds to lead one to expect that appropriations to the fund would be made unless it was entirely convenient to do so.[1] As a result there can hardly

[1] *Cf.* Geo. N. Browne, *The Sinking Fund*, Second Edition (Boston, 1880), "The best way to sink a debt is to pay it," p. 10. For a comprehensive collection of official material on the question of funding prior to 1845, see, Jonathan Elliot, *The Funding System of the U. S. and Great Britain* (Washington, 1845).

fail to exist an element of uncertainty, which is perhaps aggravated in the minds of prospective investors. Because of this it is impossible for us to evaluate the effect of such provisions upon the task of placing securities.

Furthermore, most of the sinking funds are ordinarily tied up with the refunding programs, and thus come too late to be of material assistance at the time when they are most needed as an adjunct of the financing program. However, the second salutary effect of the sinking fund may appear in that purchases, even during peace times, affect the market for bonds during that time, and in that successful debt retirement improves the status of government credit generally. At least such developments may be expected to supply a happy experience, the memory of which serves the Treasury in good stead at the time of any subsequent crisis.

Specific Appropriations

The policy of appropriating certain sources of revenue for the repayment of the loan, constitutes another method of assuring its solvency. The practice in this respect may be divided into several types.

Before 1802, the loan acts specifically appropriated all revenue over and above a certain minimum which was retained for the annual expenses of the government. A modification of this idea appears in the modern plan of setting aside any revenues not otherwise appropriated, and in the older plan of appropriating excess revenues. These steps amount to the same thing as the other, except that there is no specification of the amount which is to be otherwise appropriated.

Beginning in 1802, a specified sum was to be appropriated annually. A variation of this plan of appropriating a definite amount is to be found both in the Civil War, and the World War, when amounts equivalent to 1% and 2½% of the respective debts were set aside for their redemption.

Still another variation combines both of the previous methods and is to be found in the 1817 provision for setting aside ten million dollars and all surplus over and above two million dollars. None of these provisions amounted to anything more than a promise to pay if the government found itself in a position to do so. None added much to the assurrance of repayment.

A final form of specific appropriation on the other hand, gives an assurance commensurate with the certainty of the revenue appropriated. Such measures are to be found in the appropriation of the proceeds of the sale of lands for the retirement of the public debt, and in the specification that dividends from bank stock were to be set aside for the repayment of the bank loan, (1794). Still another principle is found in setting aside a part of the proceeds of a loan for the purpose of paying interest thereon. The practice of appropriating specific taxes for the payment of certain loans likewise constitutes an example of definite appropriation.

Very similar to the specific appropriation was Hamilton's plan of an 8% amortization fund. Under this arrangement, a definite amount was to be appropriated annually and applied to the specific loan regardless of whether or not any sums were being set aside for the repayment of other obligations.

Taxation

Insofar as the receipts from taxes are specifically appropriated for the retirement of bonds, taxation comes in for a very direct influence upon the solvency of obligations. Even where such direct appropriations are absent, however, taxation has an admitted influence in connection with adding to or subtracting from the general confidence in the government's ability and willingness to meet its obligations. The connection becomes the more evident when we recall the failure of sinking funds and alleged specific appropriations to do anything more than merely promise payment provided funds are available.

The failure to provide adequate taxation has ordinarily been considered as a predominant reason for the financial difficulties of the 1812 period. Again, the attempt to finance the Civil War on a basis of no more taxation than enough to pay interest and ordinary expenditures, undoubtedly contributed to the difficulties of the period.

Even the peace-time period of 1837 witnessed difficulties which might have been avoided by a wiser and more extensive use of the taxing power of the government. The lessons learned from the experiences of these periods undoubtedly aided in avoiding similar mistakes during the World War.

A program of heavy taxation is ordinarily thought to act as a curb on extravagance and thereby prove beneficial entirely aside from the resulting direct increase in revenue.

A mere enumeration of features which have been discussed in other sections will be sufficient to call attention to the manner in which they added to the security of a loan. Short maturity, the conversion privilege, receivability, and of course the legal tender privilege, each potentially improves the security or solvency of an obligation.

VI. PRICE MAINTENANCE

An important aspect of war financing, especially in the modern period has had to do with maintaining prices of outstanding securities. The attempt has resulted in a number of provisions.

Sinking Fund Operations

We have already pointed out that the operations of the sinking fund do not necessarily have a very definite connection with the financing during the war periods. However, since its operations may be thought to have a material effect upon the position of the government's obligations in the market, it is important in the following discussion to review the developments.

Around 1807, securities were above par, and could not be purchased. The same situation prevailed in the late 20's, until an act of 1830 authorized purchase at above par. In the middle 50's, when the government was most active in the purchase of securities, it at one time paid as high as 21% premium.

These illustrations are important in that they show that the government was apparently in no wise attempting to keep up the price. As a matter of fact the resulting increase in price actually interfered with the retirement operations, so extensively, in fact, that at certain times purchases were made through agents in order to avoid the effect which the Treasury's presence in the market had on the price of securities.

Furthermore, in purchasing securities at a premium, the government was opposing the idea that bonds should not be bought at above par. Thus, it would seem that we may dispose of these purchases as having nothing to do with the attempt to maintain price.

On the other hand, most purchases in the market have been made at less than par. Since the major operations have not come at a time when the government was selling bonds, but when it was attempting to redeem the debt, however, we seem hardly justified, even under these conditions, in ascribing to the officials of the sinking fund any intention to benefit the market value of the outstanding securities.

Direct Purchase and Similar Operations

In early financing, Hamilton provided (1790) for a two million dollar loan for the purpose of buying the domestic debt. The objective was that of maintaining the domestic price in order to prevent the flow of the securities abroad. A similar provision was found in connection with World-War financing when the Five Per Cent Fund was established to be used in purchasing outstanding obligations. At this time the object was solely to maintain market prices. Other provisions stipulated that the proceeds of the franchise tax from the Federal Reserve banks, and from foreign governments in repayments were to be used in purchasing Liberty bonds. These various arrangements for direct purchase, as well as their equivalent in the provisions that bonds would be received at par in payment of estate taxes, and another to the effect that bonds would be acceptable on the same basis in the repayment of foreign loans, were designed with the idea that they would assist in maintaining prices at par.

In addition to these measures we must mention a number of features which, if not designed to maintain price, at least had the incidental effect of influencing the status of bonds on the market. The circulation privilege, exemption (especially contingent exemption), the conversion privilege, the various methods employed to create a demand for government obligations, as well as the numerous bank provisions which contributed to the usefulness of the bonds, all continued to influence the attractiveness of the affected securities and combined to maintain the prices of government securities at a satisfactory level.

Price Maintenance as a Policy

It is worth notice that measures specifically designed to maintain prices were not utilized to any great extent before the World War. The reasons for this are not hard to find. Before 1812, the only successful loans were practically of a compulsory nature. During the 1812 period a situation peculiar to American war finance resulted in the loans being placed on a business basis. The underlying theory of financing did not at that time require sales at par and political pressure did not compel it. The deals accordingly represented coldblooded transactions in which, if we now be permitted to make the charge, the best men got the better of the bargain. Under such conditions, the Government was under no obligation to these purchasers who had bought the securities on satisfactory terms and who had even inveigled the Government into adding features which assured them of future safety. It is of equal interest to observe that the Government apparently did not even attempt to do what strong business firms have frequently been known to do, namely, peg the market in the interest of forthcoming issues.

Subsequent history likewise furnished relatively little occasion for price-maintenance activities. From 1837 to 1841 the treasury notes depended for their market price in a large measure upon the receivability feature and on their position as currency. There was accordingly no problem of maintaining prices.

From this time until just before the Civil War, the security market was usually so strong that such efforts would have been superfluous. During the Civil War, bonds were quoted in paper money, and as a result of the continued depression of this currency, never went so far below par as to incite any drastic attempts to force the government to take any action. Moreover, in a large part of its operations the Treasury had ceased to pretend that the government obligations were to be considered as investments. During the World War, the situation was somewhat different. While pretending that the securities were on an investment basis, the government's appeal to patriotism, coupled with social pressure, had forced the acceptance of securities on such terms that it could not be hoped they would be retained.

Consequently, since the outstanding bonds did not carry a sufficient interest rate to justify their retention as a par-value investment, the inevitable result was that they decreased in value when patriotism waned, or when the force of necessity compelled certain holders to part with them. When this inevitable result materialized, the cry came up that the Government, in allowing the bonds to go below par, had perpetrated a rank injustice on the American people. More important than this, however, from the Government's standpoint, was that in preparing for the sale of new issues, likewise on a non-business basis, the Treasury was forced to apply some stimulant to all previous issues. This necessity was first occasioned by the fact that it would have been difficult to place new issues when old ones were at a discount on the market. In the second place, the conversion feature forced the Treasury to utilize some method which would ensure the placement of new issues at a low figure in order to avoid a large subsidy to holders of outstanding convertible securities.

On the whole, therefore, we see that the effort to maintain market prices is a logical, even though undesirable, consequence of the policy of placing bonds on a non-business basis as well as a means of continuing such a policy in forthcoming issues.

Viewed in one light, therefore, any inconvenience as a result of that pressure which characterized both the war and the post-war periods and which occasioned the frantic search for means of maintaining market prices must be considered as an undesirable consequence of the adoption of the specific bond features and financing devices. These financial tactics, while attractive from the standpoint of expediency, are not necessarily desirable when the financial rather than political considerations are brought into our purview.

VII. CONCLUSIONS ON FINANCING

Surprising as it may seem, the greatest obstacles to financial strength, especially in modern times, have appeared not as a result of failing resources, present or prospective, but as a consequence of weak financial policies.[1] That this statement, in and of itself, is not necessarily a harsh criticism of those who have been responsible for the unfortunate results, becomes evident when we recall the peculiar situation in which Treasury officials and legislators have found themselves.[2] Ruled directly or indirectly by the masses, the Treasury's every action must fall in line with the plea of the "people" or be justified before the court of popular appeals. The public, alas, is so untutored in finance, that its orders often run counter to the dictates of sound finance. It is for this reason that Treasury officials are put in the position of one who is called upon to serve two masters.[3] Consequently, their actions may be evaluated from two points of view. First, we may pass judgment on whether they followed our preference as to the master they tried to serve. In the second place, we may evaluate the effectiveness of their service.

We may dispose of the first by saying that from the vantage point of one who looks back on history in an attempt to evaluate in terms of ultimate results, there is hardly any

[1] *Cf.* John Foster Bass and H. G. Moulton, *America and the Balance Sheet of Europe* (New York, 1921). The writers point out that the abuse of credit, the use of the printing press and other such measures, are not to be ascribed merely to the difficulty of balancing budgets. "It is almost as much because the lessons of sound finance have been forgotten," p. 40.

[2] *Cf.* Haig, *op. cit.*, "To be wise a financial policy must fit its environment" (p. 4) and Adams, *Public Debt, op. cit.*, "The first lesson in practical finance is that circumstances alter cases," p. 52.

[3] *Cf.* Jacob H. Hollander, *Annals Am. Acad. of Phil. and Soc. Sci.*, vol. lxxv, Jan., 1918, p. 104.

doubt that political expediency has played an altogether too important part, and that greater attention should have been given to establishing the Treasury on a sound financial basis.

When we come to evaluate the effectiveness of the financing measures employed, nothing stands in the way of a clear-cut criticism of the action of treasury officials. On this point, we feel justified in making a generalization of wide scope:

In not a single major period in American finance has the Treasury manipulated matters so as to avoid the unfortunate confusion and the costly results which follow in the wake of badly used financing tactics. The misuse of both security features and financing devices may accordingly be described as characteristic of American financing. This unfortunate situation cannot be explained in any terms other than those describing ignorance of the principles of finance, lack of knowledge of financing tactics, and unfamiliarity with the operation of adopted measures. The only consolation we get out of this thought is that there is some chance that the future will witness the elimination of the defects of the past.

A	B	C	D	E
	Loan	Authorizing Acts	Amounts Authorized	Amounts Issued
1	Loan from Farmers-General of France	Dec. 23, 1776	$10,000,000	$181,500
2	French Loan of 18,000,000, livres	Dec. 3, 1777	10,000,000	3,267,000
3	Spanish Loan 1781	Sept. 28, 1777	5,000,000	174,017.13
4	French Loan of 10,000,000, livres	Oct. 26, 1779	10,000,000	1,815,000
5	French Loan of 6,000,000, livres	Sept. 14, 1782	4,000,000	1,089,000
5x	Balance of supplies due France			
6	Holland Loan of 1782	Oct. 26, 1779	10,000,000	2,000,000
7	Holland Loan of 1784	Oct. 26, 1779	10,000,000	800,000
8	Holland Loan of 1787	Oct. 26, 1779	10,000,000	400,000
9	Holland Loan of 1788	Oct. 26, 1779	10,000,000	400,000
10	Holland Loan of 1790	Aug. 4, 1790	12,000,000	1,200,000
		Aug. 12, 1790	2,000,000	
11	Holland Loan of Mar., 1791	Aug. 4, 1790	12,000,000	1,000,000
		Aug. 12, 1790	2,000,000	
12	Holland Loan of Sept., 1791	Aug. 4, 1790	12,000,000	2,400,000
		Aug. 12, 1790	2,000,000	
13	Antwerp Loan of 1791	Aug. 4, 1790	12,000,000	820,000
		Aug. 12, 1790	2,000,000	
14	Holland Loan of Dec., 1791	Aug. 4, 1790	12,000,000	1,200,000
		Aug. 12, 1790	2,000,000	
15	Holland Loan of 1792	Aug. 4, 1790	12,000,000	1,180,000
		Aug. 12, 1790	2,000,000	
16	Holland Loan of 1793	Aug. 4, 1790	12,000,000	400,000
		Aug. 12, 1790	2,000,000	
17	Holland Loan of 1794	Aug. 4, 1790	12,000,000	1,200,000
		Aug. 12, 1790	2,000,000	
18	Debt due Foreign Officers	Res. Jan.22.1784 May 8, 1792	Indefinite	186,988.78
19	Temporary Loan of 1789	No authority	No authority	191,608.81
20	Temporary Loan of 1790	Mar. 26, 1790	Indefinite	55,000
21	6% stock of 1790	Aug. 4, 1790	Entire Dom. Debt	30,088,397.75 (estimated)
22	Deferred 6s of 1790	Aug. 4, 1790	Dom. Debt	14,649,328.76 (estimated)
23	Threes of 1790	Aug. 4, 1790	Dom. Debt	19,718,757.01 (estimated)
24	Subscription Loan of 1791	Feb. 25, 1791	2,000,000	2,000,000
25	Temporary Loan from Bank of N. A.	Mar. 3, 1791	312,686.20	156,595.56
26	Temporary Loan of 1792	May 2, 1792	523,500	400,000
27	Temporary Loan of 1793	Feb. 28, 1793	800,000	800,000
28	Temporary Loan from Bank of N. Y.	Mar. 20, 1794	1,000,000	200,000
29	Temporary Loan of Mar., 1794	Mar. 20, 1794	1,000,000	1,000,000
30	Temporary Loan of June, 1794	June 9, 1794	1,000,000	1,000,000
31	Temporary Loan of Dec., 1794	Dec. 18, 1794	2,000,000	2,000,000
32	Temporary Loan of Feb., 1795	Feb. 21, 1795	800,000	800,000

APPENDIX

FEDERAL LOANS

F_2	G	H	J	K_1
nterest				Terms of
Issued	Length of Loan Authorized	Date of Redeemability	Date of Maturity	Authorized
5	Not less than 10 years	No mention	Indefinite	No mention
5	Not less than 10 years	No mention	3–15 years after peace	No mention
5	No mention	No mention	Indefinite	Best terms
4	No mention		10 annual instal. from Nov. 5, 1787	
			1797–1802	
5				
5			1793–7	
4		Jan. 31, 1801	Jan. 31, 1801–7	
5			June 1, 1798–1802	
5			June 1, 1799–1803	
} 5	Not over 15 years Not specified		Feb. 1, 1800 to 1804	
5	Not over 15 years	Any earlier date	(Mar. 1) 1802–6	
5	Not over 15 years	Any earlier date	1802–6	
4½	Not over 15 years	Right to redeem sooner—no date	1802–6	
4	Not over 15 years		1802–6	
4	Not over 15 years		1803–7	
5	Not over 15 years		1803	
5	Not over 15 years		1805–9	
6	Not specified		Indefinite	
6	No authority	As per contract	Indefinite	
6	Not specified		As per contract	
6	Not specified	2% yearly	None	Exchange at par
6		2% yearly	None	Exchange at par
3		At pleasure of U. S.	None	Exchange at par
6	10 years	At pleasure of U. S.	1792–1801	
None			As per contract	
5	At pleasure of U. S.	At pleasure of U. S.		
5	Pleasure of U. S.	At pleasure of U. S.		
5			June 8, 1796	
5	At pleasure of U. S.	Pleasure of U. S.		
5		Pleasure of U. S.	July 1, 1795	
5	Pleasure of U. S.		Jan. & Apr. 1, 1796	
6			4 instalments, Dec. 31, 1796 9	

K_2	L	M	N_1	N_2
Sale	Receivability	Tax Exemption	Agent's Commissions	
Sold			Authorized	Paid
Par	No mention	No mention		
Par	No mention	No mention		
Par	No mention	No mention		
Par			Best terms	
Par			Best terms	4½
Par			Best terms	4½
Par			Best terms	8
Par			Best terms	8
95½				4½
96				4
96				4
96		From all taxes forever		4
94½				5½
95				5
96½				3½
96				4
Par				
Par				
Par				
Par				
Par				
Par				
Par				
Par				
Par				
Par				
Par				
Par				
Par				
Par				
Par				

	O_2	
Conversion		Comments
‹ority ct	P. M. Conversion Act	
	For 5½ % stock of 1795 Mar. 3, 1795	
	Ex. for 4½% stock of 1795 Act Mar. 3, 1795 for 5½% stock of 1795 Act Mar. 3, 1795	Authorized employment of fiscal agent in Holland.
		Authorized to employ agents on best terms.
		Authorized to employ agents on best terms.
		Authorized to employ agents on best terms.
		Authorized to employ agents on best terms.
		{ Note—No authorization in either act for the employment of agents. However they were employed and liberal commissions paid.
		Issued in payment of services.
		Principal and interest payable in Paris.
		Issued without any authority.
		Issued in exchange for evidences of the Domestic and State Debts.
		Issued in exchange for evidences of the Domestic and State Debts.
		Issued in exchange for evidences of the Domestic and State Debts.

A	B	C	D	E
	Loan	Authorizing Acts	Amounts Authorized	Amounts Issued
33	Temporary Loan of Mar., 2795 A	Mar. 3, 1795 § 1 18/433 ch. 45	$1,000,000	$500,000
34	Temporary Loan of Mar., 1795 B	Mar. 3, 1795 18/439 ch. 46	1,469,439.29	500,000
35	Temporary Loan of Mar., 1795 C	Mar. 3, 1795 18/439 ch. 46	1,469,439.29	500,000
36	5½% stock of 1795	Mar. 3, 1795 § 2 18/433 ch. 45	For Debt	1,848,900
37	4½% stock of 1795	Mar. 3, 1795 § 2 18/433 ch. 45	For Debt	176,000
38	Temporary Loan from Bank of N. Y.	May 31, 1796	5,000,000	320,000
39	Temporary Loan of 1798	Mar. 3, 1795 § 10 18/433 ch. 45	1,000,000	200,000
40	6% stock of 1796	May 31, 1796	5,000,000	80,000
41	Navy 6% stock	June 30, 1798	Indefinite	711,700
42	8% Loan of 1798	July 16, 1798	5,000,000	5,000,000
43	8% Loan of 1800	May 7, 1800	3,500,000	1,481,700
44	Louisiana 6% stock	Nov, 10, 1803	11,250,000	11,250,000
45	Exchanged 6% stock of 1807	Feb. 11, 1807	Indefinite	6,294,051.12
46	Converted 6% stock of 1807	Feb. 11, 1807	Indefinite	1,859,850.70
47	Loan of 1810	May 1, 1810	Indefinite	2,250,000
48	6% Loan of 1812	Mar. 14, 1812 July 6, 1812	11,000,000	8,134,700
49	Temporary Loan of 1812	Mar. 14, 1812 July 6, 1812	11,000,000	2,150,000
50	Treasury Notes of 1812	June 30, 1812	5,000,000	5,000,000
51	Exchanged 6% stock of 1812	July 6, 1812	Indefinite	2,984,746.72
52	$16,000,000 Loan of 1813	Feb. 8, 1813	$16,000,000	18,109,377.43 (531,200)
53	Treasury Notes of 1813	Feb. 25, 1813	5,000,000	5,000,000
54	$7,500,000 Loan of 1813	Aug. 2, 1813	7,500,000	8,498,581.95
55	Treasury Notes of Mar., 1814	Mar. 4, 1814	10,000,000	10,000,000
56	$10,000,000 Loan of 1814	Mar. 24, 1814	25,000,000	9,919,476.25
57	$6,000,000 Loan of 1814	Mar. 24, 1814	25,000,000	5,384,134.87
57a	Undesignated Loan of 1814	Mar. 24, 1814	25,000,000	746,403.31
58	Mississippi Stock	Mar. 31, 1814	5,000,000	4,282,036.92

	F_2	G	H	J	K_1
f Interest					Terms of
d	Issued	Length of Loan Authorized	Date of Redeemability	Date of Maturity	Authorized
6	6	One year	30 days notice	Jan. 1, 1797	
n	6			Redeem on or before 1 year	
n	6			Dec. 31, 1797 Oct. 1, 1796	
sent	$5\frac{1}{2}$	Pleasure of U. S.	Pleasure of U. S.		Exchanged at par
sent	$4\frac{1}{2}$	Pleasure of U. S.	Pleasure of U. S.		Exchanged at par
6	6	Pleasure of U. S. after Dec. 31, 1819		July 1, 1797	
6	6	Pleasure of U. S.	30 days notice	Jan. 1, 1803	Not below par
6	6	Pleasure of U. S. after Dec. 31, 1819	After Dec. 31, 1819		
6	6	Pleasure of Congress	Pleasure of Congress		for ships
n	8	Not over 15 years	After 15 years		
n	8	Not over 15 years	After 15 years		
6	6	4 annual installments permitted		1818–1821	
6	6	Pleasure of U. S. 6 months notice	Pleasure of U. S. 6 months		Exchange at par
6	6	Pleasure of U. S. 6 months notice	Pleasure of U. S. 6 months		Exchange at 65 for 100-3s
6	6	Not over 6 years from Jan. 1, 1911 or at pleasure of U. S.	Dec. 31, 1811		Not below par
6	6	Not over 12 years from Jan. 1, 1813	After Jan. 1, 1825		Not below par
6	6	Not over 12 years from Jan. 1, 1813	Various dates according to contract		Not below par
$5\frac{2}{5}$	$5\frac{2}{5}$	One year after issue		One year after issue	Not below par Issue to or at par
6	6	At pleasure of U. S. after Dec. 31, 1824	Pleasure of U. S. after Dec. 31, 1824		Exchange at par
on	6 ($7\frac{1}{2}$)	Not over 12 years from Jan. 1, 1814	Jan. 1, 1826		No mention
$5\frac{2}{5}$	$5\frac{2}{5}$	1 year after issue		1 year after issue	Not below par
on	6	Not over 12 years from Jan. 1, 1814	After Jan. 1, 1826		Not below 88
$5\frac{2}{5}$	$5\frac{2}{5}$	1 year after issue		1 year after issue	Not below par
on	6	Not over 12 years from Jan. 1, 1815	After Dec. 31, 1826		No mentlon
ion	6	Not over 12 years from Jan. 1. 1815	After Dec. 31, 1826		No mention
ion	6	Not over 12 years from Jan. 1, 1815	After Dec. 31, 1826		No mention
rest	None	Out of sale of land in Mississippi Territory		As provided for by Statute	

K_2	L	M	N_1	N_2
Sale	Receivability	Tax Exemption	Agent's Commissions	
Sold			Authorized	Paid
Par				
Par				
Par				
Par				
Par				
Par				
Par				
87½				
Par				
Par				
At 105.6 or .056% prem.				
Par				
Par				
Par				
Par				
Par			⅛ of 1%	
Par			⅛ of 1%	
Par	All taxes, duties and lands			
Par				
88 (Par)			¼ of 1%	¼ of 1%
Par	For all dues, etc.		¼ of 1%	
88¼			¼ of 1%	⅛ of 1%
Par	For all dues, etc.		¼ of 1%	¼ of 1%
80			¼ of 1%	¼ of 1%
80			¼ of 1%	¼ of 1%
80–95			¼ of 1%	¼ of 1%
Par	At par for 95% of value of public lands			

	O_2	
Conversion		Comments
…hority …ct	P. M. Conversion Act	
		Issued in exchange for foreign debt—new stock ½% higher.
		Issued in exchange for foreign debt—new stock ½% higher.
		Issued in exchange for vessels sold to Government.
		Note—Stock sold by subscription.
		Note—Stock sold by subscription.
		Issued in payment of Louisiana.
		Exchanged at par for unredeemed amounts of 6s of 1790 and deferred 6s.
		Exchanged at par for 3s of 1790 —3s being taken at $65 for $100 face value.
		§ 2 made 6% stock of 1807 exchangeable.
		Supplementary Act of July 6, 1812, authorized the employment of agents and the payment of ⅛ of 1% commissions—no data.
		Supplementary Act of July 6, 1812, authorized the employment of agents and the payment of ⅛ of 1% commissions—no data.
		Issued in exchange at par for unredeemed amounts of 6s of 1799 and deferred 6s.
		Issued in settlement of land claims—to be paid out of land sales.

A	B	C	D	E	
	Loan	Authorizing Act	Amounts Authorized	Amounts Issued	
59	Temporary Loan of 1814	Nov. 15, 1814	$3,000,000	$1,450,000	
60	Treasury Notes of Dec., 1814	Dec. 26, 1814	10,500,000	8,318,400	
61	Direct Tax Loan	Jan. 9, 1815	6,000,000	200,000	
62	Temporary Loan of Feb., 1815	Feb. 13, 1815	500,000	225,000	
63	Treasury Notes of 1815	Feb. 24, 1815	25,000,000	4,969,400	
64	Treasury Note Stock of 1815	Feb. 24, 1815	25,000,000	1,505,352.18	
65	Small Treasury Notes of 1815	Feb. 24, 1815	25,000,000	3,392,994	
66	7% Stock of 1815	Feb. 24, 1815	25,000,000	9,070,386	
67	Temporary Loan of Mar., 1815	Mar. 3, 1815	13,452,800	1,150,000	
68	6% Loan of 1815	Mar. 3, 1815	18,452,800	12,288,147.56	
69	5% Loan of 1816	April 10, 1816	7,000,000	7,000,000	
70	5% Loan of 1820	May 15, 1820	3,000,000	999,999.13	(a) (b)
71	6% Loan of 1820	Mar. 15, 1820	3,000,000		(a)
				2,000,000	(b)
72	5% Loan of 1821	Mar. 3, 1821	5,000,000	4,735,296.30	
73	Exchanged 5% Stock of 1822	April 20, 1822	26,000,000	56,704.77	
74	1st 4½ Loan of 1824	May 24, 1824	5,000,000	5,000,000	
75	Ex. 4½ Stock of 1824	May 26, 1824	15,000,000	4,454,727.95	
76	2nd 4½% Loan of 1824	May 26, 1824	5,000,000	5,000,000	
77	Ex. 4½ Stock of 1825	Mar. 3, 1825	12,000,000	1,539,336.16	
78	Treasury Notes of 1837	Oct. 12, 1837	10,000,000	10,000,000	
79	Treasury Notes of 1838	May 21, 1838	10,000,000	5,709,810.01	
80	Treasury Notes of 1839	Mar. 2, 1839	10,000,000	3,857,276.21	
81	Treasury Notes of 1840	Mar. 31, 1840	5,000,000	7,114,251.31	
82	Treasury Notes of 1864	Feb. 15, 1841	5,000,000	7,529,062.75	
83	Loan of 1841	July 21, 1841	12,000,000	5,672,976.88	
84	Treasury Notes of Jan., 1842	Jan. 31, 1842	5,000,000	7,959,994.83	
85	Loan of 1842	July 21, 1841 April 15, 1842 Aug. 31, 1842	12,000,000 additional 5,000,000	8,343,886.03	

	F_2	G	H	J	K_1
interest					Terms of
	Paid	Length of Loan Authorized	Date of Redeemability	Date of Maturity	Authorized
	6–7 (400,000 at 7)	Not over 12 years from Dec. 31, 1814		Indefinite	Not limited
	$5\frac{2}{5}$	1 year after issue		1 year after issue	Not below par
)	6	No mention	Receipt of tax		No mention
o	6	No mention		Indefinite	No mention
	$5\frac{2}{5}$	Indefinite	By conversion		Not below par
	6	Redeemable after Dec. 31, 1824	After Dec. 31, 1824		Conversion Exchange
	None	Indefinite	By conversion		Not below par
	7	Redeemable after Dec. 31, 1824	After Dec. 31, 1824		Conversion Exchange
	6	Not over 12 years from Dec. 31, 1815		Indefinite	No mention
	6	Not over 12 years from Dec. 31, 1815	Redeemable after Dec. 31, 1827		No mention
	5	Pleasure of U. S.	Pleasure of U. S.		Par—Exchange
5% 6%	5	(a) After Jan. 1822 (b) Pleasure of U. S.	After Jan. 31, 1832		Not below par
5%		(a) Redeemable after Jan. 1, 1831			Not below par
6%	6	(b) Pleasure of U. S.	Pleasure of U. S.		
	5	Redeemable after Jan. 1, 1835	Jan. 1, 1835		Not below par
	5	Redeemable at pleasure after Dec. 31, 1830, 1, and 2	Dec. 31, 1830, 1831 and 1832		Exchange
½	4½	Redeemable after Jan. 1, 1832	Jan. 1, 1832		Not below par
½	4½	Redeemable after Dec. 31, 1832 & 1833	Dec. 31, 1832–33		Exchanged at par
½	4½	After Dec. 31, 1831	Dec. 31, 1831		Not below par
½	4½	Dec. 31, 1828–29	Dec. 31, 1828–29		Exchanged at par Not below par
%	.01%–6%	1 year		1 year after issue	Not below par
%	6	1 year		1 year after issue	Not below par
%	2 and 6	1 year		1 year after issue	Not below par
%	2 to 6	Within 1 year on 60 days notice	60 days notice	1 year after issue	Not below par
%	2 to 6	1 year after issue		1 year after issue	Not below par
%	$5\frac{2}{3}$ to 6	6 months notice or after Jan. 1, 1845	Jan. 1, 1845		Not below par
%	2 and 6	1 year		1 and 2 years	Not below par
%	6	6 months notice or 20 years after Jan. 1, 1863	Jan. 1, 1863		Below par after adopted Not below par

K_2	L	M	N_1	N_2
Sale	Receivability	Tax Exemption	Agent's Commissions	
Sold			Authorized	Paid
Par			¼ of 1%	
Par	For all dues, etc.		¼ of 1%	
Par			No mention	
Par			No mention	
Par	For all dues, etc.		No mention	
By conversion			No mention	
Par to 4% premium	For all dues, etc.		No mention	
Conversion			No mention	
Par			¼ of 1%	
95 to par Over 95¼			¼ of 1%	¼ of 1% 1815 Rep.
Par				
Par			⅛ of 1%	
			⅛ of 1%	
2% premium				
5.147-8% premium			⅛ of 1%	
Par—Exchange				
Par				
Par—Exchange				
Par				
Par				
Par	All dues, etc.			
Par	All dues, etc.			
Par	All dues, etc.			
Par	All dues, etc.			
Par	All dues, etc.			
Par			1/10 of 1%	
Par	All dues, etc.			
			1/10 of 1%	
97.50 below par				

	O_2	
Conversion		Comments
…hority …ct	P. M. Conversion Act	
		Treasury notes due and pay before Jan. 1, 1815, were made receivable in pay of stock at par value of Treasury notes.
…tock …5	Same act	No provision for payment other than by conversion—or receivability. Issued on conversion or $5\frac{2}{5}\%$ treasury notes.
tock …815	Same act	No provision for payment other than by conversion or receivability. Issued on conversion of small (non-interest bearing) treasury notes. Treasury notes actually issued before law enacted and by law a charge on the Sinking Fund were authorized and were made receivable in payment. Treasury notes actually issued before statute passed and by law a charge on the Sinking Fund were authorized receivable in payment. Exchange made on basis of $95 treasury notes for $100 stock. Issued in payment of subscription of U. S. to stock of Bank of U. S.
		Issued in exchange for 7s of 1815 and 6s of 1812–15 inclusive.
		Issued in exchange for 6s of 1813.
		Issued in exchange for 6s of 1813 of both loans.

A	B	C	D	E	
	Loan	Authorizing Act	Amounts Authorized	Amounts Issued	
86	Treasury Notes of Aug., 1842	Aug. 31, 1842	$6,000,000	$3,025,554.89	N
87	Treasury Notes of 1843	Mar. 3, 1843	Indefinite	1,806,950	N
88	Loan of 1843	Mar. 3, 1843	Indefinite	7,004,231.35	N
89	Treasury Notes of 1846	July 22, 1846	10,000,000	7,687,800	N
90	Loan of 1846	July 22, 1846	10,000,000	4,999,149.45	N
91	Mexican Indemnity Stock	Aug. 10, 1846	320,000	303,573.92	
92	Treasury Notes of 1847	Jan. 28, 1847	23,000,000	26,122,100	
93	Loan of 1847	Jan. 28, 1847	23,000,000	28,230,350	N
94	Bounty Land Scrip	Feb. 11, 1847	Indefinite	223,075	
95	Loan of 1848	Mar. 31, 1848	16,000,000	16,000,000	
96	Texas Indemnity Stock	Sept. 9, 1850	10,000,000	5,000,000	
97	Treasury Notes of 1857	Dec. 23, 1857	20,000,000	52,778,900	N Low
98	Loan of 1858	June 14, 1858	20,000,000	20,000,000	
99	Loan of 1860	June 22, 1860	21,000,000	7,022,000	
100	Treasury Notes of 1860	Dec. 17, 1860	10,000,000	10,010,900	
101	Loan of Feb., 1861	Feb. 8, 1861	25,000,000	18,415,000	
102	Treasury Notes of 1861	Mar. 2, 1861	10,000,000 Indefinite	22,468,100 12,896,350	
103	Oregon War Debt	Mar. 2, 1861	2,800,000	1,090,850	
104	Loan of July and August, 1861	July 17, 1861 Aug. 5, 1861	250,000,000	50,000,000 139,321,350	
105	Old Demand Notes March 17, 1862—legal tender	July 17, 1861 Feb. 12, 1862 Aug. 5, 1861	50,000,000 10,000,000	60,030,000	N N
106	Seven-Thirties or 1861	July 17, 1861 Aug, 5, 1861	250,000,000	139,999,750	
107	Five-Twenties of 1862	Feb. 25, 1862 Mar. 3, 1864 Jan. 28, 1865	500,000,000 11,000,000 [illegible],000,000	514,771,600	
108	Legal Tender Notes	Feb. 25, 1862 July 11, 1862 Mar. 3, 1863	150,000,000 150,000,000 150,000,000		

	F_2	G	H	J	K_1
Interest					Terms of
	Paid	Length of Loan Authorized	Date of Redeemability	Date of Maturity	Authorized
	6%	1 year		1 and 2 years	Not below par
	.01 and 4%	1 year		1 year	Not below par
	5%	Not over 10 years	July 1, 1853		Not below par
	.01–5.4%	1 year	1 year		Not below par
	6%	Not over 10 years	Nov. 12, 1856		Not below par
	5%	5 years		5 years from date	Payment of claim
	$5\frac{3}{5}$ and 6	1 and 2 years	1 and 2 years issue		Not below par
	6	Redeemable after Dec. 31, 1867	Dec. 31, 1867		Not below par
	6	Pleasure of U. S.	Pleasure of U. S.		Bounty
	6	20 years from July 1, 1848	July 1, 1868		Not below par
	5	Redeemable after 14 years	Jan. 1, 1865		Payment of claims
o over	3–6	1 year		1 year from date of issue	Not below par
	5	Not over 15 years from Jan. 1, 1858	Jan. 1, 1874		Not below par
	5	Not over 20 nor less than 10 years	Jan. 1, 1871		Not below par
	6–12	1 year	1 year after issue		At par
	6	10 to 20 years	Dec. 31, 1880 Jan. 1, 1871		No mention
	6	Redeemable after 2	2 years		
	6	years from date of Act	60 days		
	6	Redeemable in 20 yrs.	July 1, 1881		Payment of claims
	6	Redeemable at pleas.	June 30, 1881		None below par
	6	After 20 years	June 30, 1881		In each at rate equivalent to par for 7s
t	None	Demand	Demand		Not below par
t	None	Demand	Demand		
3	7 3	3 years		3 years after issue Aug. 19 and Oct. 1, 1864	Not below par
	6	Redeemable after 5 and pay after 20	May 1, 1867	May 1, 1882	Market value
	None	No time limitations		Demand	
	None				
	None				

K_2	L	M	N_1	N_2
Sale	Receivability	Tax Exemption	Agent's Commissions	
Sold			Authorized	Paid
Par	All dues, etc.			
Par	All dues, etc.			
1 to 3¾% premium			No commission	
Par	All dues, etc.			
Par to .277% premium			No commission	
Par				
Par	All dues, etc.			
1¼–2% premium				
Par				
3.02 to 4.05 premium				
Par				
Par	All dues, etc.			
3.59% average premium				
Par to 1.45% premium				
Par	All dues, etc.			
89.03				
Par to 1.27% premium	All dues, etc.			
Par				
At par for 7s				
Par each				
Par				
	All dues and customs			
	All dues and customs			
Average Premium of .465%				
Average premium of 3.55%		Exempt from all state and municipal taxation		
Par	All dues, etc. except customs received for loans			

	O_2	
Conversion		Comments
…ority …ct	P. M. Conversion Act	
		Approp. to pay interest and principal—Stock issued in settlement of claims.
…ock …47	Same act	
		Some issued in conversion of Treasury Notes of 1847 and of (1846)?
		Issued as a military bounty.
		Public offering for subscription required. Coupon Bonds.
		Issued in payment of claims of State of Texas.
		Public advertisement required to determine rate of interest.
		Advertisement and invitation of bids required. Secretary to accept most favorable bids.
		Advertisement and invifation of bids required.
		Advertisement and invitation of bids required to determine interest rate.
		Advertisement and invitation of bids required. Acceptance of bids not compulsory.
		Stock authorized by same act or bonds in lieu of which Treasury Notes issued.
		Issued in payment of claims provided for in Act.
		Some issued in exchange for 7.3% notes. Amount authorized by Act of Aug. 5 limited to amount of 7.3s.
		Note—Legal tenders authorized in lieu of Demand Notes.
…f 1861	By Act of Aug. 5, 1861	
…rtible …5–20s		Act of Mar. 3, 1863, limited conversion privilege to July 1, 1863. Notes legal tender except for duties on imports and for interest on public debt.

A	B	C	D	E	
	Loan	Authorizing Act	Amounts Authorized	Amounts Issued	
109	Temporary Loan Certificates of Deposit	Feb. 25, 1862 Mar. 17, 1862 July 11, 1862 June 30, 1864	$25,000,000 25,000,000 50,000,000 50,000,000	$116,099,247.16 (1881)	
110	Certificates of Indebtedness	Mar. 1, 1862 Mar. 17, 1862	Indefinite	561,753,241.65	
111	Fractional Currency	July 17, 1862	Indefinite	368,720,079.51	
		Mar. 3, 1863 June 30, 1864	50,000,000		
112	Loan of 1863	Mar. 3, 1863 June 30, 1864	900,000,000 75,000,000	75,000,000	
113	One Year Notes of 1863	Mar. 3, 1863	400,000,000	44,520,000	N
114	Two Year Notes of 1863	Mar. 3, 1863	400,000,000	166,480,000	N
115	Compound Interest Notes	Mar. 3, 1863	400,000,000	17,993,760	N
		June 30, 1864	200,000,000	248,601,680	I
116	Ten-Forties of 1864	Mar. 3, 1864	200,000,000	196,118,300	
117	Five-Twenties of Mar., 1864	Mar. 3, 1864	200,000,000	3,882,500	
118	Five-Twenties of June, 1864	June 30, 1864	400,000,000	125,561,300	
119	Seven-Thirties of 1864 and 1865	June 30, 1864 Mar. 3, 1865	200,000,000 600,000,000	829,992,500	I Not no
120	Navy Pension Fund	July 1, 1864 July 23, 1868	Indefinite	14,000,000	
121	Five-Twenties of 1865	Mar. 3, 1865 April 17, 1866	600,000,000 Indefinite	203,327,250	Not Not
122	Consols of 1865	Mar. 3, 1865 April 12, 1866	600,000,000 Indefinite	332,998,950	Not nor
123	Consols of 1867	Mar. 3, 1865 April 12, 1866	600,000,000 Indefinite	379,618,000	Not no

	F_2	G	H	J	K_1
Interest					Terms of
	Paid	Length of Loan Authorized	Date of Redeemability	Date of Maturity	Authorized
	5	Not less than 30 days	On 10 days notice		Deposit of U. S. notes
	{ 4, 5 & 6	Same	Same		
	6	1 year earliest	Pleasure of U. S.	One year from date of issue	Par
	6	Pleasure of U. S.			
	None	None		On presentation	
	None	None		On presentation	
	6	Not less than 10 nor more than 40 years	July 1, 1881		Terms deemed advisable
%	5	Not over 3 years	One year after issue		Best terms
%	5	Not over 3 years	2 years from date		Best terms
%		Not over 3 years	June 10 1867 and May 15, 1868		Best terms
3	6% comp.	Not over 3 years	After 3 years		Best terms
	5	Redeemable after 5–8 Pay not over 40	Mar. 1, 1874	Mar. 1, 1904	Best terms
	6	Redeemed after 5 and not over 40	Mar. 1, 1869	Mar. 1, 1884	Best terms
	6	Redeemable 5–30 yrs. Pay not over 40	Nov. 1, 1869	Nov. 1, 1884	Best terms
3	7.3	Not over 3 years	Aug. 15, 1867		Best terms
coin ful	7.3	as Secretary may deem expedient	June 15–July 15, 1868		Best terms
	3	Indefinite			
coin awful	6	Redeemable 5–40 yrs. Pay not over 40 years	Nov. 1, 1870	Nov. 1, 1885	Best terms
coin wful	6	Redeemable 5–40yrs. Pay not over 40	July 1, 1870	July 1, 1885	Best terms
coin ful	6	Redeemable 5–40yrs. Payable not over 40 years	July 1, 1872	July 1, 1887	Best terms

K_2	L	M	N_1	N_2
Sale	Receivability	Tax Exemption	Agent's Commissions	
Sold			Authorized	Paid
Par				
Par				
Par				
Par				
Par				
Par	All dues less than $5			
Par	All dues except imports less than $5			
Average premium 4.453%		All state and local taxes		
Par	All dues except customs			
Par	All except customs			
Par	All except customs			
Par to 7% premium		State and local taxes		
Par		State and local taxes		
2.531 premium		State and local		
.038% average premium	All except customs			
Par				
Average premium of 2.547%		State and local		
Average premium of 3.691%		State and local		
Average premium of 1.62%		State and local		

	O_2	
Conversion		Comments
…ority …ct	P. M. Conversion Act	
		Conversion privilege of legal tenders extended to certificates of deposit by act of July 11, 1862, 12 Stat. at Large 532, Chapter 142, § 3 at 533.
		Conversion privilege of legal tenders extended to certificates of indebtedness by Act of July 11, 1826, 12 Stat. at Large 532, Chapter 142, § 3 at 533.
		Each for U. S. Notes in sums of $3.
		Principal and interest payable in coin.
		Principal and interest payable in lawful money. Treasury notes a legal tender for face amount.
		Convertible at discretion of Secretary.
		Act of April 12, 1866, extended Act of Mar. 3, 1865, so as to make treasury notes convertible into bonds at the discretion of the Secretary.
		Navy Pension Fund invested in U. S. securities.

A	B	C	D	E	F₁
					Rate of Interest
	Loan	Authorizing Act	Amounts Authorized	Amounts Issued	Authorized
124	Consols of 1868	Mar. 3, 1865	$600,000,000	$42,539,350	Not over 6% coin nor 7.3 lawful money
		April 12, 1866	Indefinite		
125	Three % Certificates	Mar. 2, 1867	50,000,000	85,155	Not over 3%
		July 25, 1868	25,000,000		
126	Certificate of Indebtedness of 1870	July 8, 1870	678,362.41	678,362.41	Fixed at 4
127	Five % Loan of 1881	July 14, 1870	200,000,000	486,043,000	Fixed at 5
		Jan. 20, 1871	300,000,000		
			20,000,000		
		Dec. 17, 1873	Indefinite	13,957,000	
		Jan. 14, 1875	Indefinite	17,494,150	
		Mar. 3, 1875	Indefinite	500,000	
128	4½% Loan of 1891	July 14, 1870	300,000,000	185,000,000	Fixed at 4½
		Jan. 20, 1871			
		Jan. 14, 1875		65,000,000	
129	4% Loan of 1907	July 14, 1870	1,000,000,000	710,430,950	Fixed at 4
		Jan. 20, 1871			
		Jan. 14, 1875		30,500,000	
130	Refunding Certificates	Feb. 26, 1879	Indefinite	40,012,750	Fixed at 4
131	Continued Loan of 3½			178,055,150	
				401,503,900	
132	Loan of July 12, 1882	July 12, 1882	Indefinite	305,581,250	Fixed at 3
133	Funded Loan of 1891			25,364,500	
134	Loan of 1904	Jan. 14, 1875	Indefinite	50,000,000	Fixed at 5
				50,000,000	Fixed at 5
135	Loan of 1925	Jan. 14, 1875	Indefinite	62,315,400	Fixed at 4
				100,000,000	
136	Loan of 1898-1908	June 13, 1898	400,000,000	198,792,660	Fixed at 3
137	Consols of 1930	Mar. 14, 1900 § 11	839,146,340	646,250,150 (1909)	Fixed at 2
138	Panama Canal Loan	June 28, 1902	130,000,000	30,000,000	Fixed at 2
			Balance repealed	24,631,980	Fixed at 2
		Dec. 31, 1905	Aug. 5, 1909	30,000,000	Fixed at 2
		Aug. 5, 1909	295,569,000	50,000,000	Not over 3
		Mar. 2, 1911			
139	Certificate of Indebtedness	June 13, 1898	100,000,000	15,436,500	Not over 3
		Aug. 5, 1909 § 40	100,000,000		
140	Postal Savings Bonds	June 25, 1910	Indefinite	14,812,380 (1928)	Fixed at 2½
141	Conversion Bonds	Dec. 23, 1913	Indefinite	28,894,500 (1917)	Fixed at 3
142	Conversion Notes	Dec. 23, 1914	Indefinite	27,362,000 (1917)	Fixed at 3

—*Continued*

G	H	J	K₁	K₂	L	M
			Terms of Sale			
ength of Loan Authorized	Date of Redeemability	Date of Maturity	Authorized	Sold	Receivability	Tax Exemption
eemable 5–40 yrs. not over 40 years	July 1, 1873	July 1, 1878	Best terms	.045 average premium		
less than 30 days	Demand		Deposit of U. S. notes	Par		
5 years		Sept. 1, 1875	In payment of claims	Par		
eemed at pleasure after 10 years	May 1, 1881		Not below par in coin	Par		State and National taxes
			In each			State and National taxes
			Not below par in coin	Par		
			In payment of claims	Par		
eemable at pleas- e after 15 years	Sept. 1, 1891		Not below par in coin	Par		State and National taxes
				Par to 1½% premium		
eemable at pleas- e after 30 years	July 1, 1907		Not below par in coin			State and National taxes
				Par to ½% premium		
Indefinite	By conversion into 4%s		In exchange for lawful money	Par		
	Pleasure of U. S.			Par		State and National taxes
easure of U. S.	Pleasure of U. S.		Not below par	Par		State taxes
	Pleasure of U. S.			Par		State and National taxes
edeemable after 10 years	Feb. 1, 1904		Not below par	117.223		State and National taxes
	Feb. 1, 1904		Not below par	117.077		
edeemable after 30 years	Feb. 1, 1925			104.495		State and National taxes
				111.166		
eemable after 10 Pay 20 years	Aug. 1, 1908	Aug. 1, 1918	At par Under par if not subscribed at par	Par		
edeemable after 30 years	April 1, 1930		Exchange at rates	Par to 103		State and National taxes
eemable after 10	Aug. 1, 1916	Aug. 1, 1936	Not below par	104.036		State and National taxes (for these four rows)
Pay 30	Aug. 1. 1916	Aug. 1, 1936		102.99		
	Aug. 1, 1918	Aug. 1, 1938		102.436		
Pay after 50		June 1, 1961		102.582		
One year	Nov. 20, 1908			Par		
edeemable 1 year or pay in 20	One year	20 years		Par		State and National taxes
30 years		30 years from date of issue	In each	Par in exchange for 2s		State and National taxes except those imposed by this Act (for these two rows)
Not over 1 year		1 year from date of issue	In each	Par in exchange for 2s		

FOOTNOTES FOR TABLE

The table was made from original sources. When a number of Treasury Reports are cited, any intervening reports not mentioned retain the figures quoted for the last one mentioned. A new report is cited only when it quotes figures different from those of preceding citations.

Where Statutes at Large and other sources differ on the subject of authorizations, the Statutes are relied upon and no mention is given of the discrepancy in the footnotes.

The numbers refer to the numbers opposite the loans.

LOAN NO.

1. Bayley, p. 99, and *Treasury Report*, 1876, p. 24, says "payable as per contract"—Nothing to indicate what this was.
2. *Journals of Cong.*, vol. ii, p. 359—Bayley, p. 99—"for a term not less than ten years, with permission, if practicable, to pay the same sooner if it shall be agreeable to these states, giving twelve months' previous notice to the lender of such intention to return the money."
2. Bayley, *op. cit.*, p. 100—"payable as per contract."
2. *Treas. Report*, 1876, p. 24 states that these obligations were redeemable 14 years after peace.
3. Bayley, *op. cit.*, p. 100, and *Treas. Report*, 1876, p. 24, "payable as per contract."
3. *Journals of Continental Cong.*, vol. xv, p. 1119, Sept. 28, 1779 reads "and to solicit a loan of five millions of dollars, upon the best terms in your power, not exceeding six per cent per annum", p. 1120, footnote 1—the actual instructions in using words "best terms" did not refer to interest in any way.
4. The money was raised in Holland but only after the King of France guaranteed payment. Under the contract, the money borrowed became due to France—Bayley, *op. cit.*, p. 13.
5. Bayley, *op. cit.*, p. 14 states that the contract provided for six annual payments on Jan. 1 of 1785-1790 inclusive. Bayley, *op. cit.*, p. 101, and *Treas. Report*, 1876, p. 25, quote the dates as being 1797-1802.

6-9. The price at which the loan sold is stated as par both by Bayley and by the Secretary of the Treasury in his report for 1876, although commissions were allowed on all loans.

7. Interest was stated as 4% (Bayley, *op. cit.*, p. 102), but the *Treas. Report* of 1876, p. 25 gives 5%. Obligations issued bore 4% but in

order to sell the loan, it was necessary to give certain bonuses and gratifications. What the actual rate of interest was does not appear, but Bayley (*op. cit.*, p. 19), indicates that it was less than 6¼%. This method of selling the loan was resorted to because John Adams felt himself bound by the act to limiting the interest to 6% (Bayley, *op. cit.*, p. 18).

7. Bayley, *op. cit.*, p. 102—"By the terms of the contract for this loan, the charges were equivalent to a discount of 6.65%."

7–12, 14–17. Obligations were issued in guilders. Those of 1788 were in florins.

8. The charges really constituted a deduction from par—See Bayley, *op. cit.*, p. 21, where he says the U. S. received $92.00.

9. Bayley, *op. cit.*, p. 21, says the amount of discount and expense does not appear, but (on Bayley, p. 20) Jefferson's account shows that his estimates were based on a commission of 8%.

10–17. Since loans were made under authorization of both acts (See numerous statements in *American State Papers*, vol. i: Finance) the limitations of either act applied. Apparently, there were no authorizations for the use of agents, but they were used, and commissions were paid to them.

10–17. Terms of sale—Bayley, *op. cit.*, pp. 104-107, and *Treas. Report*, 1876, pp. 25-26, show that the sales were below par. This seems to be based on a deduction of commission from par. Merely a different form of statement from that appearing in loans 6-9 *supra*.

10. The 1876 *Report*, p. 25, says that payments were from March 1, 1802.

12. Apparently this loan was also redeemable before maturity as final payment was made in 1905.

13. Bonds issued in Florins.

15. Bayley, *op. cit.*, p. 26—an issue of 3,000,000 guilders ($1,200,000) was offered but for some reason subscriptions were closed at 2,950,000 guilders ($1,180,000).

15. Bayley, *op. cit.*, p. 106, places the price at which bonds were sold at 96. This is undoubtedly an error as the commission was 5%.

18. Resolution of Jan. 1784 made the interest on the certificates payable annually in Paris, at the house of M. Grand, broker, 5%. The act of May 8, 1792, authorized the redemption of the certificates.

19. No statutory authority existed for this loan. It was made entirely on the authority of the Secretary of State—Bayley, *op. cit.*, p. 108.

19. The contract for repayment, given in Bayley, *op. cit.*, p. 108, shows that by the terms of the contract with the Bank, these advances were repayable out of the first moneys which accrued in the State of New York, from the duties on imports and tonnage. The same terms were made with the Bank of North America for repayment out of

the first moneys which accrued in the state of Pennsylvania from a like source.

20. Section 7 of the Act of Mar. 26, 1790, authorized the President to empower the Secretary of the Treasury to make such loans as might be necessary to carry into effect certain specific appropriations made by the act. Bayley, p. 30, contains a copy of the express authorization of President Washington limiting the amount to $100,000.

20. The authorization limited the rate of interest to not over 6%.

20. Bayley, *op. cit.*, p. 108—Contract of loan provided for repayment in manner detailed under loan 19.

20–2. Amounts issued—*Treas. Report*, 1876, pp. 27-28, says these are estimates.

21–23. The amount of the loan authorized as stated by Bayley, and *Treas. Reports* are indefinite, but authorization under Section 3, and 13, of the Act of Aug. 4, 1790 was (1) to the full amount of the domestic debt and (2) $21,500,000 to cover the state debts.

21. *Treas. Report*, 1876, p. 27—Amount issued estimated at $30,088,397.75.

21–3. The Act of Aug. 4, 1790, provided no dates of maturity but stipulated that the 6% loan of 1790 could be redeemed by payments not to exceed 8% of the face value, to include interest and principle. The same provisions applied to the deferred 6's. The 3's were simply "subject to redemption whenever provision should be made by law for that purpose."

21–3. Sections 3, 4, 5 and 13 of Act of Aug. 4, 1790, specified the basis of exchange of the old debt for the new and enumerated the securities which were exchangeable.

22. In the *Treas. Report* for 1876 (p. 28) the amount issued was estimated at $14,649,328.76.

22. Interest on loan was not to begin until 1800.

23. In the *Treas. Report* for 1876 (p. 28) the amount issued was estimated at $19,718,751.01.

25. Bayley, *op. cit.*, p. 112—"This loan was made without interest in consideration of the advantages gained by the bank in having a large amount of bills of exchange on Amsterdam remaining on deposit."

31. Bayley, *op. cit.*, p. 114 states that the obligations were redeemable at the pleasure of the U. S., see also, *Treas. Report*, 1876, p. 30.

31. The 1876 *Report*, p. 30, places the rate of interest at 6%.

32. Bayley, *op. cit.*, p. 115, says that the obligations were redeemable at the pleasure of the U. S.—Also 1876 *Treas. Report*, p. 30.
Par-Loan from the bank of the U. S.—The U. S. got in payment 6% stock which was later sold in Europe at less than the equivalent of par—Bayley, *op. cit.*, p. 39—citing Secretary Wolcott in *American State Papers*—"Foreign relations," vol. i, p. 555.

33. Act was Act of March 3, 1795. Section 6—authorized one million dollars annually.
33. The *Treas. Report*, 1876, p. 30, states that the obligations were redeemable at the pleasure of the U. S.
34. The *Treas. Report* of 1876, p. 30, says they were redeemable at the pleasure of the U. S.
34. Bayley is inconsistent—He says, p. 30, that the date of the loan was Jan. 1, 1796, and the date of maturity Dec. 31, 1797—on p. 116 he says that the length of the loan was one year, and that the loan was redeemable as per contract.
35. The 1876 *Treas. Report*, p. 31, says that the loan was redeemable at the pleasure of the U. S.
38. Bayley, *op. cit.*, p. 117—Length, one year, redeemable as per contract. See also, *Treas. Report*, 1876, p. 31.
The confusion arising as a consequence of a variation between the terms actually given and those authorized in the *Act of May 31, 1796* (1 Stat. L. 488, chap. 42), leads us to doubt that the loan was issued under this authority, as both Bayley and the Secretary of the Treasury claim. It is possible that the loan was negotiated under the *Act of May 30, 1796*, 1 Stat. L. 477, chap. 41, which authorized a loan of $324,539.06. This act included the provision for repayment at the pleasure of the U. S.
39. Bayley, *op. cit.*, p. 118, makes no mention of redeemability prior to Jan. 1, 1803. He says, p. 40, that the loan was redeemable on one month's notice, and cites the American State Papers as his authority.
41. Amount authorized limited to cost of 12 vessels—Bayley, *op. cit.*, p. 119.
42. Bayley, *op. cit.*, p. 44, says that the stock was to bear interest at 8% to Dec. 31, 1808, and thereafter at like interest during the pleasure of the U. S. The loan was redeemable after 15 years, p. 119.
43. Bayley, *op. cit.*, pp. 45 and 119, says the premium was almost 5¼% —The amount of the premium was $183,529.24, p. 45. The *Treas. Report*, 1876, p. 32, used 105.6.
44. "Provided however, that the Secretary of the Treasury may, with the approbation of the President of the United States, consent to discharge the said stock in four equal annual instalments, and also shorten the periods fixed by the convention for its reimbursement." 2 Statutes at Large 246.
Report of Gallatin for 1803, p. 264, assumes payment in four annual instalments—Same in 1806 report, p. 335, where there appears the statement "The Louisiana stock cannot be reimbursed before the period fixed by the contract." Bayley, *op. cit.*, p. 45, indicates four annual instalments merely permissive—(The convention provided

for annual payments of over 3,000,000). The report of Secretary Crawford for 1817, p. 291, indicates that he had the same opinion as Bayley, and further indicates that payment would be made in two instalments.

45. Indefinite. The amount authorized was equal to the unredeemed 6's and deferred 6's. See Act, p. 416, "Provided that no part of the stock thus created, shall be reimbursable without the assent of the holder or holders of such stock until after the whole of the 8% and 4½% stocks, as well as all the 6% stock which may be created by virtue of the preceding section, shall have been redeemed."

47. The amount authorized was equal to the amount of the public debt stock at 65% of the stock converted. Redeemed at the pleasure of the U. S. but only after 8's, 4½'s, and exchanged 6's of 1807 had been redeemed—Bayley, *op. cit.*, p. 47.

Act. "a sum not exceeding the amount of the principal of the public debt which will be reimbursed, according to law, during the present year, by the commissioners of the sinking fund."

47. The amount authorized was equal to the amount of the public debt to be redeemed during 1810—Bayley, *op. cit.*, p. 122.

Bayley, p. 48, states that the loan was redeemable at the pleasure of the U. S. *Treas. Reports*, vol. i, 1790-1814, pp. 424 and 441, Articles of Agreement, indicates that the loan was redeemable on December 31, 1811, but gave the bank in the event of non-renewal of the charter, the right to call for earlier redemption on giving three months notice.

48–49. No data on the employment of agents.

51. The full amount of old 6% and deferred stocks was authorized.

52. Bayley, *op. cit.*, p. 50, "Under this bill $15,468,800 was obtained on subscriptions and sales of $100 in stock for $88 in money, and $531,200 at par, by giving an annuity of 1½% for thirteen years in addition to the interest. As the bill contains no provision for offering annuities in addition to the interest, it must have been done under the unlimited authorization given by the bill to raise money without restricting the means." The apparent overissue may be explained by the fact that the Act authorized the borrowing of sixteen million dollars, and the issue of stock therefor. In the *Treas. Report*, vol. i, p. 488—Gallatin says (June, 1913) that subscribers were given the option of 1½% annuity for 13 years or a purchase price of 88.

52. A commission was allowed on subscriptions of $100,000. Bayley, *op. cit.*, p. 125. Also, no proposal for less than $100,000 would be considered. *Treas. Report*, vol. i, p. 497.

53. An additional issue of five million dollars as a part of the loan was authorized during the same session of Congress.

54. The apparent overissue is to be explained by the fact that the bill authorized a loan of that amount and the issue of stock therefor.

54. Commissions were allowed on subscriptions of $100,000 — Bayley, *op. cit.*, p. 126, *Treas. Reports*, vol. i, p. 520. No subscriptions less than 100,000—*Treas. Reports*, vol. i, p. 520.

55. The act authorized an issue of five million dollars and a further issue of five million dollars was authorized as part of the loan to be authorized during the same session.

56. The amounts given vary. Figures in the table are those given by Bayley, *op. cit.*, pp. 523, 127-9, and the Treasury Report (*Treas. Reports*, vol. i, p. 527. Offers for $9,229,056 were made and later $566,000 additional was accepted making the total $9,795,056. Subsequently there was a failure of about $900,000. Bolles, agrees with the figures of the Treasury report but cites no authority. This figure includes supplemental stock, Bayley, *op. cit.*, p. 53.

56. This loan was issued at 88 but the issue was subject to the condition that if more favorable terms were given for any other part of the $25,000,000 loan, these subscribers were to receive the same terms. Bayley, *op. cit.*, p. 53, says $7,935,581 was later received on a basis of 80.

56. Subscriptions were limited to $25,000 on which ¼% was allowed, *Treas. Report*, vol. i, p. 535.

57. The figures are from Bayley: The 1814 *Treas. Report*, vol. i, p. 528, states that $2,723,300 was first accepted and later an additional $207,000 making $2,930,300 which was reduced to $12,520,300 by failure of $410,000 of subscriptions.

57. Bayley, *op. cit.*, p. 53, states that $4,307,307.90 was received for this loan at 80.

According to *Treas. Reports*, vol. i, p. 539, Commissions of ¼ of 1% were allowed on minimum subscriptions of 25,000. *Cf.* Bayley, *op. cit.*, p. 128.

No mention was made in the Treasury Reports of 1814-1815 or by Bolles—But 1815 *Report*, vol. ii, p. 17, lists subscriptions to 6% loans of 1814 (lumped) showing $12,551,511.87 cash received at 80 (largely) 85, 90%, and 90¾ for $15,661,818.54 stock. No explanation given but these figures are larger than those given in the 1814 report for loans 56 and 57.

Bayley, *op. cit.*, pp. 53 and 129, gives $652,534.36 as the amount received in cash.

58. The 1876 *Treasury Report* places the amount issued at $4,282,151.12.

59. According to Bayley, *op. cit.*, p. 131, $400,000 was borrowed at 7% and the balance at 6%.

59. No stock was issued. The money was borrowed from banks on special contracts. Bayley, *op. cit.*, p. 56.

59. Bolles claims that payment was accepted in bank bills worth 65%, necessitating as late as 1855 issues of stock to supplement loans 56 and 57. He cites no authority. The treasury reports for 1855-56 make no mention of the matter. See, however, discussion and citations, *supra*, chap. ii.

60. The act authorized an amount—for so much of the $28,000,000 authorized under the Acts of Mar. 24, and Nov. 15, 1814, as shall not have been effected, not to exceed $7,500,000. Another section authorized $3,000,000 additional.

63. Reissue was permitted. The $25,000,000 was limited to the amount outstanding at any one time. The reissue power was repealed Mar. 3, 1817.

63. Bayley, *op. cit.*, p. 133, states that the obligations were redeemable at the pleasure of the U. S.

63. Reissue of treasury notes permitted by Statute.

65. Premium received on part of issue—$32,793.73. Bayley, *op. cit.*, p. 134.

65. Reissue of treasury notes was permitted by the act.

66. Reissue of small notes explains amount of conversion. Knox, *United States Notes*, p. 65.

68. Treasury notes were received on the basis of $95 treasury notes for $100 stock. A prior offering had been withdrawn by Dallas because of low bids 75-89. Bids ranged from 95 to 100 in cash due to the fact that Dallas increased the rate as the amount subscribed at a particular place approached the amount needed to redeem Treasury notes. *Treas. Report*, vol. ii, pp. 26-7, Bayley, *op. cit.*, p. 59, states that $11,699,326.63 were received and that there was an average discount of $4\frac{4}{5}$%.

68. The 1876 *Treas. Report*, p. 39, says the obligations were redemeable after Jan. 1, 1830.

70–1. Note alternative provisions combining rate and maturity.

70. In the *Treas. Report* for 1820 (p. 178)—the amount issued is given at one million dollars, whereas the 1821 report gives the amount which appears in the table.

71. Bayley, *op. cit.*, p. 137, quotes the premium as $40,000.

72. Bayley, *op. cit.*, p. 137, and the Treasury report of 1876, p. 40, give the premium as in the table. On page 63 it is given as over 5½%. Pages 63 and 138 give the amount of the premium as $264,703.70. The 1821 *Treas. Report*, p. 204, says the average premium was 5.59%.

73. Stock issued in exchange for 6's was to be redeemable: one-third after Dec. 31, 1830, one-third after Dec. 31, 1831, and one-third after Dec. 31, 1832. Stock issued in exchange for 7's was to be redeemable after Dec. 31, 1833. None was ever issued.

73. Subscriptions were authorized to an amount of twelve million dollars in 6's and 7's of 1812 and $14,000,000 in 6's of 1813, 1814, and 1815.

75. Bolles says that only $3,308,307 were exchanged. Bayley and *Treas. Reports* (in several places) give the amount quoted in the table.

75. Subscriptions were authorized to an amount of $15,000,000 in 6's of 1813.

76. According to the *Treas. Reports*, vol. iii, pp. 283-4, there was an offer by the bank to take five million dollars at par. Other offers to the amount of $2,554,585.37 were at rates from par to 4½% premiums. Individual offers averaged .97⅓ of 1% premium. The offer of the bank was actually equivalent to a premium of 4¾%, however, on account of the government's interest in the bank.

77. Subscriptions were authorized to the amount of $12,000,000 of 6's of 1813.

77. The 1825 *Treas. Report*, p. 316, gives the amount exchanged as $1,585,138. Later reports show the amount which appears in the table.

77. The *Treas. Report* of 1876, p. 41, says the securities were redeemable at the pleasure of the U. S.

79. The authorization was to issue notes in place of those of Loan 78 which had been paid into the Treasury and cancelled.

80. The act merely extended the date of issue to June 30, 1839, and did not authorize an additional ten million dollars of treasury notes. Acts had permitted the issue up to a limited date only. Knox, *op. cit.*, p. 45, quotes to the effect that the whole amount outstanding was limited to ten million dollars, which seems to apply to amounts under this and previous acts.

81. Amount authorized was five million dollars, outstanding at any one time in lieu of those which had or might be redeemed. Reissue permitted.

82. Amount authorized was five million dollars, outstanding at any one time and irrespective of the volume outstanding under other acts.

83. Bayley, *op. cit.*, p. 41, quotes rates of 5⅖, 5½ and 6% and, p. 142, says $16,155 at 5⅖%; $3,213,791.86 at 5½%; $2,443,030.02 at 6%.

83. The *Treas. Report* of 1844, p. 658, states that the interest was 5½%. *Treas. Report* of 1876, p. 43, says interest was at 5%.

83. Footnote for Loan 82, *supra*, apparently applies here.

84. The *Treas. Report* of 1876, p. 43, describes notes as issued at one and two years. Bayley, p. 140, (not specific as to each issue) has notes as issued for one and two years. Act of Oct. 12, 1837, permitted issues for one year only, and all subsequent acts including this one, refer back to Act of Oct. 12, 1837. Apparently no authorization for a two-year treasury note.

85. Act of April 15, 1842, extended and modified the act of July 21, 1841, and added an authorization of five million dollars.

85. Sale below par was to be permitted only after the loan had been advertised for a reasonable length of time and proposals for subscriptions invited. The authority to sell below par was terminated by the Act of Aug. 31, 1842.

85. Bayley, *op. cit.*, p. 142—$1,700,000 was sold at 97.50—Discount $42,417.80.

86. See footnote. Loans 82 and 84 *supra*.

87. The authorization apparently includes the authority to reissue treasury notes of previous acts redeemed before July 1, 1844.

88. The *Treas. Report* of 1843, p. 600, describes the loan as one of seven million dollars—also 1843, p. 629, table of offers accepted shows $7,000,000 offers accepted—But the 1844 *Report*, p. 658, shows the amount appearing in the table.

88. Bayley, *op. cit.*, p. 143, quotes the premium at $76,632.35. *Treas. Report* of 1843, p. 629, gives the premium at $72,367.40, and quotes rate of 1.01% to 2.37½%.

89-90. The amount outstanding at any one time under both loans was limited to ten million dollars. Power to reissue treasury notes, was given.

90. Bayley, *op. cit.*, p. 144, cites a premium of $1,007.75.

90. The *Treas. Report* of 1876, p. 44, states that the loan was made at par.

91. See *Treas. Report* of 1876, p. 45.

92-3. The right to reissue treasury notes was given but the volume outstanding at any one time under both loans was limited to $23,000,000.

92. The *Treas. Report* of 1876, p. 44, says they were redeemable after 60 days notice.

93. The apparent overissue is explained by the fact that other treasury notes were convertible into and actually were converted into this stock. The limitation of $23,000,000 applied to operations of 1874 only.

93. Interest: Section 13 of the act, p. 121, provided for conversion into stock with interest fixed at 6%—Section 16, p. 121, provided for the issue of stock at not over 6%.

93. Bayley, *op. cit.*, p. 146—"The premium realized from 1847 to 1850 on a portion of the stock issued amounted to $74,884.98.

93. The *Treas. Report* of 1876, p. 4, says that $28,207,000 were issued. The 1881 report (and after) places the amount at $28,230,350.

94. The *Treas. Report* of 1876, p. 45, says redeemable from July 1, 1849 to 1881, at the pleasure of the U. S.

95. Bayley, *op. cit.*, p. 147, gives the premium as $487,191.16, citing treasury reports. *Treas. Report* of 1848, p. 303, places the amount of the premium at $487,168.66.

95. Note provision requiring advertisement for subscriptions.
95. Apparently the use of agents was authorized as section 3 limited the expenses for agents and other expenses to not over $16,000.
97. $20,000,000 authorized outstanding at any particular time.
97. Interest: $6,000,000 authorized to be issued at not over 6%. Balance to be issued at par to those bidders willing to take at the lowest rates of interest not over 6%. Bayley, p. 149, gives amounts issued at each rate from 3 to 6%. *Treas. Report* of 1876, p. 45, has rates at 5 and 5½%. The 1881 report has rates at 3 to 6%.
98. *Treas. Report* of 1876, p. 46, states that sale was at par. The 1877 report, p. 25, describes the sale as being at .0205 to .0703 premium. Bayley, p. 74, says premium was 2 to 7%. The 1881 report (and after) has average premium of 3.059%.
99. According to the *Treas. Report* of 1860, $10,000,000 was offered on September 8, 1860, and the entire amount was subscribed but some subscribers defaulted.
99. Bayley, *op. cit.*, p. 150, places the amount of the premium at $33,-216.20. The 1876 report, p. 46, says that the sale was at par. The 1877 report says the sale was at par to .0145 premium.
100. Section 2 authorized the issue of 6% notes. Section 4 authorized the issue of notes at such rates as might be offered by the lowest responsible bidders after due advertisement.
101. Bayley, *op. cit.*, p. 76, declared that the discount amounted to $2,-019,776.10. The 1876 Treasury *Report* claims that the sale was at par. Subsequent reports (1880 and later) give the rate as 89.03.
102. Indefinite. Section 4 of act allowed the President to substitute treasury notes for any loans then authorized but not used.
102. The 1876 *Report*, p. 46, claims that the issue was at par, while the 1881 report (and after) describes the sale at from par to 1.27% premium.
104. Amount of $50,000,000 issued for stock sold, while $139,321,350 was issued in exchange for 7–30's.
104. The 1861 *Report* shows sale at par for 7's.
The 1877 *Report*, p. 27, and subsequent reports say $50,000,000 6's were issued at a discount of $5,338,768.09 being equivalent to par for a 7% security. The 1862 *Report* described the sale as one at par for 7%. After 1882, the price was always quoted at par.
105. Bayley and Treasury Reports after 1881 give issue as $60,030,000 including reissues. Apparently no authority for reissues amounting (from 1876 to 1880) to $60,000,000.
105. Made legal tender by Act of Mar. 17, 1862, Section 2.
106. The 1876 *Report*, p. 47, places the amount issued at $140,094,750. The amount given in the table appears in the report for 1881 (and after).

106. The 1876 *Report*, p. 47, states that the issue was at par. The 1881 report refers to a .465% premium and the 1891 report, to one of .165%. According to Bayley, p. 165, $650,324.44, was the amount of the premium.

107. The act did not expressly authorize the employment of agents. Chase apparently justified employment under general expense authorization. The same is true of other loans.

107. According to Bayley, *op. cit.*, p. 156, there was a premium of $1,826,868.75. The 1876 *Report*, p. 47, says that sale was at par. The 1881 report (and after) shows premium of .355.

108. The highest amount outstanding was that of $449,338,902, on June 30, 1864, Bayley, *Report* of 1877, p. 27.

108. The conversion privilege terminated July 1, 1863.

109. The highest (given in table—1881 report) amount outstanding was that of $149,500,000, June 12, 1864—Bayley, *op. cit.*, p. 158.

109. *Act of Mar. 3, 1863*, chs. 73, 128, 709—Section 2, at p. 710—interest on certificates hereafter issued payable in lawful money.

111. *Act of Mar. 3, 1863*—$50,000,000 included postage and revenue stamps.

111. The 1876 *Report*, p. 49, says that the amount issued was $223,625,663.45. The 1877 *Report*, p. 29, places the amount at $49,102,660.27 (apparently highest amount outstanding). The 1881 report has this amount in its table.

112. *Act of Mar. 2, 1864*, authorized issue of $9,000,000. Section 3, of *Act of June 30, 1864*, repealed except as to $75,000,000 already offered.

112. Bayley, *op. cit.*, p. 160, says that the amount of the premium was $3,339,751.70. The 1876 *Treasury Report* gives the average premium as 4.13%. This statement continued until 1881 when 4.453% came to be given as the premium.

113–114. Interest payable in lawful money.

115. Interest payable in lawful money.

113-115. Legal tender for face value.

116. The 1876 *Report*, p. 50, has the amount issued as $196,117,300. Later reports after 1881 have same amount as in table.

116. Bayley, p. 164, has premium as $659,422.78. The 1876 *Report*, p. 50, refers to the sale at par. Premium appears in report for 1877.

118. Bayley, p. 165, says there was a premium of $3,178,710.81. The 1876 *Report*, p. 50, says the issue was at par. A reference to the premium appears in the report for 1881. The 1891 report and after places the premium at 2.521%.

119. The 1878 *Report*, p. 30, places the amount authorized and issued at $830,000,000. Reports after 1881 give the figures which appear in the table.

119. Interest payable in lawful money.
119. Legal tender for face value.
119. Bayley, p. 166, states that a premium of $316,876.14 was realized on a portion of loan. The 1876 *Report*, p. 50, describes the issue at par. The premium appears in the report for 1881 as .038%. In later reports as 2.038% (1889). The 1896 report cites a premium of 2.058%.
120. Interest payable in lawful money.
121. Bayley, *op. cit.*, p. 167—Premium was $15,179,393.07. The 1876 *Report*, p. 51, refers to the issue at par. The report for 1881 gives the premium at 2.547% and reports for 1891 and after give the premium as 3.547%.
122. Bayley, p. 168—Premium was $12,291,531.54. The 1876 *Treasury Report* has the issue at par. The 1881 report gives the premium as 3.691%. The 1891 *Report* (and after) gives the premium at 1.691%.
123. The *Treas. Report* of 1876, p. 51. Amount issued $379,616,050. The 1877 *Report*, p. 31, $379,617,750. The 1878 *Report* says $379,618,000.
123. Bayley, *op. cit.*, p. 168, has the premium as $4,031,895.77. The 1876 *Report*, p. 51, has the issue at par. The 1881 reports (and after) refer to a premium of 1.062%.
124. Bayley, *op. cit.*, p. 169. Premium on portion of stock was $19,253.40. The 1876 *Treas. Report*, p. 52, refers to the issue at par, while the 1881 report (and after) cites a premium of .045%.
125. The 1876 *Report*, p. 52, describes an issue of $85,150,000. In the 1878 (and after) report, the amount is given as $85,155,000.
125. Interest not over 3% in lawful money.
126. Principal and interest payable in lawful money.
127. *Act of Dec. 17, 1873.* The amount authorized was equal to the amount of the 1858 loan.
127. De Knight, *History of Currency and Loans*, p. 103, states that the loan sold at a premium of .015 of 1%, amounting to $77,265.51 (p. 104).
128. De Knight (p. 105) gives premium as $750,000.
129. Under the Act of Dec. 17, 1873, there were issued $260,000 in 4's.
129. According to De Knight (p. 107) a premium of $746,948.28 was realized on this loan.
129. Amounts issued vary in different *Treasury Reports*. Tables for dates show these amounts. 1879 report, XVIII. Issues to date, $710,345,950

1879—$636,529,900.	1880—$708,980,800.	1890—$710,313,600
1891—$710,327,350.	1896—$710,888,100.	1910—$710,417,500
1905—$710,430,950.	1922—$710,398,200.	1928—$710,438,100.

De Knight (p. 107) gives the total amount issued as $740,898,200 of which $710,398,200 was under the refunding act.

131. Continuation of 5's of 1881 at 3½% apparently no statute authorizing.
131. 1881 *Report XXV* says $401,504,900 in 5%'s and $178,055,150 6's continued.
De Knight, p. 103, gives the amount as $401,503,900.
132. Pleasure of the U. S. — but not while bonds of the U. S. redeemable at the pleasure of the U. S. and bearing a higher rate are outstanding.
132. The 1833 *Report*, p. 9, says $305,581,250 was issued.
133. Continuation of 4½%'s of 1891 at 2%. Apparently no statutory authority.
134. Offered at 117.223. Premium received was $8,660,917.63 which is at the rate of 117.322. De Knight claims (p. 112) that $50,000,000 sold at 117.266.
135. Actual premium was $11,166,246.51. *Treas. Report*, 1896, p. 29.
135. De Knight (p. 114) claims there was a premium amounting to $2,800,844.62 additional on another portion of the loan.
136. The 1898 *Report*. Table gives issue as $198,678,720. The 1900 report says $113,920 additional was issued and table shows issue as $198,-792,640. Shown in table for 1905 as $198,792,660.
136. Popular loan. Public subscription required.
136. According to De Knight's Appendix (p. 243) the amount issued was $199,308,880.
137. Issued in exchange for other bonds at various rates of exchange, based on present values at specified rates of interest.
138. The premium on the first, $30,000,000 issue was $1,210,817.95—1906 *Report*. The premium on $50,000,000 was $1,291,274.19—1911 *Report*.
138. The first act did not grant the circulation privilege. The *Act of Dec. 31, 1905*, gave to the bonds the circulation privilege. According to the *Act of Mar. 2, 1911*, the Bonds issued under the *Act of Aug. 5, 1909*, were to have no circulation privilege.
138. The Act of Aug. 5, repealed the unexercised authority of previous acts and authorized the issue of $295,569,000 (in addition to amount already borrowed).
140. No circulation privilege.
141. No circulation privilege.

SOURCES

In the main, the materials of the study have been drawn from official sources falling under the following classes or titles:

American State Papers
Abridgement of Debates in Congress
Annals of Congress
Congressional Debates
Congressional Globe
Congressional Record
Journals of Continental Congress
Treasury Reports
Hearings, especially before the House Committee on Ways and Means, the Senate Committee on Finance, and the House Committee on Banking and Currency.
House and Senate Documents.
United States Statutes at Large.

Complete citations appear at the proper places in the text.

The following governmental reports are catalogued under the name of the author:

1. Bayley, Rafael A., *The National Loans of the United States from July 4, 1776, to June 30, 1880*, Washington, 1881, 2nd ed.
2. Noyes, A. D., *History of the National Banking System*, National Monetary Commission, 61st Cong., 2nd Sess., Senate Doc. No. 572.
3. Davis, A. Mc.F., *The Origin of the National Banking System*, National Monetary Commission, 61st Cong., 2nd Sess., Senate Doc. No. 582.
4. Kinley, David, *The Independent Treasury*, National Monetary Commission, 61st Cong., 2nd Sess., Senate Doc. No. 587.

The following secondary sources have been referred to in connection with some aspect of the study.

Adams, Henry, *Public Debts*, New York, 1890.

Bankers Magazine.

Bass, John Foster and Moulton, H. G., *America and the Balance Sheet of Europe*, New York, 1921.

Beckhart, Benjamin H., *The Discount Policy of the Federal Reserve Bank*, New York, 1924.

Bolles, Albert S., *The Financial History of the United States from 1789 to 1860*, New York, 1883.

——, *The Financial History of the United States from 1861 to 1885*, New York, 1886.

Brief and Speech of Mr. Jacob Barker of New Orleans.

Browne, Geo. N., *The Sinking Fund*, 2nd ed., Boston, 1880.

Clarke, Matthew St. Clair, *Legislative and Documentary History of the Bank.*

Dalton, Hugh, *Principles of Public Finance*, 5th ed., London, 1929.

De Knight, *History of Currency and Loans.*

Delano, F. A., *The Economic World*, vol. x, Oct. 2, 1915, pp. 432-34.

Dewey, D. R., *Financial History of the United States.*

Elliot, Jonathan, *The Funding System of the United States and Great Britain*, Washington, 1845.

Federal Reserve Bulletin.

Gallatin, James, *Financial Economy of the United States.*

——, *Government Finances and Currency.*

——, *Letters to Daniel Wilmot*, Hall, Clayton and Medale, 1862.

——, *Letters to S. P. Chase*, New York, 1861.

——, *National Debt, Taxation, Currency, and Banking System*, New York, 1864.

——, *The National Finances, a Reply to a Speech in Congress by Samuel Hooper*, New York, 1864.

Gibbons, James G., *The Public Debt of the United States*, New York, 1867.

Haig, R. M., *The Public Finances of Post-War France*, New York, 1929.

——, "Should Banks be Taxed and How," *Bulletin of the National Tax Association*, vol. 44, no. 5, Feb., 1930, pp. 134-141.

Hardy, *Tax Exempt Securities and the Surtax*, New York, 1926.

Hart, Albert Bushnell, *American Statesmen, Chase*, New York, 1899.

Holdsworth, J. Thom, *The First Bank of the United States.*

Hollander, Jacob H., *Annals, American Academy of Phil. and Social Science*, vol. lxxv, Jan., 1918, p. 104.

Hunts Magazine.

Jensen, Jens P., *Problems of Public Finance*, New York, 1921.

Knox, John J., *United States Notes*, New York, 1888.

Love, Robert A., "The Use of Liberty Bonds in Payment of Estate Taxes," *American Economic Review*, vol. xv, no. 2, June, 1925, pp. 275-283.

The Liberty Loan of 1917. Campaign Text Book.

Lutz, H. L., "The Evolution of Section 5219, United States Revised Statutes," *Bulletin of the National Tax Association*, vol. xiii, no. 7, April, 1928, pp. 205-212.

Mitchell, Wesley C., *A History of the Greenbacks*, Chicago, 1903.

McCulloch, Hugh, *Men and Measures of Half a Century*, New York, 1889.
Moulton, H. G. See Bass, John Foster.
Noyes, A. D., *War Period of American Finance*, New York, 1926.
——, *Forty Years of American Finance*, New York, 1909.
——, "The Treasury Reserve and the Bond Syndicate Operations," *Political Science Quarterly*, vol. x, no. 4, p. 573.
Pigou, A. C., *A Study of Public Finance*, London, 1928.
Saxe, Martin, "The Threatened Discrimination in Banking Taxation," *Bulletin of National Tax Association*, vol. xii, no. 6, March, 1928, pp. 166-175.
Scott, William A., "Bond Issues and the Money Market" appearing in *Financial Mobilization for War*, Chicago, 1917.
Charles Sumner's Speech in the Senate, July 11, 1868, Washington, 1868.
Seligman, Edwin R. A., *Currency Inflation and Public Debts*, New York, 1921.
——"Our Fiscal Policy" in *Financial Mobilization for War*, Chicago, 1917.
——, *Studies in Public Finance*, New York, 1925.
Spaulding, *Financial History of the War*, 2nd ed.
Sherman, John, *Recollections of Forty Years*, New York, 1895.
Spear, Samuel J., *The Legal Tender Acts*, New York, 1875.
Walker, Robert J., *Review of Our Finances*, Dec. 19, 1862.
Williams, J. E., *The War Loans of the Associated Banks to the Government*, Letter to Congressman Kelly, Feb. 14, 1867.
Willis, H. Parker, *The Federal Reserve System*, New York, 1923.

INDEX

Adams, Henry, 37 fn.; 222 fn.; 239 fn.
Adams, John, negotiated loan, 21; lowered nominal rate, 23
Advertising, of loan, 72; plan of, 147
Agents, abandoned, 72; versus direct sales, 215
Agriculture, plans for improving, 266
Annuity offered, 44
Anticipation of specified revenues, 27
Appropriation, of special revenue, 26; methods of, 27; of proceeds of land proposed, 74; for debt retirement, 198; of all revenue, 232; of specified sum, 232

Bank, bought issue at low figure, 54
Bank, first of U. S., 24, 30, 33; dividends large, 32; stock disposed of, 33
Bank, of North America, 23, 24, 242
Bank notes, proposed issue with Liberties as base, 206
Banking, changes in, 213
Banks, arrangement with, to avoid conversion, 48; relations with, 54 and 83; objections to, 57; and exemption, 112; special contract with, 124; used as depositories, 129; use of, 214
Banks, Federal Reserve, rates of rediscount, 134 fn.
Banks, National, compelled to purchase securities, 115
Barings, fear of loan from, 58
Barker, 47, 49, 50; set terms, 46
Bass, 239 fn.
Beckhart, 151 fn.
Biddle, 58
Bills of Credit in disrepute, 17
Bolles, 50, 51, 246, 247; footnote reference to, 19, 28, 49, 54, 57, 62, 97, 103, 110, 112, 116, 118, 119
Bond, houses used, 119
Bond, syndicate operation, 120 fn.
Borrowing, to pay principal and interest, 18 fn.
Boutwell, 125 fn.; recommends exemption, 112
Browne, 231 fn.
Building lots, income from, appropriated, 26

Calhoun, 58 fn., 60, 61
Campbell, opposed claims, 47; questioned borrowing policy, 52
Carlisle, appeal to banks, 120
Certificates, of indebtedness introduced, 95
Chase, 76, 77; interpretation of "Market Price," 78 and 102; legal tender, 80; specie and subtreasury, 84; difficulties with conversion, 102; inability to dispose of bonds, 103; decision by, 113 fn.; justified expense, 251
Circulating, medium, in demand, 39
Circulation privilege, 126-128; on Panama Canal bonds, 127 fn. and 128 fn.; denied to Liberties, 148 and 155; term misunderstood, 153 fn.
Clarke, Matthew St. Clair, 17 fn., 31 fn.
Clarke, Comptroller, 112
Cobb, 74 fn.
Coin payment, 120; proposed, 41; of interest, 108; of principal, 109
Collamer, 80
Commission, of 4½%, 20; resort to, 21; of 8%, 23; not to be paid, 72
Competitive bidding, 45, 52, 71
Competing media eliminated, 86, 87
Compulsory loans, 216
Compulsory purchase, considered, 190
Conversion, efforts to avoid, 37; notes into bonds, 42; only pro-

vision for repayment, 42; prevents circulation, 43; results of, 47; pecuniary loss from, 49; expected, 100; difficulties of Chase, 102; right repealed, 104; of first Liberties, 149; limited to first opportunity, 156; abandoned, 167; necessity of avoiding, 177; of 3½'s possible, 186; exchange of two types of securities, 191; of notes into bonds, 222; two-way type, 223; into future issues, 224; complete, 224; criticism of, 225; post mortem, 35, 101, 227
Cooke, 104, 110 fn.
Coupon bonds, introduced, 72, 147
Coupons clipped, 97
Currency, 37, 82, 137; Whig attempt to make notes acceptable as, 68; treasury's need of, 86; proposal to exchange for bonds, 206; manipulation of, 212
Credit, conditions in post-revolutionary period, 17, 18 fn.
Creditors, issue of securities to, 24; payment to, 94

Dallas, 39 fn., 50, 247; proposed coin payments, 41; acceded to demand, 47
Dalton, 140 fn.
Davis, 83 fn., 87 fn.
Debt, reduction, 70
Debt, retirement, 53, 198; definite amount appropriated for, 27
DeKnight, 252, 253
Delano, 116 fn.
Demand notes, 68, 93; affected by receivability, 91; resemble receivable notes, 94
Democrats, dependence upon treasury notes, 59
Denomination, small, 147
Deposit, left with banks, 33; amount of bank's subscription left on, 55; with banks and states, 57; proceeds of loan left on, 118; of funds in banks, 129
Deposits, of notes, accepted, 106
Depositories, security required of, 131
Dewey, footnote references to, 18, 19, 27, 32, 39, 41, 50, 55, 68, 70, 97, 100
Direct loan, 120; versus agents, 215
Discount, sale at, 20, 68, 74; sales at prevented, 78
Discretionary power, 187
Dividends, from bank stock appropriated, 27
Domestic, loans, 24
Duration of loan, 228; reduced, 64
Dutch loans, 20

Elliot, 231 fn.
Estate taxes, receivability of bonds for, 170
Ewing, favored long period, 64, 67; on terms, 66
Exempt and non-exempt bonds proposed, 162
Exemption, 30, 111, 218; gain or loss from, 219; status of, 113 fn.; on First Liberties, 150; reasons for abandoning, 161; changed in second loan, 157; of specified amount, 162; proposals to list, 163; retained in third loan, 167; on bank holdings, proposed, 172; possibility of using, 177; contingent, 178; supposedly limited but practically complete, 180; on one type, 190; of bonds, 207 fn.
Expenses of selling Liberties, 146, 155
Exchangeability, 148

Federal Reserve Notes, field for, enlarged, 137; issued on basis of commercial paper, 138; based on War Finance Corporation bonds, 144; proposed issue with Liberties as base, 206
Federal Reserve System, and financing, 129; burden of corporate financing borne by, 144
Fessenden, on coin payments, 110
Financial needs not met, 66
Financing, final conclusion on, 239
France, took loans at par, 20; finances of post-war, 203 fn.
Franchise tax of reserve banks, 199
Freeman, 223 fn.
Foreign exchange, interest and principal payable in, 20
Foreigners, attempt to prevent purchases by, 28
Funded debt, antipathy toward, 57; increased at expense of floating debt, 197

Gallatin, Albert, 36, 37, 38, 44; recommends purchase at market, 30; on relations with banks, 31 fn.; opinions conservative, 39
Gallatin, James, 107; footnote references, 39, 76, 77, 79, 82, 84, 85, 86, 98, 112
Gibbons, 72 fn.
Glass, 185; objected to compulsion, 190; unwilling to purchase, 197
Gratifications, offered by Adams, 21

Haig, footnote references, 115, 203, 228, 239
Hall, resolutions introduced by, 39
Hardy, 220 fn.
Hamilton, 17 fn., 18, 19, 23, 24, 27 fn., 28, 29, 31 fn., 32 fn.
Hart, 79 fn., 81 fn., 87 fn.
Holdsworth, 32 fn., 34 fn.
Hollander, 239 fn.
Houston, 196-198
Hooper, 80

Import duties, appropriated, 26; paid in bank notes, 34
Incomes, in high brackets grow, 176
Income taxes, raised to enhance exemption, 176
Indents of interest, 18 fn.
Indirect method of issue, 139
Inflation, 137, 212
Interest, amendment to do away with, 61; continued on notes, 68; bias on question of, 79; payable in Europe, 125; obstacles to a remunerative rate, 186
Interest rate, limitation on, 17, 24, 207; left to discretion of secretary, 62, 43, 164; not remunerative, 62; and failure of loan, 67; decreased one point, 105; treasury policy on, 151; increased, 168

Jefferson, 23 fn., 242
Jensen, 230 fn.
Johnson, 110 fn.

Kings County, N. Y., holdings of Liberties in, 180 fn.
Kinley, footnote references, 71, 120, 122, 123, 124
Kitchin, favored conversion, 156; justified opposition to conversion, 168; favors receivability, 170; misinterprets bill, 173; on conversion, 187
Knox, footnote references, 17, 62, 63, 69, 72, 248

LaFollette, presents resolution, 203
Leffingwell, 188; supports contingent exemption, 178; favored control over transaction, 181
Legal tender, 96; proposed for notes, 39; used as threat, 79; receivability of, 89; substitutes for, 99; proposals for, 126
Liberty bonds, used in paying estate taxes, 201; holdings by large estate, 201; proposed plans for aiding holders, 206-207
Liberty Loan, the first, 146-154; second, 155-166; third, 167-175; fourth, 176-184; fifth, 185-192
Loans, dependence upon, 36; to bond holders proposed, 206; compulsory, 216
Louisiana stock, 244
Lutz, 115 fn.

Market, furnishing a, 116
Market transactions, efforts to control, 181
Marketing technique, 118
Marshall, decision by, 113 fn.
Maturities, poorly arranged, 70; leaving to secretary, 164, 182
McCulloch, 76 fn., 81 fn., 105 fn.; urged coin payment, 110; on exemption, 112
McAdoo, 152; stated purpose of corporation, 141; reason for wanting low interest, 154; reasons for change on exemption, 157; opposed exemption, 161; opposed two types, 162; proposed to list exemptions, 163; requested freedom to fix terms, 164; favored low rate, 169; lamented state of market, 176; promised low rate, 187
Mexican war financing, 69
Middle class, appeal to, 161
Mitchell, footnote references, 75, 77, 78, 81, 82, 84, 85, 86, 98, 99, 100, 103, 104, 106, 108, 116
Morrill, 121
Moulton, 239 fn.

Nassau County, holdings of Liberties in, 180 fn.
National Banking System, 87
Necessity, argument of, 98
New York County, holdings of Liberties in, 180 fn.
Nominal taxes defended, 161
Notes, defined, 19 fn.; as means of anticipating revenues, 38; issued instead of bonds, 187
Noyes, footnote references, 120, 121, 124, 125, 126, 137, 203

Panama Canal bonds, doubt as to circulation privilege on 1902 issue, 127 fn.; 1911 3's offered without this privilege, 128 fn.
Par, 33; purchase not permitted above, 28, 30; prices above, 36, 70; prices below, 37; provision for sale below, 67; sale at less than, 68; purchases above, 71; sale at, but bidders insert rates, 71; no permission for sale below, 78; restriction repealed, 78; sale at, 148; no sale below, on Liberties, 155; proposal to prevent brokers selling at less than, 204; significance of sale at, 209
Patriotism, decline of, 185; appeal to, 211
Penrose, 188
Pigou, 139 fn.
Policy, problems of, 208
Political strategy, 58, 167, 188
Popular loans, 119
Preferential rates, 133
Preparation of the field, 211
Price maintenance, 28, 189, 193, 234; activities of war finance corporation, 194; sentiment in favor of, 203; by direct purchase, 235; as a policy, 236
Prices of securities low, 198
Public lands, proceeds from sale of, appropriated, 26; paid for in securities, 34
Purchase, by the Treasury, 70; to benefit business, 71, 122; requirement removed, 136; with five per cent of proceeds, 171, 195; continued by fourth loan, 182; from proceeds of franchise tax, 199; from repayment of foreign loans, 199; to maintain prices, 235

Railroads, issues to help, 93
Receivability, of securities in payment of bank stock, 34; of securities in payment of land, 34; of bank notes, in payment of import duties, 34; proposed for notes, 39; to make notes current, 40; ineffective, 42; discontinued, 42; for all dues, 62; results in retirement, 63; of notes, 89; omitted from first Civil War notes, 89; for import duties denied, 90; of old for new securities, 90; effect of, 91; of bonds in repayment by railroads, 93; and coin payments, 123; of bonds for estate taxes, 170, 200; continued in fourth loan, 182; of bonds in repayment by foreign governments, 200; operation of feature of, 201; proposed, 204; of Liberties for income and excess profit taxes, 204; of Liberties in payment of internal revenue, 205 fn.
Redeemability, 124
Rediscount rates, 134 fn.; decrease proposed, 206
Reserve of legal tender, 95, 107
Reserve requirements, not to apply, 130; changed, 135
Reserves depleted, 124

Saxe, 115 fn.
Scott, 120 fn.
Security, definition, 18 fn.
Security features, 218
Seligman, 140 fn., 150 fn., 220 fn.
Sherman, 74, 94 fn., 119, 121, 123, 125 fn.
Sherman, Silver Act, 124
Short-term financing, 37
Short-term obligations, reasons for, 230
Silver, not on par with gold, 120
Simmons, 183
Sinking fund, 122, 231; unable to meet obligations, 28; 2½% provision, 198; operations for price maintenance, 234
Sloan, against conversion, 156
Soldiers, pay docked, 217
Solvency, assuring, 231
Spain, took loans at par, 20

Spaulding, 79, 84, 99 fn., 103 fn., 104 fn.
Spear, 98, 105 fn., 125 fn.
Specie, laws prior to 1860, 83; payment to Sub-Treasury, 84
Stock, defined, 19 fn.
Sub-Treasury, and specie payments, 83, 84; and receivability, 89; abolished, 129 fn.
Subscriptions, bonds disposed of by, 119; size of, 159 fn.
Sumner, 110 fn.
Surplus, invested in bonds, 195
Suspension, effect on financing, 85

Taxation, attempt to avoid, 36; advocated, 52; inadequate, 82; failure to provide, 233
Ten percent limit removed, 133
Terms left to Secretary, 188
Theory, problem of, 208
Treasury note, 69

Victory Loan, 185-192

Walker, 84 fn.
War psychology, 17
War Finance Corporation, reasons for, 141; how purpose was attained, 143; price maintenance operation, 194
Webster, 60
Whigs, attempt to fund debt, 63
William, 76 fn.
Willis, 129 fn., 130 fn.
Windom, 121
Wisconsin, resolution from, 203
Wolcott, 32, 243

Bei Fragen zur Produktsicherheit wenden Sie sich bitte an:
If you have any questions regarding product safety,
please contact:

Walter de Gruyter GmbH
Genthiner Straße 13
10785 Berlin
productsafety@degruyterbrill.com